American Federalism

American Federalism

A Concise Introduction

Larry N. Gerston

M.E.Sharpe
Armonk, New York
London, England

Library of Congress Cataloging-in-Publication Data

Gerston, Larry N.
  American federalism : a concise introduction / by Larry N. Gerston.
    p. cm.
  Includes index.
  ISBN-13: 978-0-7656-1671-5 (cloth: alk. paper)
  ISBN-10: 0-7656-1671-8 (cloth: alk. paper)
  1. Federal government--United States. 2. United States--Politics and government. I. Title.

JK311.G47 2007
320.473'049—dc22   2006022798

For Selma Heller,
Not only my mother, but my first teacher of politics

Contents

Preface

Few topics are as difficult to "wrap your arms around" as American federalism. Designed as a governing mechanism for the union at the Constitutional Convention in 1787, this concept is both a fundamental prerequisite to understanding the operations of American governments and a value statement about the use of authority. The Framers did not make it easy. There is no section of the Constitution titled "Federalism." Yet, through their efforts to simultaneously amass, distribute, and restrict political power in the United States in a manner that would provide strength with flexibility, the Framers developed a unique system of governance.

Writings on the topic of federalism are almost as diverse as approaches to the concept itself. Over the more than thirty years that I have been dealing with the topic, I have seen books that focus on structure without political context, normative discourses that speak to one view of power or another, and technical explanations dry enough to make the Mohave desert seem like a lush garden paradise. Switching from book to book over the years, I told my students repeatedly that "federalism is really interesting, honest." Yet the chasm between the written material and my protestations never narrowed. Left with no choice, I embarked on my own effort to describe the topic, culminating with the completion of *American Federalism: A Concise Introduction.*

Fundamentally, federalism addresses the intersection of people, policies, and political power. It is a mechanism that helps to guide the actions of various governments on endless topics of importance. Food content labels, smokestack emission rules, public education systems, immigration regulations, and domestic partner relationships are some of the many subjects whose management is structured by federalism. How various levels of governments see the dispositions of these and other issues helps to explain the uses of power and influences our lives. And given that governments often clash about what should be done and by whom, federalism helps to bring order to an otherwise messy political environment. Viewed from this perspective, federalism, I believe, is downright fascinating.

As with all of my books, I have tried to make *American Federalism: A Concise Introduction* user-friendly and intellectually interactive. In no way have I sought to minimize the value of the theories that frame the topic. However, I have attempted to illustrate each theoretical theme with numerous examples that give context and reality to the discussion. Some may object that I give too little attention to the body of theoretical literature, not to mention the mountains of statistics compiled by policy wonks that revel in detail. No disrespect is intended in either case. Instead, I have sought my own middle ground, striving to show the linkages between historical events and contemporary political arrangements that frame our everyday lives.

Throughout this effort, I have leaned on people for support and, in some cases, a little guidance. Constantine Danopoulos (San José State University) and Stephen Schechter (Russell Sage College), though a continent apart, were my intellectual bookends on theoretical matters that set the federalism table. At San José State, additional thanks go to colleagues Terry Christensen, Ken Peter, and Frances Edwards for pointing the way at particular moments of curiosity or ignorance by providing valuable information and insight. A Norton research grant from the Political Science Department at San José State University facilitated part of my off-site research.

Putting together materials for any book is always a challenge. Students Lisa Day Krenzel and Joel VanderVeur dedicated great amounts of energy to this task, for which I am grateful.

At M.E. Sharpe, special thanks go to Patricia Kolb, editorial director and vice president, for her support of this project. Ana Erlic served as the production editor who moved the book to completion, and Richard Gunde as copy editor displayed extraordinary skills in the final shaping of the manuscript.

Finally, there is the person behind the scenes who offers the "reasonableness" test. That job continues to fall to Elisa, my wife, who through every one of my written odysseys, has been the one to say, "I get it" or "I don't get it." As always, she is my canary in the mine shaft.

All of these people and others helped me in one way or another, but the final product is mine alone and a work for which I take full responsibility. And if this book helps students "get it," then it will have been a journey well worth traveling.

American Federalism

Part I

Creating a New Nation

1

☆ ☆ ☆ ☆

The Great Political Experiment

Defining Federalism and Organized Power in the "First New Nation"

In the "over the top" drama of twenty-first century communications, hyperbole often tramples reality. "Best ever" replaces "good"; "critical moment" supplants "difficult time"; "unique" substitutes for "different." So when American federalism is described as "the great political experiment" in representative democracy, it is easy to see why such a claim might be dismissed as just another example of the language excesses that commonly sprinkle our daily conversations. But unlike characterizations that often exaggerate beyond the pale without any basis or fact, American federalism *is* a great political experiment—a novel design that has resulted in a template for countless other governments throughout the world to emulate over the past two centuries.

Federalism refers to the multifaceted political power relationships between governments within the same geographical setting. Its origin lies in the Latin word *foedus,* which refers to a lasting voluntary association among equals. The application of modern federalism has evolved to the extent that voluntary associations have been replaced by government units. Thus, today federalism frames the ways that various governments simultaneously influence, depend upon, and push away from each other. The use of power is the most important aspect of government, particularly for democracies, because government is the official coercive authority for so many decisions that affect people, values, and resources. Representative governments award, deprive, and rearrange our lives with our consent, even though we may not always agree with what they do or how things turn out. Federalism, then, is the organizational mechanism through which governments manage power.

The United States is not the only nation to embrace federalism.[1] In fact, in recent years, several nations have relied upon federalism as a "middle ground" for distributing political power. Thus, in 2005, as Shiite, Sunni, and Kurd blocs attempted to create a new arrangement of political power in post–Saddam Hussein Iraq, representatives relied upon federalism to parcel out power on governmental topics ranging from domestic oil revenues to foreign trade.[2] Meanwhile, a continent away in Africa, Kenyans considered constitutional reform, with the most important issue being the extent to which political power should be shifted from the central government to the outlying provinces.[3]

Modern international applications notwithstanding, federalism is a singularly American invention described by one political scientist as "the greatest of American contributions to the art of government."[4] The concept was born out of political necessity, an unanticipated offspring of the American Revolution. With the leaders of the "first new nation"[5] accepting national government organization on a scale wider than ever before, they struggled for a way to develop meaningful representation.[6] Federalism is an outgrowth of that effort.

Opportunities for Participation

In addition to dispersing power and authority, federalism provides a way for ongoing citizen involvement in the political process. In the United States, opportunities for participation have expanded over time through constitutional amendments, particularly through enfranchisement of African Americans (13th, 14th, 15th), women (19th), and young people 18–20 years old (26th). Numerous voting rights laws enacted by Congress, executive orders signed by presidents, and decisions handed down by the United States Supreme Court along with laws passed at the state levels have further guaranteed avenues for participation.

Sometimes, participation takes place through voting; other times, it occurs through a variety of other means including campaign contributions, letters to elected officials, political marches and demonstrations, interest group activity, and citizen meetings with those in positions of power. The interests, capabilities, and resources of political participants may differ, but the opportunities to converge upon the various governing layers of the federal system are many. Further, as different combinations of expressed interests make themselves heard, policy outcomes sometimes change accordingly.[7] From city hall to the halls of Congress and other national institutions, federalism assures endless opportunities for people to participate in the political process. And they do.

Avenues for Representation

With so many layers of government responsible for managing policy issues, citizens can express themselves through "channels of political participation"[8]

Figure 1.1 **The Federalism Grid in the United States**

		Horizontal		
V	National	Executive branch	Legislative branch	Judiciary
e				
r				
t	States	Executive branch	Legislative branch	Judiciary
i				
c				
a	Local		County boards of supervisors	Judiciary
l				
	Local	Mayors	City councils	

in several political decision-making arenas. Multiply these access points times endless issues and the various governmental doors available—the executive branch, legislative branch, judiciary, and numerous regulatory agencies—and the concept of federalism quickly becomes a fascinating enterprise both to watch and to practice. Further, Theodore Lowi observes, as the roles of government have expanded over the past two centuries, so have the gateways for groups to pursue their needs at whatever level necessary to succeed.[9]

Under American federalism, countless opportunities exist for interested parties to influence the political process. Thus, if someone seeks to address a toxic waste problem, theoretically he or she could petition authorities at the local, state, and even federal levels, depending upon the specific characteristics associated with the issue, the places of power to which he or she has access, and whether he or she wanted more or less regulation of the problem. Moreover, to the extent a grievant is unhappy with the outcome at a lower level of government, he or she might well be able to gain a more favorable result by taking the issue to a higher level, although, to be sure, there are no guarantees. On this note it is fair to say that the federal arrangement is far more complicated today than in the early years of the Republic.

The existence of so many sources of power, while often confusing, allows people to pursue political ideas to the point of exhaustion, yet satisfaction that at least they have been heard. E.E. Schattschneider describes this process as the "socialization of conflict," where people and their ideas compete for the attention of public policymakers at whatever levels of government necessary to assure success.[10] Other observers of the system are not so positive in their assessments. G. Ross Stephens and Nelson Wikstrom argue that "the multidimensional maze of federal, state, and local political and administrative jurisdictions . . . makes the federal system so amorphous, it's amazing it works at all."[11] It is messy, for sure, and replete with overlapping governmental responsibilities and inconsistencies, but the nature of American federalism permits political claims to be heard and vetted in ways not commonly seen in other governmental arrangements.

Endless Nuances

The uniqueness of federalism is a lot more than meets the eye. Imagine a three-dimensional game of tic-tac-toe and you begin to get an idea of the complex dimensions of American federalism. At the very same time that decision makers from two or more governments may be cooperating with each other in one policy area, they may be competing with, or even battling against, one another in a different policy area. Thus, Congress and the state governments may work together to solve problems resulting from issues such as toxic waste or mining regulations. At the same time, state legislatures and the federal courts may differ widely over the constitutional conditions related to Internet taxation or education policy. Such shifting relationships may be difficult to follow at times, but the overall result is a collective "equilibrium" of sorts that leaves various governments competing with one another for the public trust.[12]

Sometimes, significant differences in approach to a problem exist within the same level of government. Within the national executive branch alone, the president and his assistants may have one set of views regarding management of an issue that differs markedly from the approach taken by a majority of the legislative branch. Other fissures persist as well. For example, not all members of Congress draw the line between federal and state responsibilities the same way, with differences often occurring not only along political party lines, but also by geography, the needs of unique political constituencies, and philosophical values among the legislators themselves.[13] Within the federal judiciary, changing combinations of judges over time may contribute to different majorities in one direction or another about which levels of authority should do what; on other occasions the same issue can attract different opinions from the same court!

As if to complicate matters more, states differ with each other over a host of policy issues ranging from public benefits for illegal immigrants to methods of funding public education. The fact that the collective values of states within the same political union can be so different has often been viewed as a justification for political autonomy, with each state adopting different approaches to the same problem or policy issue.[14] Sometimes, adjoining states can differ on the same question, such as the ways that Washington State and Oregon treat taxation or the responses of Michigan and Ohio to the issue of capital punishment.

Much like magnetic fields that simultaneously draw and repel particles within the same physical environment, federalism generates simultaneously changing tug and pull political relationships among government units. In a nation of 300,000,000 people who are served by nearly 88,000 governmental units, the ramifications of these transactions take on dizzying proportions.

In some respects, federalism is more flexible than other political systems of governance. At one extreme, many nations operate with unitary systems, where virtually all decisions of importance are determined at the national level; Great Britain is often cited as the classic example of unitary government. At the other extreme, some nations are cobbled together through local jurisdictions, with the "national" government having little real power; post-Taliban Afghanistan may well fit into this model. Federalism splits the difference, however, with two or more levels holding and sharing real power. But even federalism can be employed in different combinations. The types of arrangements may vary from nation-centered dominance to state-centered control to distinct divisions between levels with no overlap, but in each case power is distributed among two or more levels of governments.[15]

The Four Characteristics of Federalism

Hardly a concept with precise, well-defined boundaries, American federalism takes on different combinations of characteristics depending upon the circumstances, values, and players associated with each issue. Fundamentally, however, federalism is molded by four key characteristics: consensus, cooperation, conflict, and chaos. Typically, these characteristics interact with values, issues, and policymakers in distinct combinations or patterns. Further, sometimes different issues will simultaneously draw out different constellations of government actors, making it all the more difficult to define a political era or explain the outcome of a particular situation. For these and other reasons, the functions of governments tend to be anything but predictable over time, even though the frameworks of governments are well defined.

Consensus

A hallmark of the American political system is the extent to which political actors at all levels of governance share core values. The more that citizens and leaders alike at the national, state, and local levels embody a basic vision about political issues and approaches to resolving those issues, the more that they exhibit consensus. In the United States, societal commitments to equality, individualism, majority rule, and representation represent a few of these core values that transcend both political institutions and individual concerns. To be sure, such tenets are not universal, yet they resonate throughout the political system.

Consensus means that regardless of the outcome, most people attach themselves to dealing with a series of core issues in generally agreed-upon ways. Response of the American government to the terrorist attacks of September 11, 2001, exemplified such a political environment. In the aftermath of this horrific event, political authorities at all levels committed to protecting Americans wherever and however possible; meanwhile American citizens shared the desire to give authorities the necessary opportunities to help us feel safe in a suddenly unsafe world.

Consensus is usually most obvious on broad questions such as public safety or the general welfare—issues that are valued similarly by almost everyone. Determining how to guarantee these values, to what extent, and under what conditions can lead to deep divisions, however. For example, does promotion of the "general welfare" mean that governments should see to it that all people have the same opportunities to study for college degrees or the same degrees irrespective of their capabilities? Does the commitment to Social Security mean that the under-funded program should continue in the wake of the federal government taking the "trust fund" for uses other than retirement pensions, or should a different funding mechanism be employed? Moving from theory to reality can quickly erode consensus, yet the concept is valuable in federalism, particularly as it applies to the general proposition that all citizens have the right to be heard.

Cooperation

Less commonplace but fairly prominent in American federalism is the attribute of cooperation. With this characteristic, government units may be competitive regarding a particular situation or public policy issue but realize that benefits will accrue to each only through cooperation. Under these circumstances, states may realize that working together to solve a joint problem will produce results far more beneficial than by either going it alone or getting caught up in a costly battle with an uncertain outcome or potentially harmful result. In some cases, states will team up with the federal government to deal with the issue.

A shared vision of Internet taxation stands out as a case in point. Consumer purchases via the Internet now approach $200 billion annually.[16] As such, these transactions represent potential state sales tax revenues in the tens of billions of dollars—revenues that tax-starved states would accrue if the purchases were made at a traditional "brick and mortar" store. But with commerce increasingly "on-line," it becomes difficult to determine where the purchase actually takes place as well as the physical location of the seller. Today, close to forty states have banded together to design a "protocol" for Internet taxation that would distribute revenues among the states in a way acceptable to all.[17] The leaders of this effort hope that with this consensus in hand, Congress will ratify their plan.

In the aftermath of Hurricane Katrina, a devastating storm that rocked the Gulf Coast in 2005, the Federal Emergency Management Agency struggled to restore power, empty floods from New Orleans and nearby cities along the Gulf of Mexico, remove thousands of destroyed buildings, and help the area infrastructure begin the long road back to normal. In the interim, more than thirty states accepted hundreds of thousands of refugees as temporary residents, providing assistance from housing to public education. True, the governments at various levels had difficulty coordinating services, but their intent on cooperation for the greater good was present from the first hours of the disaster.

Conflict

"Politics," Harold Lasswell once wrote, "is the struggle over who gets, what, when, and how."[18] When something of value is in short supply, struggle and conflict are inevitable. Such strains among governments to control scarce resources range from the flow of water to the movement of international trade. Likewise, states squabble over tax breaks to attract new industries or assembly plants. Under such circumstances, sometimes the "winner" loses because the giveaways exceed any benefits from the new industry.

In the parched West, states compete for the control of water sources and their aquifers, or underground reservoirs that transcend politically defined boundaries. Similar struggles have emerged over the growing reliance upon international trade, with some groups often benefiting at the expense of others. No one complains about clothing at a fraction of the price he or she paid years ago because of the low foreign labor costs, unless that person worked for the U.S. company that either had to close or outsource production to the foreign location. In both of these cases, the residents of some states may gain, while those in others may pay a dear price.

Conflict does not have to be of the economic variety. States that refuse to honor the laws of nearby states exhibit conflict. For example, civil unions between two consenting adults of the same sex have become battlegrounds in many states. Not only have states taken different stances on the same issue, but some states will not honor the arrangements in others. Commonly these decisions are made by legislatures, but sometimes the public makes policy through state initiative elections. In the case of civil unions, President George W. Bush also expressed his opinion on the issue, asking for a constitutional amendment to define marriage as a union only between a man and a woman.

Sometimes, conflict occurs when the states refuse to honor federal rule. Numerous Southern states opposed Supreme Court and lower federal court orders to desegregate in the late 1950s and 1960s, leading to the presence of National Guard or U.S. Army troops to enforce the Court's decisions. Similarly, several states have adopted legislation that permits the use of "medical" marijuana, claimed by some to greatly reduce pain associated with several serious diseases. At the same time, the federal Food and Drug Administration has declared marijuana an illegal drug, leading to cat-and-mouse enforcement games between state and federal authorities. Such situations can spark tension and occasional violence, although the instances are relatively few in American society.

Chaos

Finally, there are those times when governments and their leaders suffer almost irreconcilable differences over resources, values, or other sources of division. In these situations, great anguish reigns because of conflicting management approaches or solutions to often sensitive issues.

In the early years of the twenty-first century, governments are struggling over how to manage the issue of an individual's rights in the waning moments of terminal illness. One state, Oregon, has gone so far as to enact legislation allowing terminally ill individuals to receive physician-prescribed drugs to facilitate a less painful death. Officials in other states, among them Florida, have enacted laws that forbid anyone from interfering with life support or other forms of patient assistance. Given these wide-ranging policy responses to the same fundamental issue—life—from state to state and between some states and the federal government, medical practitioners and patients alike are uncertain of their rights and obligations. Such incongruity leaves people confused about the roles of governments in their lives. Further, the executive branch of the national government has challenged through the courts the question of physician-assisted suicide, and some members of Congress have taken positions on the matter of life support.[19]

Disagreements between levels of governments have also attended the emergence of stem cell research, thought by many scientists to offer hope for problems ranging from currently incurable diseases to organ replacements. While some nations have moved aggressively on the issue, President George W. Bush has supported only minimal research at the federal level. Meanwhile, several states have undertaken research initiatives that place them squarely in opposition to the president's policy.

In the wake of Hurricane Katrina, chaos quickly became the word most often explaining bungled government efforts to address the tragedy. Officials at all levels of public authority pointed fingers at each other for letting down Gulf Coast residents in their time of need.[20] Six months after the disaster, three-fourths of the 480,000 residents living in New Orleans had not returned either because of destroyed homes or a ruined infrastructure. Eight months after the tragedy, only 18 percent of the public schools and 39 percent of the retail establishments had reopened, despite promises of federal assistance. Cumulatively, the elements associated with the slow recovery of the area led many to accuse the federal government of abandoning an entire region of the nation.[21]

Chaos-related situations occur periodically in American society, although rarely to the extent of something like Hurricane Katrina. On a practical basis, however, the responses to them represent cornerstones of federalism. Efforts to solve difficult problems often pit leaders of the national government against the states, and sometimes the states against one another. Other levels, such as regional or urban governments, become part of the mix as well. The outcomes of these crises become even more baffling when people in the same level of public authority clash over which level of government should deal with a given issue.

Fluidity and Continuity

Perhaps one of the most impressive aspects of American federalism lies in the ability of government institutions to adapt the concept to changing times, issues, and conditions. Today's highly urban, post-industrial, high tech society is a world away from the slow-paced, remote, agrarian environment that characterized the United States in its earliest years. Although our basic governing structure remains remarkably similar to the framework drawn up in Philadelphia in 1787, the capabilities, distributions, and uses of authority by various governments have changed markedly.

To be sure, over the past two hundred twenty years, the powers of some institutions have been clarified, while the resources of others have evolved considerably. Even more remarkable, some power relationships have shifted over time, revealing a profound flexibility within the American government framework. More times than not, such shifts in power have not occurred with unanimity. In fact, great debates over the appropriate assignments of government functions continue to this day.[22] Nevertheless, the basic elements of American federalism remain in place, even if the applications are different. And other than the Civil War nearly one hundred fifty years ago, the political "operating system" of the nation has functioned without serious bloodshed.

Along with resilient adaptability, American federalism has demonstrated a great sense of continuity. Other nations, particularly those in the midst of rapid transformation, remake their governing mechanisms as times and circumstances dictate, sometimes allowing expediency and charismatic leadership to overpower longstanding values and historical themes.[23] However, in the United States the times and circumstances continuously reshape the operations of our political system while keeping it intact. Credit the Framers, writes Joseph Zimmerman, who "understood the importance of a fundamental document that would permit mid-course changes in direction as experience was gained and new developments occurred."[24] This elasticity is a hallmark of American federalism. It underscores the dual—and sometimes conflicting—properties of change and perpetuity within the same governmental structure.

Outcomes of Federalism

You may ask, "What does all of this have to do with me? After all, I'm just one person out of 300,000,000, and far removed from many of these centers of political power."

The answer might surprise you. Federalism is all around us; nevertheless, we just do not always see it at work. One of the biggest problems with our understanding of government today is that, absent something like a local city council meeting where one can drop by and watch what happens, we rarely observe firsthand the relationship between "cause and effect." In other words, while we are impacted by policies such as a new tax law or a court decision that declares an executive order unconstitutional, we do not necessarily understand the linkage between the values and power relationships associated with those policies or their consequences. Nor do we necessarily appreciate which level of government can assume responsibility for a given decision, or why.

The fact is, however, that public decision-making bodies at all levels of political organization play active roles in our lives, and the outcomes of their interactions can differ greatly, depending upon which levels prevail on which issues. Accordingly, we see these impacts of federalism play out in the political, economic, and social realms.

Political Consequences

Determining conditions in the workplace, the rules for abortions, acceptable levels of factory smokestack emissions, allocations of precious resources such as water, and assistance to states that guard against terrorism are all aspects of federalism. In these and countless other instances, the political circumstances of our daily routines are framed by the conditions under which governments operate. Consider water pollution. If the national government sets the standards, all parts of the nation would need to comply with the same rules; as a result, those states that use voluminous amounts of water for manufacturing or other forms of production would be pressed more than non-manufacturing states to the extent that they have pollution issues. However, if the states set their own separate standards, the meanings of "acceptable" levels of pollution could vary greatly; should tainted water bring harm to certain groups, such as small children or pregnant women, the political fallout could be tremendous. More often than not, federalism is a zero-sum game with one level of government prevailing at the expense of another. That is, to the extent that a particular government authority has the power to dispose of public resources or manage a given policy area, another may not.

Economic Impacts

In addition to political consequences, federalism can have economic impacts on people in very real ways, and the outcomes may differ by state or region. For example, although there exists a federal minimum wage, some states have higher minimums than the floor established by Congress. As a result, their residents accrue economic benefits not necessarily available elsewhere. Likewise, a few states now allow their residents to buy prescription drugs from Canada and other nations at prices much lower than those in the United States for the same drugs, while most others do not afford such opportunities to their residents. This situation is no small consequence to poor or elderly people on fixed incomes who have expensive prescriptions. Again, some populations benefit more than others. And there is another angle—along with the state-to-state differences, you can imagine that state laws allowing prescription purchases from outside the United States do not set well with U.S. pharmaceuticals, which would be much happier if these purchases were under tighter federal control.

Social Outcomes

Federalism also has social consequences. Consider the fact that in recent years, the U.S. Congress has wrestled away from the states the power to establish the minimum age for the legal consumption of alcohol, and has set the age at twenty-one—something that has had varying impacts on some states where people once could drink if they were as young as eighteen. Then there is the question of abortion. Some believe that the U.S. Supreme Court settled the issue in 1973 when, in *Roe v. Wade,* the Court declared that a woman has the right to choose the fate of her pregnancy during the first trimester without any interference from government. Nevertheless, since the decision, several states have denied insurance coverage for abortions, others have stipulated waiting periods or mandatory counseling, and others still have required parental notification by minors.[25] Again, the outcomes of these differences can have tremendous consequences on various populations, leaving some with different sets of opportunities than others.

Truth be told, our lives are tied directly to the vertical and horizontal relationships among the various levels of government. And we are not always affected the same way or with the same results.

Follow the Bouncing Ball—The Uncertainties of Federalism

The very factors that make federalism so fascinating to some leave others totally frustrated. Inasmuch as many decisions are bounced up and down the federal decision-making ladder, people can easily become confused about how policies are made and issues are decided. Perhaps the federalism puzzle becomes a bit easier to understand if certain principles are kept in mind:

1. **Federalism is open to interpretation**. Determining which levels of government should bear responsibility, if any, for a given policy or task is less a matter of capability or capacity and more a matter of beliefs, values, and political will. Governments can do almost anything, but absent any constitutional issues, political justification for their actions determines what they will do. Consider the issue of welfare reform. The Personal Responsibility and Work Opportunity Reconciliation Act passed by Congress in 1996 reflected more a transfer of responsibility to the states (welfare would no longer be the province of the national government) than a question of individual capability. With this act, Congress decided that states would be better at managing the welfare issue. Beyond the economics, the new law reflected a major shift in political values.[26] Moreover, just as the national government took over control of welfare in large part during the Great Depression, it is entirely possible that responsibility might shift again in the future.

2. **Federalism is inconsistent**. The same political, social, and economic issue may often be resolved by governments in dramatically different fashion. To the extent that governments move in different directions on the same issue, their actions may well speak to their respect for local political values. No example stands out more than the issue of gay rights. In 2004, eleven states enacted laws that forbade marriages

between two people of the same gender. At the same time, states such as Hawaii and Massachusetts enacted laws that approved domestic partnerships between people of the same gender. How could such differences occur? Because whatever their distinctiveness in geography or heritage, states have unique political cultures that often lead them to take different positions on the same issue.[27] Yet they manage to operate within a large national political framework.

3. **Federalism is incomplete**. As society evolves, issues once not even anticipated by governments must be addressed by these decision-making entities. To do otherwise would leave people at risk in various ways. Until a few years ago, few people were aware of stem cell research and the microbiological analysis of human cells and their human applications. For some, stem cell research represents new hope in combating terrible diseases and regenerating damaged organs. For others, it represents an assault upon life, since many of the "lines" come from human embryos. Nowhere in the Constitution is there reference to the management such an issue, yet people are troubled by a series of social, ethical, and political questions.[28] Today the national and state governments are struggling to determine which level should have responsibility for overseeing this new area of science. At the same time that the George W. Bush administration has made a determined effort to restrict stem cell research at the national level, several states led by California have undertaken massive efforts to explore the new scientific area.[29] Such collisions show that there are always new vistas for federalism.

4. **Federalism changes with the growth of technology**. Values that are at one time treasured by most people may be reconsidered at another time as a result of advances, causing applications of federalism to change as well. The issue of capital punishment stands out as an example. For many years a large number of states used the death penalty as a response to the most heinous crimes. However, with the technological ability to analyze DNA from people associated with a crime, some states began reconsidering use of the death penalty without first relying on this new evidentiary source to affirm that those convicted have actually committed the crime.[30] Innovations such as the RU-486 "morning after" contraceptive pill have brought on similar debates at the state and national levels,[31] with technology raising new questions related to individual rights, regulation, and political decisions by governments at various levels of authority.

The fact is, two hundred and twenty years after the creation of the Constitution, uncertainty remains about the political resolution of numerous issues. Moreover, although the government responsibilities relating to the current crop of issues may be resolved today, others will appear tomorrow. Just as modern societies are anything but static, so it is that governmental arrangements face new challenges as well. Recognition of this ambiguity may not always be comforting, but it is a reflection of the realities in today's world.

Looking Ahead

The remaining chapters of this book are dedicated to understanding the bouncing ball of federalism. We will consider the topic both in terms of its origins and present-day applications, with attention to the evolution of American institutions of governance. Along the way, we will examine federalism in vertical and horizontal contexts, bearing in mind the numerous agents who try to influence power relationships. Further, we will consider outside factors that affect American federalism today, ranging from domestic economic interests to international crises and issues.

More than two hundred years after its creation, American federalism remains the curious combination of a concrete organizational framework that houses a somewhat unpredictable and complex political structure. Much like a Frisbee that sails in an unintended direction seemingly without explanation or a comet that veers off course unaccountably, federalism can be a vexing element of the political system, but it is an element that the American political system cannot afford to do without. Our challenge is to understand how it works.

2

☆ ☆ ☆ ☆

Reordering the Rules on Power and Governance

Questioning the Traditional Rules on Power and Governance

American federalism emerged as a by-product of the deteriorating relationship between the colonists and the British in the New World. Several European countries—notably Great Britain, the Netherlands, France, and Spain—laid claim to parts of North America in the 1600s, but the British quickly emerged as the dominant power. From within the framework of the loosely fashioned new political territory would develop the foundation of federalism, a form of shared powers and authority among various governments.

Initially, most of the authoritative capabilities in the new political arrangement were left with the colonists, who were awarded limited self-government as part of the package of benefits associated with their settlement. Over time the once-common bonds between the British and colonists became unglued, and the colonists slowly began to consider alternative arrangements, particularly with respect to more comprehensive self-governance. The most radical idea was claiming an independent, sovereign authority. We need to fully grasp the falling out between the colonists and British, for without that split, there would have been no need to invent American federalism.

Early Political Arrangements

Whatever their reasons for coming to the New World, the colonists shared at least one trait: They wanted different lives from those of Europe, and particularly England. Whether because of religious concerns, economic limitations, or rigid social standings in their former environment, the colonists looked to their new homes as sources of previously missed opportunities. With that impetus, the newest inhabitants of North America slowly crafted their own separate traditions, creating various blends of old values and new beliefs. For the first century, most differences between colonial residents and British authorities did not interfere with a generally strong economic partnership that seemed to benefit both sides of the Atlantic. But the political relationship would be tested from the 1750s on, especially as the British increased their military presence in areas contested by their French rivals.

So restless were the British and the colonists over the many threats to domestic security that in 1754 Britain's key foreign ministers asked the colonists to organize a meeting to provide for their common defense against the French and their Indian allies. The assembly was held in Albany, where Benjamin Franklin proposed a General Council of all the colonies, whose allocation of members would be decided in proportion to the taxes paid by each to a general treasury. Franklin also designed a means of common colonial defense against hostile forces. These proposals, known as the Albany Plan, were rejected unanimously by the delegates for taking too much power from the individual colonies and by the British for potentially creating a unified force among the colonies that might one day become hostile to the throne.[1] Yet Franklin's proposals served as early springboards for future colonial organization and ultimate British fears.

Meanwhile, the crown struggled to keep its footing in an otherwise uncertain economic environment and deteriorating political climate. As a condition of maintaining an army to protect both the population and their economic investment, the British demanded assistance from the colonists in the form of taxes to support their costly ventures. The more the colonists rejected British demands for compensation, the more that the British attempted to force compliance by passing legislation such as the Revenue Act in 1764 (also known as the Sugar Act) and the Stamp Act in 1766. Enacted without the agreement of the colonies, these economic moves generated criticism from the king's subjects. But criticism became outrage after Parliament passed four Coercive Acts in 1774, placing severe economic and political constraints upon the colonists. Suddenly, the colonies had more in common than not—strong aversion to authoritarian British rule.[2]

Nowhere were the reactions more profound than in the concept of governance, particularly in terms of representation. Several colonial legislatures condemned the new wave of legislation as laws made without their consent or agreement. Although spokesmen for the crown argued that the colonists had "virtual representation" in Parliament, the colonists considered such linkages as all too indirect, if not meaningless.[3] That fundamental difference would later emerge as a cornerstone in the Declaration of Independence.

These struggles occurred in anything but an orderly environment. The political systems of the colonies during the 1600s and 1700s were hardly like those in the United States today. There was no official "union" of colonies to speak of until the First Continental Congress was assembled in 1774, although leading individuals from various locations sometimes saw the need to meet on particular issues of mutual interest. Collectively, however, the general values of the colonial residents were considerably different from those in England and elsewhere on the east side of the Atlantic Ocean.

One of the sharpest thorns regarding the presence of the crown lay in the nature of conflicting governing structures. All the colonies had legislatures with limited powers of self-taxation and other capabilities relating to autonomous rule. At the same time, the crown had its own appointed governor on-site in each colony to oversee the needs and expectations of the king. Clearly, the two sides were not on the same page, especially when it came to issues relating to scarce financial resources such as profits from various ventures. The demands from a centralized government three thousand miles away for colonial cooperation and deference, combined with an increasingly menacing British military presence in the colonies, eventually drove the two groups apart.

As they neared the moments leading to the Declaration of Independence, the revolutionary zeal of the colonists focused upon more than simply breaking away from the British—it centered on the need to create a new form of representative government that would acknowledge the value of individuals while appreciating the benefit of limited government. The potential clash between the needs of individual freedom and the value of government authority later would become one of the hallmarks of federalism, as well as a source of occasional adjustment and refinement.

After years of failed negotiation, civil unrest, economic losses, and lessened political autonomy, the individuals from the once-autonomous colonies organized and declared their independence from England on July 4, 1776. From that point on, the Revolutionary War began in earnest.[4]

New Theories and the Old Regime: Sowing Seeds of Change

Great ideas often gain their stature because they percolate through history and survive the test of time. So it was with the march toward American federalism, which occurred in an evolutionary and unpredictable manner. Complicating the development of federalism was the fact that the concept was ancillary to the larger struggle for freedom. There was no template in another country for the colonists to emulate or borrow. Rather, as the colonists first reconsidered, then rejected the idea of British rule, they also had to figure out what form of governance they would use in place of the only system they knew.

The thinkers of the seventeenth and eighteenth centuries slowly cobbled together various thoughts about the political relationships between men and representative governance. Their exploration was more a zigzag journey of pensive, passionate, and persistent dialogues than an organized linear progression of crisp ideas. Some of the early discussions centered on acquired property as a physical definition of individual freedom, in itself a radical thought given that ownership in Europe was largely a preordained arrangement dependent upon one's connection to royalty and little else. And while much of the discourse covered the inherent conflicts from correlating individualism, arbitrary rule, and the need for order, these considerations served as the forerunners of debates about political power among free people and their governments. After all, what good was a debate about the powers of governments if people had no influence on the management of those governments?

Part of the answer to this question would come through determining new relationships between the people and their leaders—relationships that would be based upon connecting public sentiments with authority through free elections, rather than preordained hierarchies that denied widespread public involvement. From there, the organizations of various governments would follow. Although scores of political philosophers touched on the issue, Locke, Montesquieu, and Jefferson collectively represent much of the thinking that contributed to the development of the new nation during this fertile period of history.

John Locke

Several philosophers began questioning the concept of automatic royalty as the basis of political authority as early as the thirteenth century, but it was not until much later that the subject took on a more compelling look.[5] John Locke wrote that citizens, particularly gentlemen of the nobility, had a duty to be educated and participate in the well-being of the country. Such awareness would be of value to the kingdom, rather than a threat. But individual participation was more than simply an aid to the crown. In his *Second Treatise on Government*, Locke argued that individuals had the right to acquire property and that governments were obligated to respect such ownership. Such a claim to the "natural rights" of individuals challenged the traditional concept of hierarchy and order based upon royalty. Written in 1690, this essay on economic freedom in Europe eventually helped to frame the values of political freedom for the American colonists. Locke's writings were particularly influential on Thomas Jefferson.[6]

Baron de Montesquieu

The colonists were not the only subjects struggling with their political framework. In France, Baron de Montesquieu moved along the discussion. Writing about the virtues of a republic—a political entity where individuals would contribute to their own governance—he attempted to construct the outlines of the new political arrangement that would benefit society. The discussion of federalism is broached in Montesquieu's *Spirit of the Laws*, which appeared in 1748. In this book, he wrote that if free citizens in small political units agree to be part of a larger society, this political arrangement would discourage corruption and other dangers.[7] Thus, Montesquieu was among the first to contemplate intertwining governments at various levels of authority, an ingredient essential to the concept of federalism. In a related vein, Montesquieu contributed to the design of the Constitution by advocating an independent judiciary, apart from separate legislative and executive branches, as the essence of guaranteeing true liberty.[8] Such ideas would be an integral part of the organizational mix nearly forty years later in Philadelphia and the philosophical underpinning of "checks and balances."

Thomas Jefferson

As the primary author of the Declaration of Independence, Jefferson knew a thing or two about the necessity and value of freedom. Jefferson wrote that free government was the only way to guarantee that each individual could reach his potential, yet he also worried that government organization might place restraints upon the individual. It is that very conundrum that led Jefferson to discuss particular government arrangements that would simultaneously promote freedom without restricting the well-being of the individual. A prominent Virginian, Jefferson viewed the colonies as the best sources of protection against excessive power and of support for individual rights.[9] Later, as the colonies became states of the new union, he cautioned that political liberty was best guaranteed "by guarding each man against his associates, and them against him."[10] Appreciative of a new form of government, he was also wary of it.

Many other scholars, visionaries, and activists contributed to the emerging body of political thought leading to a new design of American self-governance. However, the writings of Locke, Montesquieu, and Jefferson serve as a representative sample of the thinking that went into the justification for revolution and development of a new government network. Turning their words into political systems would be another task altogether. Terms such as "self-government" and "popular sovereignty" sounded wonderful to those who had neither, but designing a new arrangement that replaced well-established royalty with popular consent, and centralization with "something else," would be a taxing enterprise. That chapter unfolded in earnest with the successful outcome of the Revolutionary War.

The Articles of Confederation: The First Effort at
Self-Governance

As the colonists struggled to break free of England, it seemed that the revolutionaries were more certain of what they *did not* want than what they *did* want. In 1777, shortly after the Declaration of Independence and long before the end of the Revolutionary War, delegates to the Second Continental Congress, an elected legislative assemblage of the thirteen colonies, crafted the Articles of Confederation. This document became the first set of rules for the new nation. Bearing in mind what the colonists believed to be English excesses and abuses, the Articles granted few real powers to the new national government. Instead, they focused on limiting national government and authority.

Under the terms of the new operating arrangement or "league of friendship," the colonies turned states agreed to autonomous self-governance. The aversion to strong centralized governance was understandable, given the bad taste from the endless, and seemingly arbitrary rules laid down by the British with little regard for the states. Yet there was a larger lesson as well: The dramatic swing from one direction (strong central authority) to the other (weak central authority) would be the first of many twists and turns in the development and management of American federalism. Too, there was an inescapable irony that accompanied the desire for minimalist national government. As Seymour Martin Lipset notes, "in spite of working and fighting together in the seven year struggle for independence, the best governmental structure which the Americans could devise was a loose federal union."[11] Whatever their collective commitments to new government, the revolutionaries were in no mood to issue blank checks in the form of another strong central government that could become as harmful as the one they fought to remove.

The new national governmental structure contained neither an executive nor independent judiciary; instead the governing body mimicked the legislature-based organizations of the states. The operating rules called for unanimous votes of the Continental Congress for almost any decision of significance, guaranteeing that the weak national government would have no real power on any policy area over which any single state took issue. So impotent was the government under the Articles that it had no standing army, relying instead upon the state militias in cases of emergency. In fact, the new leaders wanted it that way. The rule of unanimity almost guaranteed inertia. Thus, when Congress asked the states for the right to impose duties on imports as a means of controlling trade, two states refused, thereby assuring demise of the proposal.

The Continental Congress was given limited authority, including the power to wage war and sign treaties. Nevertheless, the Articles provided no mechanism to raise the revenues necessary to carry out any national initiatives including war. With few responsibilities other than an almost ceremonial presence, the Congress became a place of debate and little else. States all but ignored the "national" government, something easy to do since the national government was hardly in position to make any laws or public policies.

Limited horizontal linkages between the states underscored another element of the power relationships during the reign of the Articles of Confederation, where competition seemed more common than cooperation. More often than not, the only scintilla of coordination among the states occurred in their military mobilization against the British prior to and during the Revolutionary War. After the war's end in 1781, with British rule repulsed, the states focused upon maximizing the benefits from their individual existences.

Quickly, the new "union" became state-centric. With the Continental currency deemed worthless by 1781, each state issued its own currency, which also lost value almost immediately. Because states were trying to present themselves as creditworthy trading partners with nations, they passed taxation laws that were particularly onerous, often leading to foreclosures of property, with their owners thrown into debtors' prison.[12] The results were not pleasant, with large numbers of people ultimately rebelling against state governments that responded to deteriorating economies with increased taxes.

Meanwhile, the inability of the states to defend themselves against foreign attack was a cause for further concern. As a sign of their independence, states conducted individual foreign policies and pretty much disregarded the needs and/or well-being of all others. So autonomous were these political jurisdictions that nine states actually operated their own navies. In a span of a few short years, national unity became little more than a vague concept. Within a decade of the fight for independence, angry citizens wondered whether the cure—state sovereignty—was worse than the disease—British rule.

The weak national government notwithstanding, an even more fundamental question remained, namely in times of conflict between the two levels, which would prevail? On the one hand, the question seemed almost moot, given that any action on the part of the national government required unanimous agreement among the states. On the other hand, the issue of dominance could still emerge in a time of crisis. As dysfunctionalism of the states increased, concern about the proper location of power began to tug at the thoughts of greater numbers of leaders at both levels of governance.[13]

With an all but nonexistent national government and increasingly tyrannical state governments, an ever-swelling cadre of political leaders realized the necessity of new political arrangements.[14] At first, they tried to amend the Articles when the members of the Continental Congress organized a hastily called meeting in Annapolis in 1786. But the effort quickly fizzled when only twelve delegates from five states showed up. With political conditions fast deteriorating, a few months later the Continental Congress authorized representatives to meet in Philadelphia to consider possible revisions to the Articles. This time, twelve states sent representatives, with only Rhode Island refraining from participation.

The Constitutional Convention: The Second Effort at Self-Governance

The fifty-five delegates who assembled in Philadelphia to correct deficiencies in the Articles of Confederation realized the extraordinary moment before them. They gathered in large part to address a series of problems, not the least of which concerned the imbalance between the national and state governments. Whatever the other issues, clearly the Articles had failed to organize power in such a way that advocates of both the national and state levels of government would take comfort; in fact, the Articles had benefited the states disproportionately, to the detriment of the national union. Yet, as the principal sources of political and economic power, the states had performed miserably in two respects. On the one hand, the state leaders had failed to support the national economic needs expressed by the new Congress by rejecting several badly needed tax proposals. One the other hand, they had pursued oppressive taxation policies and ruthless economic competition with one another at the expense of their own angry citizens.[15] Combined, these twin disappointments became the urgent impetus for reform.

No one articulated the issues of the day more eloquently than James Madison, who in a long pre-Convention memorandum to fellow delegates promoted the idea of stronger national government organization because "one could hardly expect the state legislatures to take enlightened views of national affairs."[16] True enough, inventions such as "checks and balances," and the Great Compromise balancing representation of small and large states in a bicameral legislature, would emerge during the summer of 1787 at Philadelphia, as well as the general yet critical concern for limiting government. But from the standpoint of federalism, the readjusted relationship between the states and national government was the most significant ingredient in the recipe for political change.

Getting this fractious group to make any meaningful alterations to the Articles seemed more than daunting, even though they readily agreed that the Articles were ineffective and potentially harmful to the future of the republic. Yet Madison's voice would be heard throughout the Constitutional Convention as well as during the trying period of ratification after the meeting. Despite his concerns with the process and some elements of the Constitution itself, he became a persistent nurturing force and compromising voice throughout the four month assembly.[17]

As the summer wore on, the delegates realized the necessity of tossing out the Articles of Confederation altogether and beginning anew. Central to the thinking of most was the idea of a stronger national government, particularly as envisioned in the Congress. True, there would also be a chief executive with some powers and a judiciary with still undefined responsibilities, but the reorganization of Congress alone as a representative body with two newly constituted houses of legislation—the House of Representatives and the Senate—empowered to legislate on behalf of the people was enough to signal a change in the balance between the national government and the states. Other substantive changes would follow.

By the meeting's end, the delegates had crafted a new relationship between the national government and the states. Yes, the states would still legislate for their own populations in numerous policy areas, as well as agree to new, better coordinated relationships of mutual respect and accommodation, thereby affirming a strong vision of valued horizontal linkages. But more would need to occur for the nation to avoid the serious deficiencies stemming from the Articles. The most fundamental change would take place in the formation of a national government considerably stronger than its predecessor in its powers relative to the states. Just *how* strong would be the subject of endless debates that continue to this day, but few dissented from the proposition that the new national government needed to have more clout for the nation to remain unified and strong.

Key Themes at Philadelphia

Embedded within the general proposition that national survival depended upon substantive change were the specific flashpoints of serious constitutional debate. Of the many themes that resonated throughout the Philadelphia meeting, those that stirred the most discussion were the approaches to representation, the distribution of power and authority, and the tension between liberty and equality. Collectively, the outcomes of these concerns at the Constitutional Convention would frame the organization of American federalism. Curiously by today's standards, slavery was broached more from the perspective of counting bodies for purposes of representation (hence the three-fifths rule) than any sense of discrimination or inequality.[18]

Representation

Anyone who is familiar with the game of baseball understands the phrase, "three strikes and you're out." Of course, the possibility of failure at Philadelphia augured consequences far more serious than losing a game—at stake was the uncertain future of a struggling nation. Bearing in mind the dictatorial hierarchy under the British crown and the near anarchy that followed under the Articles, the delegates were down to their "third strike" in their efforts to successfully link the people with their government. These linkage issues are key to the workings of federalism, for without a more acceptable way to manage the relationship between the citizenry and those selected to govern them, the system would surely collapse.

By definition, representation means that a few people are given authority to govern on behalf of the many. Such a responsibility implies a strong relationship between those who confer the trust and those who carry out the mandate to rule.[19] In a democracy, this political covenant takes on a special significance because those who are selected to govern bear responsibility to those who have placed faith in them.[20] But exactly who would be given these responsibilities, under which circumstances, and with what guarantees that they would not abuse the public good or trust with their new powers?

The answer would come in the form of a complex political arrangement that provided the mechanism to assure centralized governance while distributing the capability to govern among three sectors, or branches, of the same government. Thus emerged the concept known as **separation of powers**, meaning that each branch of the new national government would have its own specific set of responsibilities. The Congress, with two chambers by far the most defined authority in the Constitution, would focus on national lawmaking. The president would assume the dual capacities of chief executive and head of state; the first role would center on proposing and approving national legislation, while the second would highlight ceremonial functions related to national unity. The judiciary, by far the least developed authority at the 1787 meeting, would see to it that the laws were managed fairly, although its true powers would not emerge until 1803 with the Supreme Court's assumption of **judicial review**, the ability to determine whether laws and other commitments of government met the requirements of the Constitution.

Key to the functions of the three branches of the strengthened national government would be the means of policymaker selection. States would have direct roles in selecting the Congress, with voters electing members of the House of Representatives, a group whose composition depended upon the number of people in each state, while state legislatures initially chose two senators each. Presidents would be less directly chosen, thanks to the creation of an entity known as the Electoral College. Judges would have no direct or indirect connection with the public; instead, they would be nominated by the president and considered by the Senate. The bottom line is this: Two of the three branches had ties to the states and their populations, while the composition of the third would depend upon the wills of the individuals selected by state populations.

Distribution of Power

The new national government clearly was designed to be more powerful than its predecessor under the Articles of Confederation. But how much power would be desirable? Given the animus toward the centralized regime under Great Britain and the failure of a state-centered arrangement after winning the American Revolution, the answer to this question would be difficult to divine and critical to the creation of federalism. Yet, the debate would be played out during and after the Philadelphia meeting through the statements of the **Federalists**, who saw the need for a stronger national government, and the **Anti-Federalists**, who viewed such a proposition as a New World version of the dictatorial arrangement ordained by the British crown.

Many leaders of the day moved cautiously on this front, afraid of repeating the costly history lesson of excessive centralized British rule. For example, Thomas Jefferson looked to the states "as the real arenas [of] government and society."[21] While he acknowledged the need for a new political relationship with a different balance than that under the Articles, Jefferson still considered "the fundamental powers [of government] as residing in the states,"[22] which he perceived as the repositories of the people's rights and needs and the rightful centers of power. Interestingly, Jefferson was the foreign minister to France during the Convention, and therefore absent from the Philadelphia meeting. Nevertheless, his values weighed heavily on many of the delegates, and they became the backbone of Anti-Federalist thought, a viewpoint that sought to limit national power. Other Anti-Federalists' criticisms centered on the lack of a bill of rights (corrected shortly after the Constitutional Convention), excessive national dominance, the potential of aristocratic rule, a return to taxation "without representation," and the possibility of a national army intruding upon state sovereignty.[23]

The Anti-Federalists were countered by others who fretted that a weak national government would be the death knell to a young nation that had barely survived a precarious first decade intact. At the extreme was Alexander Hamilton, an outspoken Federalist, who viewed national supremacy as key to the endurance of the union and authored a plan with a considerably stronger central government than that eventually approved by the delegates.[24] Many delegates were suspicious of Hamilton, who often expressed admiration of British conventions and the value of order. Yet, when it came to signing the document, all but three of the remaining forty-two delegates (thirteen of the fifty-five had returned to their states) joined Hamilton.

However, the primary architect of national supremacy came to be James Madison. Much less willing than Hamilton to honor the new national government as a reincarnation of British domination, Madison still argued strongly for a unique form of new national authority. However, he made his case in a way that included the states as part of the solution, rather than the source of the problem, often negotiating his way through tricky political currents in private meetings.[25] Madison suggested that the new political arrangement should be contingent upon ratification by the states which, by their assent, would establish the national government as the preeminent national authority.[26] What may have seemed almost a nuance—sowing more a voluntary relationship between the national government and the states—became the means through which many of the differences among the delegates were patched up enough to ensure passage of a final proposal.

Ultimately, the most trying of all conflicts between the Federalists and Anti-Federalists centered on their differences over the appropriate use of power. Placement of this precious commodity simply in the hands of one level or another would neither solve the problem of authority nor assure a strong enough role for the people, the basis of that authority as conceived by the new theorists. Fundamentally, the people would be in charge of their fate, but their control would come via the complex, and sometimes overlapping, uses of power at different levels of governance. This was the genius of the new system according to Robert Dahl: "Instead of a single center of sovereign power, there must be multiple centers of power, none of which is or can be wholly sovereign."[27] Nevertheless, while Dahl viewed such an approach as unique middle ground between the Federalists and Anti-Federalists, few at the time characterized the division with the same accommodationist views.

The debate between the Federalists and Anti-Federalists was hardly limited to the discussions in Philadelphia in 1787, nor settled with the signing of the Constitution. In fact, the ideological conflict continued throughout the ratification period and continues to this day.

Liberty versus Equality

For many at the Philadelphia meeting, the struggle over defining government powers represented more of an attempt to find the appropriate point on a continuum rather than create a new system. Among the activists, Alexander Hamilton was much more willing to view the new version of the national government as truly supreme with respect to the states than some of his contemporaries; he spoke of Americans as "one people" rather than "thirteen separate peoples."[28] James Madison, however, saw national powers as enhanced from the days of the Articles, but still specific and defined.[29] Meanwhile, Constitutional Convention delegates such as Luther Martin continued to view the states as "immutable sovereign members of the union,"[30] with no reason to grant larger powers to another level. Whatever their differences—and there were many—virtually all delegates recognized that the new national government could not carry out "business as usual," and that some new amount of authority would be necessitated for that level. But how much?

Underlying the debate between the Federalists and Anti-Federalists, however, was a large philosophical question, notably the struggle over the values of liberty versus equality. Clearly, both elements were well developed in the Constitution of 1787, and each appealed to a different audience.

Anti-Federalists coalesced around **liberty**, in the sense that individuals and their respective states should be able to pursue their own best interests without interference from another level, thereby minimizing national goals. The physical and emotional connections between the people and their state governments offered the hope that state policies would reflect the public will. To the extent that the value of liberty prevailed, the new system would be much closer in operation to the original Articles, with some national government adjustments for currency and foreign policy responsibilities.

Federalists embraced a notion of **equality** that promoted the same guarantees to all who were now part of the revised union. Within the context of equality, the national government would set the standards for the states and their people, guaranteeing uniformity of policy applications, while protecting minorities against "the danger of fractious state majorities."[31] Such an approach elevated the "United" part of the United States to a new level of prominence. Of course, equality could only be imposed under the auspices of a strong national government.

Indeed, few conflicts have shaped the meaning of American federalism over the past two hundred years as much as the tussle between liberty and equality. In fact, these competing themes have continued as mainstays of the ideological battle to define which view of federalism, that stressing liberty or that stressing equality, should underscore the relationship between the governors and the governed.

A good deal of the debate regarding the wisdom of a strong national branch appeared in the *Federalist Papers*, a collection of eighty-five essays written by James Madison, Alexander Hamilton, and John Jay shortly after the delegates approved the new Constitution.[32] In this compendium, the authors came down hard on the side of a strong national government. And while they acknowledged that the new arrangement of authority might snuff out some individual values, the needs of the collective good made the risk worthwhile.[33]

Those who emphasize liberty focus on the desirability of the state governments to pursue interests that might very well depart from the wills of others elsewhere. Thus, the idea of one state embracing a policy different from others—perhaps racial segregation or conditions in the workplace—would be acceptable as an expression of state values. Those who emphasize equality look to the national government as the authority that defines the same opportunities and responsibilities for all states, regardless if the people in some states might feel differently from others. Defining the same voting rights for all or establishing the same definition of "life" irrespective of one's state of residence are prominent examples. These illustrations notwithstanding, it is almost impossible for the themes of liberty and equality to coexist. To the extent that government institutions promote liberty, the public policy rules are bound to differ from state to state. And to the extent that government institutions endorse equality, states are disallowed from behaving in ways unique to their individual existences. Therein lies a conundrum of American federalism.

From the Past to the Present

How do we leap from the eighteenth century to the twenty-first century on the topic of federalism? To proceed in linear fashion would probably lead to the world's longest (and most boring) book. Further, if relevance is of any value here (e.g., what does federalism mean to *me*, anyway?), we need to examine federalism simultaneously in the context of historical and contemporary applications. Traditional political values, the structures of political institutions, and social change are all woven into the fabric of federalism, which has been both stretched and tightened over time.

The vision of the Framers is every bit as important to the existence of American government today as in 1787, yet the makeup of American society is understandably quite different. How do the guideposts of the former mesh with the latter, or can they? Through coming to terms with the value of tradition in the context of a modern nation, we will better grasp the multifaceted and long-lasting significance of American federalism.

Part II

Organizing a Federal System of Government

3

✫ ✫ ✫ ✫

The Appeal of Tradition

Tradition can be a strong bond among people, especially if they have earned their way to success through overcoming adversity, as did those who prevailed in the American Revolution. Karl Deutsch describes tradition as a fundamental building block of society that, as such, can linger well beyond the circumstances initially responsible for the bond. Where inhabitants "have a political and economic 'stake in the country' and are accorded security and prestige, there are the ties to their own people, living standards, education and tradition."[1] Commitment to tradition may not necessarily be logical or rational, but it often exists because of the innate comfort people feel with conventional or established arrangements.[2]

Tradition not only holds people together, but keeps them on a proven path. When the Framers took the large steps in 1787 to create the Constitution, they fused a new political system with long-standing colonial values. Concerned about the potential of excessive power and longing to include those who had been excluded from power, the Framers designed a complex arrangement. In Richard Hofstadter's words, the new system of power "would check interest with interest, class with class, faction with faction, and one branch of government with another in a harmonious system of mutual frustration,"[3] while simultaneously providing orderly governance. Many compromises emerged, including the "checks and balances" of the three branches of national government and an awkward arrangement that put the slavery issue out of range, at least until the moments before the Civil War.[4] But when it came to the use of power of government, the debate over the distribution between the national and state units carried particular sway. Thus, the division and assignments of powers among the various levels of government became a constitutional cornerstone, although the Framers were not in complete agreement as to the details of its makeup.

But what about today? Have the powers of government tilted more toward the national government or the states, and does it matter?

No one makes the case for a state-centered federal arrangement more forcefully than Robert Nagel, who notes that the Constitution was enacted to preserve broad regulatory power at the state and local levels "to ensure a sufficient supply of centrifugal political energy to maintain a national government of limited powers."[5] Under such a system, the national government, while stronger than the first attempt at political organization, would complement enduring state authority. This approach was embraced by the Anti-Federalists, those who preferred government power to spring largely from the states, where such powers would be controlled by the people. In recent years, advocates with values along these lines have been referred to as adherents to the states' rights approach to federalism.

Nagel's claim is countered by those who see value in a growing role for the national government, even if it comes at the cost of state and local authority. The adherents of strong national power point to a society that is much different today than in the early days of the Republic. Thus, referring to the sweeping economic, social, and political changes that transformed the United States over the past two hundred plus years, Michael Reagan and John Sanzone conclude that "we have now arrived at a point in our constitutional history where no sphere of life is beyond the reach of the national government."[6] A clean environment, the safe composition of food and drugs, and a reliable highway system are but a few of the many public policy examples where the national government exercises its will. The changes associated with modernization of the United States have spilled over to political adjustments as well. This openness to an expanding role of the national government was the rallying theme of the **Federalists**. In recent years, this mantle has been assumed by those associated with the national dominance style of federalism.

Over the years, scholars, practitioners, and everyday Americans have relied upon the Philadelphia agreement as a sacred benchmark for the assignment of authoritative activities to and among governments. However, talking about federalism in grand theoretical terms can be quite different from nuts-and-bolts applications of the concept. Though most accept the tradition of federalism, many differ on its limits and opportunities today, as attested by the debate described above.

Still, whatever the intentions of the Framers, we cannot dispute the rather limited objectives associated with the earliest interpretations of American federalism. In the following pages, we will examine the constitutional framework and its inherently conservative bias. And while federalism as a concept has been subject to change at various junctures in the nation's history, such changes have come at a price from the perspective of the traditionalists.

Tradition: The Conservative Ethic in America

Whatever the anti-British fervor of the Revolutionaries, the last thing they wanted was anarchy. Thus, as they struggled to form a more open, inclusive government, they also settled on an arrangement based more on vigilance and distrust than automatic acceptance and embrace of any new authority. Historian Richard Hofstadter describes the extent to which distrust framed the new political arrangement: "Since man was an unchangeable creature of self-interest, it would not do to leave anything to his capacity for restraint. It was too much to expect that vice could be checked by virtue; the Fathers relied instead upon checking vice with vice."[7] Simply put, people could not be trusted to their own devices, lest they succumb to their darker, self-centered sides. And so began an effort to create a source of comprehensive power for the public good by dividing power among those who would use it.

Operating on a theoretical principle of "mixed government," the Framers designed an intricate system—really two systems—where there would be competition among branches *and* between levels of government.[8] James Madison articulated both the concern and the hope of multiple interests (which he called factions) expressing themselves in and out of the halls of government, ultimately leading to a balance where all views would be espoused, yet none would dominate. His theory included the execution of political power among the states. Thus, in Federalist #10, Madison wrote: "The influence of factious leaders may kindle a flame within their particular States, but will not be able to spread a general conflagration through the other states."[9] To deny the existence of such energy would be foolish, if not harmful to the nation as a whole. At least in the early going, practitioners of government at the national level realized that the demands of the states "were more popular politically than any national, centralized, tax-supported program."[10] Even Federalist Madison recognized that whatever the delicate balance of power achieved on paper in Philadelphia, the states seemed to carry more sway with the public as dispensers of power in the early days of the new arrangement.

To Trust or Not to Trust the People—Conflicting Themes

For every step the Framers took to advance the idea of a strong central government, they took another to counter the potential for excess. Intended or otherwise, it was an extraordinary balancing act that has served as a source of creative tension for more than two hundred years. Yes, the new system of governance would greatly increase national power; however, a carefully crafted division of authority among three branches would require incredible cooperation and synchronization to make and carry out decisions. Further, most of the methods of selecting leaders would be such that a few elites would temper any runaway passions of the masses.

Indirect Selection

Although the new nation's warriors fought for a system that would create a more direct representation of the governed by their governors, ultimately the Framers relied upon indirect selection and appointment as fundamental guiding principles for much of the government structure. At issue here was more than the simple division of authority into a format that would balance the use of power through a system of "checks and balances"; rather it was an effort to make sure that the will of the people would be tempered through various filtering networks that blunted any threats of radicalism.

The United States Senate

Many at Philadelphia worried that the will of the new American elites would be swept away with the zeal to bring heretofore repressed interests to America's enlarged "political table." The selection of U.S. senators by state legislatures offered the hope of keeping elite values in a prominent position of power. The appointment of U.S. senators by these bodies virtually guaranteed a national upper house with values far removed from the masses. "Bicameralism," Saul Cornell writes, "in this scheme, reflected the existence of a clear division between patricians and plebeians and embodied the virtues of both social classes."[11] The voices of "the people" would be heard unequivocally enough with the direct election of the members of the House of Representatives, the legislative body with two-year terms of office. Organization of the Senate, however, was another matter. Not only would the terms of office be relatively long at six years, but determination of the individuals chosen for this body would be through state legislators, a kind of filtering mechanism.

Selection of U.S. senators by the states also eased worries about the new national government having too much control. With state legislatures shaping composition of the upper chamber of the U.S. Congress, states enjoyed considerable direct influence over national policymaking.[12] This political arrangement continued until ratification of the Seventeenth Amendment in 1913, which established direct election of U.S. senators. Nevertheless, the constitutional mechanism set into play a tradition that allowed direct representation of state interests for more than a century.

The Presidency

The Framers set up a system where the nation's chief executive would be selected not directly by the people but indirectly by the states. Each state would be allocated a number of "electoral votes" equal to its total of U.S. senators and members of the House of Representatives; with small states having at least three electoral votes (two senators and a minimum of one representative), their influence would be strong, perhaps disproportionately so.

Members of the Electoral College were intended to reflect the results of the popular votes for president in each state. At first, states doled out electoral votes on a proportional basis, but by 1836 all of the state legislatures established bloc awards—that is, whoever captured more votes in the state than anyone else would be declared the winner and receive all of the state's electoral votes.[13] Afterward, the candidate receiving a majority of electoral votes would be declared the winner, with the candidate receiving the second highest number automatically becoming vice president. In the event that no candidate achieved a majority of electoral votes, the Framers decided that the House would select the president from among the candidates; however, each state would have one vote in the process, again giving disproportionate power to the small states.

Two outcomes emerged from indirect election of the president: First, the people would not be casting their votes directly, but rather in state blocs; through this mechanism, states would negotiate with each other to select a winner. Second, the Electoral College, the body of delegates chosen by each of the various states in accordance with their allocated numbers, would have final say over who would become president. Cumbersome, perhaps, but these mechanisms seemed to solve several problems at once. As James Pfiffner concludes, for those who favored state control, state legislatures could decide electors. For those who were concerned about too much democracy, electors would be anything but common folk.[14] Regardless, in terms of federalism, the states were given tremendous say over the selection of president. For the most part, state control of voting systems and conditions of participation continued well into the twentieth century.

Indirect Selection as the Guardian of State Influence

There was nothing haphazard about the decisions of the Framers to establish legislative involvement in the selection of two of the three branches of the new national government. Through these unique linkages, the delegates "hoped those [state] governments would accept the reduction of their state power" that had presided over—and ruined—the first organization of the United States government.[15] Clearly, the states remained a player in the federal arrangement, a condition that served as the political baseline for arguments long after the arrangement and its reshaping through the Seventeenth Amendment.

The Constitution: Assigned Powers and Early Interpretations

Aside from the thorny issues of representation, the Framers had to decide how to parcel out authority. As discussed in Chapter 2, the debates focused on finding some middle ground between the overly centralized and unrepresentative national model used by the British and the decentralized and disjointed state-centric model created under the Articles of Confederation. Carefully and deliberately, the Framers assigned some powers to the national government, some powers to the state government, and some powers jointly to both levels of government.

National Powers

Led by James Madison and Alexander Hamilton, the Framers created an instrument of government with national powers considerably greater than those of its predecessor. As initially conceived, the Constitution consisted of seven articles. In terms of federalism arrangements, the first four articles contain most of the prescriptions for the exercise of power and authority: Article I defines the powers of the national legislature, while Article II deals with the powers of the national executive. The powers associated with Article III, the national judiciary, were vaguely worded, and became the springboard for vigorous debates that persist to this very day. As for the powers and guarantees to the states, Article IV is the centerpiece for this discussion.

A cautionary note: There are areas in the remaining three articles that focus on the divisions of power as relating to the national government versus the states. Article VI, particularly, acknowledges the laws of the United States as "the Supreme Law of the Land," hardly a trivial issue in this discussion. The remaining articles will be visited as necessary; nevertheless, the focus here is on the first four articles as the most significant elements for assigning power.

Article I

Consisting of ten sections, Article I declares that "All legislative Powers herein granted shall be vested in a Congress of the United States, which shall consist of a Senate and House of Representatives" (Section 1). The article goes on to describe the selection mechanisms (Sections 2, 3, 4), internal organization (Sections 5, 6), and origins of legislation by chamber (Section 7). With respect to federalism, the most important elements of Article I appear in the last three sections.

Over the years, perhaps the greatest attention has focused upon Section 8, which describes a litany of enumerated, or listed, powers of Congress including the right to collect taxes, borrow money, regulate commerce, coin money, establish a post office, declare war, and create an army and navy. However, it is the last part of Section 8 that has caused the most stir over the past two centuries. It reads that Congress shall have the ability "to make all laws which shall be necessary and proper for carrying into Execution the foregoing Powers, and all other Powers vested by this Constitution in the Government of the United States." Known as the **elastic clause** because of its lack of clear boundaries, this section has been viewed as "the chief basis for later expansion of national authority" through repeated attention of the federal courts,[16] and a joyful clause for the Federalists.

The last two sections of Article I focus on restrictions of congressional power and the states. In Section 9, the thorny issue of slavery, on which the states were divided, is addressed through a prohibition against imports after 1808. In addition, this section prevents suspending a **writ of habeas corpus** (a petition asking a judge to show why someone has been imprisoned) and disallows passage of **ex post facto** laws (laws passed after the fact). The section denies Congress the right to tax state exports. Section 10 excludes the states from signing treaties, coining money, and charging import or export duties.

All told, Article I makes Congress a powerful player in national policymaking. Unlike the Articles of Confederation, this portion of the Constitution assigns numerous responsibilities to the legislative branch, differentiating governing obligations at the national level from those of the states. More ambiguous, however, is the extent to which Congress and the national government can undertake activities not explicitly mentioned in the Constitution.

Article II

The powers of the president, or chief executive, are defined in Article II. However, the Constitution is much less descriptive about the president's authority and functions compared to the specifics laid out for Congress in Article I.

As with the first portion of Article I, Section 1 of Article II has a "housekeeping" function, defining the method of election, requirements of the candidate, and succession should the president leave office. Section 2 centers on the president's powers, among them, his role as Commander in Chief of the military, power to make treaties (which take effect only upon acceptance by the Senate), and his right to nominate federal judges. Section 3 requires the president to report periodically to the Congress (annual State of the Union addresses) and deal with representatives from other countries. Section 4 covers the issue of and reasons for impeachment.

That the Framers intended to separate the president from the Congress through creation of a distinct set of powers is a "no brainer." Given the failings of an executive-less Articles of Confederation, this change was widely anticipated and considered necessary. Why the president's powers are not discussed in a level of detail similar to those of Congress, however, remains something of a mystery. Historian Jack Rakove suggests that the office was given a less detailed definition by the Framers because of their inability to agree on a clear set of powers, despite their desire to construct the office.[17] Regardless, given the lack of specificity, some observers contend that "the scope of presidential powers is not confined to those powers enumerated in the Constitution."[18] Given the myriad presidential activities over the years that have expanded the power of the national government, this distinction is significant.

Article III

Of the three articles outlining national power, Article III is by far the most mercurial. The general thrust of the article concerns an independent judiciary, but the lack of specificity regarding the judiciary's roles and powers left much to be desired. Section 1 speaks to the Supreme Court and the right of Congress to establish "inferior courts," which have been created as district courts, courts of appeals, and various "specialty" courts touching on unique issues such as patents, customs, and surveillance.[19] This section also provides the right of federal judges to hold their offices as long as they wish, assuming the absence of criminal behavior. Section 2 focuses on the types of jurisdiction for the courts, original and appellate. Both forms of jurisdiction relate to federalism—original, because of the Supreme Court's power in deciding cases where one state sues another, and appellate because of the Court's ability to hear cases upon appeal from lower federal courts or state courts in matters concerning issues pertaining to the United States Constitution. Section 3 defines treason and, as such, has little to do with the functioning of the judicial branch.

Considering that Article III carried the weight of a new and independent judiciary—judges independent of the other branches—brevity of the article brought about more confusion than consolation. Judicial scholars David Neubauer and Stephen Meinhold contend that the ambiguity was the natural outcome of a division of opinion between the Federalists and Anti-Federalists.

The former argued for sweeping judicial powers, including lower courts that would dispense uniform policy decisions, whereas the latter feared the Supreme Court would run roughshod over state issues.[20] Could it be that the lack of definition was the only way to prevent a major rupture at the Constitutional Convention? Inasmuch as the article "laid the foundation of the Supreme Court's ultimate right to define the nature and extent of state and national authority,"[21] conflict over the specifics of the judiciary in advance of adoption could well have become a pothole in the road to federalism. With the magnitude of the decisions handled by the Supreme Court regarding the powers of governments since the Constitution's creation, "crater" might be a better description.

Article IV

While the first three articles of the Constitution emphasize the national government and its authority, the Framers discussed state powers and the limits of those powers in Article IV. Section 1, the "full faith and credit" component, obligates the states to honor the laws of one another, thus acknowledging their political sovereignty regarding the potential encroachment of others. Section 2 further underscores the power of each state vis-à-vis the others in matters of criminality; thus, if someone commits a crime in one state and flees to another, the first state has the right to demand the individual's return. The essence of Section 3 focuses on the process for forming new states. This section also denies Congress the right to create new states from the land within existing states without permission of the affected states, something that has occurred on five occasions.[22]

Section 4 of Article IV has two major elements. First, it guarantees a "republican" form of government to each state, implying an oversight by Congress of the ways that states operate. Second, it protects the states against invasion from foreign countries, a major difference from the Articles of Confederation. Third, Section 4 gives the national government the power to intercede if the states succumb to domestic or internal violence.

Anti-Federalists hoped that Article IV would at least moderate some of the new powers handed to the national government in the first three articles. True, Article IV focuses more on the states than any other article of the Constitution. Yet a close reading shows, along with restraints against the national government, the article also emphasizes what states cannot do as much or more of the time than what they can do. Nevertheless, Samuel Beer notes "the states . . . opened to the people of the nation a second avenue, so to speak, by which to control and direct the federal government,"[23] and this was the central theme of the Anti-Federalists.[24] And whatever the shortcomings of the article, state concerns would be bolstered later on through ratification by the states of the Bill of Rights.

Collective Powers

What about changes to the Constitution, should the demands for such ever arise? Here again, the Framers trusted no one, and therefore assigned responsibility to everyone. As provided in Article V, amendments to the Constitution would be initiated only upon approval of two-thirds of each chamber in the Congress or petitions by two-thirds of the states. Ratification of any proposed amendment would occur only upon approval of three-fourths of the states. The objective here was reasonably clear: Not only did the Framers want both levels of government to share in any changes, but they made the process one that would require a near consensus for any change to occur. This requirement stemmed from the difficulties associated with extracting major compromises in Philadelphia.

The Framers certainly succeeded in limiting the possibility of changes—at least on paper. Other than the Bill of Rights, the first ten amendments, only seventeen other changes have been incorporated into the Constitution since its design.

The Bill of Rights

One would think that after all the effort at Philadelphia, everyone would take a breather before making changes to the new framework. But the agreements at the Convention, while one-sided, had left an ugly imprint in the minds of those who viewed the Constitution as tilting toward federal power to the point of threatening the freedom of individuals in the states. Convention delegate and non-signer Luther Martin made the point most emphatically when he stated, "It is the state governments which are to watch over and protect the rights of the individual."[25] The grumbles of the dissenters spilled over to the first Congress after the Convention, and soon led many Federalists, including the influential Madison, to conclude that further constitutional guarantees would be a wise investment to assuring both ratification and domestic tranquility.

Within days of the conclusion of the Convention's work, Anti-Federalists began organizing to recalibrate the newly created balance of power. By 1789, the Congress agreed to propose twelve amendments. The thrust in each case was to deny the federal government the ability to intrude on an aspect of individual life. Madison tried, and failed, to extend the guarantees against intrusion to the states as well, but his ideas would not be embraced until a series of U.S. Supreme Court decisions broadened the thrust of the Bill of Rights to the states, beginning in 1925.[26] Ultimately, the required number of states ratified ten proposed amendments, the combination of which became known as the Bill of Rights.

Curiously, individual rights were defined not by what people could do, but by what the national government could not do. Thus emerged a series of guarantees designed to placate those who feared a tyrannical national government. The First Amendment focuses on Congress guaranteeing freedoms of religion, speech, press, and assembly. The Second Amendment discusses a citizen's right to keep and bear firearms. The Third Amendment denies to the national government the ability to house soldiers in private homes without the householders' permission. The Fourth, Fifth, and Sixth amendments deal with aspects of criminal rights including protection against unreasonable search and seizure (Fourth), guarantees of "due process" when an individual is charged with a crime (Fifth), and a series of rights associated with trial (Sixth). In the Seventh Amendment, the right to a trial by jury is preserved. The Eighth Amendment assures that there will not be "cruel and unusual" punishment for someone convicted of a crime.

The two remaining amendments have loomed large in the assertion of states' rights, although one is much more famous than the other. The Ninth Amendment provides that whatever the enumerated powers in the Constitution, the document "shall not be construed to deny or disparage others retained by the people." And in the most famous component of the Bill of Rights, the Tenth Amendment, any powers not awarded to the national government "are reserved to the States respectively, or to the people." The Tenth Amendment, in particular, has been the rallying cry for Anti-Federalists at several points in American history. When one or more components of the national government have adopted or approved policies without any seemingly direct constitutional links, Anti-Federalists have seized upon the Tenth Amendment as their justification of the charge of usurpation.

Unanswered Questions

It all seemed to be such a puzzle, particularly to the extent that the division of powers between the national and state governments bordered on inconsistencies, if not outright contradictions. For all of their efforts to provide a superior form of collective governance, could not the Framers have been clearer about their intentions? Perhaps. Then again, perhaps constitutional ambiguity was preferred over political stalemate, always a possibility, given the passions of the Federalist and Anti-Federalist camps. Historian Michael Kammen suggests that the Framers intentionally chose deferral over deterioration: "The existence of various ambiguities of the Constitution meant that explication would subsequently be required by various authorities, such as the Supreme Court,"[27] even though the Framers were less precise in their description of the powers of the judiciary than the other two national branches. More than anything else, political realities seemed to dictate the behavior of the Framers. Clarification would come later.

Pitting Liberty against Equality?

The foregoing discussion points to a rational, slow, and steady movement of the nation to a mode of governance that emphasized national dominance over states' rights. Even Anti-Federalists acknowledged the need for some shift in balance, considering the lack of cohesion under the Articles of Confederation. But how much? National dominance promised a new level of equality in terms of the same general policies distributed throughout the nation. Given economic contentiousness, foreign entanglements, and the lack of political stability among the states prior to the Constitutional Convention, the promise of equality seemed a natural output of representative democracy. Such a system offered the hope that unity would flow from equality.

Yet many leaders worried that consolidating political power would come at the cost of liberty, a precious value for which many fought. Differences among the states remained in terms of agrarian versus commercial bases, different attitudes toward religion, and the ever-divisive question of slavery. Considering how the British centralized government had sapped the colonies of control and independence just a few years before the Constitutional Convention, clearly many state leaders viewed their governments as the best guarantors of liberty. After all, the people were much closer to this level of political organization than any national behemoth.

Liberty and equality are two critical centerpieces of democracy. However, in some respects these two philosophical giants stand at opposite ends of a political continuum, particularly in light of the competing sources of authority that promote them. The conflict seems all but unavoidable: The more that the national government is able to promote the same conditions and policies throughout the nation for all, the less that states can determine the well-being of their own people, hence the loss of individual liberty. Likewise, the more that states are able to design and implement policies befitting their populations, the less that the national government will be in position to apply the same policies to all people, hence the loss of same guarantees wherever one may reside. This debate was not only crucial in the days following the Constitutional Convention but remains a fundamental focal point of American politics today.

In Defense of Liberty

Anti-Federalists were known more for their opposition to the Constitution than any counterproposal, primarily because there were many sources of opposition. Some Anti-Federalists fretted that the new national government was dangerous because of the ambiguity associated with its composition. Anti-Federalist Elbridge Gerry wrote that "some of the powers of the [national] Legislature are ambiguous, and others indefinite and dangerous." He feared "that the executive had too much power over the Congress, and that the Courts would become oppressive."[28] Others viewed the states as repositories of liberty because of the large size of the federal government, an institution that could not possibly represent different needs in different locales. That said, for Anti-Federalists no concept was more treasured than liberty, for liberty focused on individual freedom, the most basic value. This theme was articulated often by Thomas Jefferson, principal author of the Declaration of Independence. Jefferson viewed the states as the repository of liberty because, in part, of the close connection between the people and their land.[29] Owning land, Jefferson said, would give people a stake in their society and connect them with the greater good. Whatever their reasons, however, Anti-Federalists shared the common belief that liberty would be best protected by the states.

The concept of liberty has remained a foundation for those who view the states as the rightful source of authority. Daniel Elazar, a leading architect in this school of thought, contends that states are historical repositories of citizen beliefs, values, and historical collective experiences. Under American federalism, although the Constitution may establish general guidelines and national institutions may forge policies, "the state governments are left to administer their own services within their own boundaries in a manner consonant with their respective policies."[30] Only extraordinary instances of compelling national need, he writes, would interfere with this foundation of power. Something akin to the terrorist attacks on the United States in September 2001 would no doubt qualify as a legitimate reason for federal intervention, but such experiences are clearly the exception to the rule.

Some scholars who praise liberty do so in the name of fending off national mediocrity. If the leaders in the national government embark on policies that impact people the same way everywhere, they will need to do so by focusing on the lowest common denominator in order to maintain tranquility. This can come at a substantial cost. Michael Greve writes that in policy areas ranging from wages to environmental protection, state policies may well exceed those reflecting any national "norm." If so, why should such states be denied? Then there is the question of differing approaches to basic social questions, to which Greve responds: "Some people do not wish to live near homosexual enclaves or in jurisdictions that permit same-sex marriages; others like a tolerant, bohemian environment. Some people feel good about themselves when banning smoking in public places; to others, such restrictions smack of creeping fascism."[31] Federalism, he concludes, should allow different populations to embrace policies consistent with their values; anything less is denial of fundamental liberty.

There is also the related question of competition among the states. While ruthless rivalries were in part responsible for bringing on the Philadelphia Convention, competition in the modern setting can provide valuable outcomes that may actually lead to national policies. Consider the use of vouchers in Wisconsin and Ohio as a way of improving the states' public education system, or health care cost containment in Oregon as a response to runaway costs. The Wisconsin and Ohio programs ultimately paved the way for national legislation providing financial assistance for a pilot program in Washington, D.C.[32] The Oregon case has contributed greatly to the national discussion on health care reform. No less a prominent spokesman for equality than former U.S. Supreme Court justice Louis Brandeis once wrote, "It is one of the happy incidents of the federal system that a single courageous State may, if its citizens choose, serve as a laboratory; and try social and economic experiments without risks to the country."[33] Competition, in this sense, brings out the best and the brightest possibilities for the states, allowing others to emulate and, perhaps, the national government to follow. Without the liberty to carry on such ways, modern Anti-Federalists argue, the nation would stagnate in mediocrity.

For states that seek to remain in control of their own destiny as much as possible, liberty is not simply a value—it is a rallying cry for sovereignty and independence. Hardly an anachronism of the 1780s, the theme resonates loudly today.

In Defense of Equality

Equality is a term with many meanings, particularly in contemporary America. For example, the debate over equality associated with affirmative action has long centered on the difference between "equality of opportunity" and "equality of outcome." Whereas in the first case government guarantees parity in advance of an event or circumstance, in the latter government assures similar conditions among individuals after an event or circumstance.[34] The great Federalist Alexander Hamilton focused on neither of these themes, instead viewing equality from the perspective of the way the national government would treat the people.

For Hamilton, the Constitution was a sacred compact between the national government and the people, not the national government and the states. Noting the failure of the states under the Articles to protect "the common defence and general welfare," Hamilton wrote in Federalist #23 that "we must abandon the vain project of legislating upon the States in their collective capacities; we must extend the laws of the federal government to the individual citizens of America."[35] That direct link was critical for the national government to succeed for the welfare of the nation, not as a means of ensuring the direct representation of individuals. If anything, Hamilton greatly distrusted the masses, but he very much favored a unified government presiding over the masses because the states were shortsighted and self-centered.[36] Only the national government could truly protect the public good.

Over the course of generations, Federalists have come to embrace the powerful national government envisioned by Hamilton as the best guarantor of equality in the sense that policies are applied universally throughout the nation. States, Federalists argue, are too likely to succumb to the self-centered demands of local pressures. Noting Madison's concerns about the perils of factions seeking to dominate one another, Michael Reagan and John Sanzone declared, "James Madison was, after all, right: The larger the area and diversity of populations encompassed in a governmental jurisdiction, the less the chance that any one faction will run roughshod over others."[37] No government in the United States is larger than the national government, and therefore no level other than the national government is more capable of dispensing policies in a uniform and fair manner. Further, the absence of national control threatens our well-being. Thus, William Hudson observes, to the extent that racial inequality, social inequality, and economic inequality are allowed to persist throughout the nation because of different state approaches, democracy is threatened.[38] The same could be said about public policies that receive radically different treatment from state to state.

Nationalization of the Bill of Rights has gone a long way toward providing similar circumstances for all Americans, particularly in terms of political opportunities. Ironically, the Bill of Rights, the first ten amendments to the Constitution, emerged largely out of concern by the Anti-Federalists that the new Constitution lacked sufficient protection for individuals against the government, particularly the national government. Yet, in a twist of application through judicial review in several cases over four decades, the Supreme Court declared the Bill of Rights a vital conduit for assuring equal treatment regardless of one's state, political affiliation, or social position. Between 1925 and the late 1960s, the Court expanded most of the guarantees against national government intrusion to the state governments as well. Thus, whatever the standards of the individual states, national interpretations would prevail.[39]

The results of this application have given life to the notion of equality in ways never anticipated by Hamilton, the Federalist. In the process of strengthening the national government, the Supreme Court has weighed in on issues ranging from abortion rights to search and seizure to capital punishment, and beyond. And even though recent Court decisions have not expanded national guarantees past the range established during the fertile four-decade period, the national government has emerged as a power player in federalism, often to the chagrin of those promoting state's rights and to the delight of those who see the national government as the protector of individual rights.

Tradition, Yes, But What Tradition?

That the United States is organized through federalism is beyond dispute; that decision was made in 1787 when the Framers committed to a new style of governance. But as the saying goes, "The devil is in the details." Setting up the new two-tiered level of governance was relatively easy compared to interpreting how the intertwined units would operate. Whatever its lack of specificity, the Constitution has assigned responsibilities. Interpreting its words over time has been another matter altogether. Even now, in the twenty-first century, there seem to be shortages of those "details."

4

★ ★ ★ ★

Institutional Change Agents
Political Wellsprings

Political institutions are the governing structures for societies. As repositories of power, they provide and enforce processes and policies for those people within their respective spheres of authority. Thus, the collections of political institutions in a city or state will have responsibilities unlike those possessed by national institutions overseeing an entire nation because they operate within different boundaries.

In addition to the differences within nations, there are differences among nations. Thus, the political institutions of democratic societies interact with their constituencies differently than those in dictatorial regimes.[1] Whereas authoritarian arrangements center upon the will of rulers and little else, democratic institutions respond to the public through a variety of mechanisms including elections within the context of well-developed rules and accepted means of application. Further, since democratic institutions dispense authority and power with some sense of accountability to the governed, they and those who serve in them are besieged by individuals, groups, and other governments to act in ways sympathetic to those interests. As Robert Dahl writes, "To influence the conduct of government is to influence the way it uses its powers of compulsion, coercion, punishment; its ability to allocate rewards, benefits, privileges, handicaps, wealth, incomes, influence, and power itself."[2] This ongoing tug-of-war characterizes the American political system not only within levels of authority but also between levels of authority.

The discussion above points to the malleability of American institutions. As our society has changed over the years, so our political institutions have changed with it—occasionally in concert with emergence of a particular issue or set of related issues, on other occasions long after the fact. Sometimes, these changes have transpired in the form of stronger national authority; other times, the changes have emerged in the form of stronger state authority. Regardless, change has occurred and continues to occur in response to changing issues and values. In this chapter, we turn to the major institutions at the national level—the courts, Congress, and the presidency—and their own changing roles in framing and reframing American federalism.

The Courts as Change Agents

Although the judiciary is the least detailed branch of the national government in the Constitution, it has changed the most over time. The evolution of national judicial power has occurred in two respects. First, the Court gave itself a prominent position in the organization of the national government by embracing the doctrine of **judicial review**. This concept allows judges to examine laws, executive orders, regulations, and other actions of governments in terms of whether they fit within the prescriptions of the Constitution, and has become a critical cornerstone of the Court's work. Second, armed with its new powers, the Court has emerged as the arbiter of claims made by the various levels of government both in terms of other levels and the people. The judicial interpretations of what policymakers in various levels can or cannot do has varied greatly over time. Unswerving, however, has been the Court's self-proclaimed right to consider constitutional issues.

Perhaps one of the greatest myths surrounding the judiciary lies in the claim that the courts have pursued a road of liberalism particularly since the 1950s, providing the way for the national government to gain power at the expense of the states. If "activism" means wielding power, such a claim has merit. However, the courts have at times exercised their power in ways that restrain all levels of government from acting against individual interests. In other instances, the courts have denied the national government authority in the name of state powers.

Judicial Review

The power of judicial review emerged in 1803 when the Supreme Court considered the case of *Marbury v. Madison.* In that case, William Marbury, a Federalist, sued James Madison, the secretary of state, to receive a judicial commission that Marbury had been awarded by fellow Federalist President John Adams in 1801 just before Adams left office and was succeeded by Anti-Federalist Thomas Jefferson. Marbury's new post, along with several others, awaited only delivery by the secretary of state. However, when Madison became Jefferson's secretary of state, Marbury's commission suddenly was no longer available. Marbury asked the Court for a writ of mandamus (an order forcing the appointment) compelling Madison to show why he should not be forced to give Marbury his appointment.

Writing for a unanimous Court, Marshall focused upon the nature of the appointment and the means by which Marbury was attempting to secure it. The Court agreed that Marbury deserved his commission. But Marshall and his colleagues concluded that the Court could not issue a writ of mandamus because this power, originating in Section 13 of the Judiciary Act of 1789, conflicted with the provisions of Article III of the U.S. Constitution. Therefore, Section 13 was unconstitutional inasmuch as Congress created policy that was beyond its authority. Out of this decision emerged the concept of judicial review.[3]

Whether the Framers intended to include judicial review as an arrow in the judiciary's quiver has been the subject of great debate between scholars almost since the first time the Court employed the concept.[4] The legality of this power is frequently questioned by those who believe its use by the Court lies beyond the Court's authority. Particularly when the Court overturns a long-held tradition or popular law, critics are most vocal. Nevertheless, judicial scholar Henry Abraham notes that "there is no longer any doubt that judicial review is a permanent fixture in the American structure and operation of government, notwithstanding the repeated frontal and guerilla attacks from both public and private sources."[5]

Arbiter of Power

The assumption of judicial review by Marshall and his colleagues gave the judiciary a place at the table of national power as a coequal branch of government. In using this tool since 1803, however, the Court also has defined the limits of government authority and drawn the line between the responsibilities of the states and the national government. Writing about judicial review, R. Kent Newmyer observes, "Not only did the Court legitimize national power but [it] also influenced the manner in which power was used to achieve policy" by the national government.[6] By affecting the capabilities of the national government, the Court, by extension, has impacted the capabilities of the state governments.

The role of the Court as the arbiter of power has been a point of dispute ever since the judiciary began using judicial review. The debate has been spirited. Writing in defense of the Court's power, Jeffrey Segal and Harold Spaeth note that "the constitutional division of governmental power between the states and Washington, as well as among the three branches of the federal government, requires some entity to resolve the conflicts that such division and separation produces." Out of necessity, they conclude, the Supreme Court gave itself that authority.[7]

Just as powerful is the argument suggesting the judiciary routinely oversteps the boundaries of federalism, denying states their due as governments close to the people. Thus, contends Robert Nagel, the Supreme Court routinely decides case by expanding individual rights at the expense of state sovereignty: "The essential task of judges, of course, is to resolve cases, and to do this they need to find some controlling authority . . . to the extent that it is definite, unambiguous, and permanent." For the justices to appreciate fully why states exist would, in their minds, undermine that national authority. That is why judges resist constitutional values in the interest of expediency.[8]

Whether the Supreme Court should play such a definitive role in determining the boundaries of federalism is clearly an argument without resolution. Regardless, almost all observers acknowledge that the Court has assumed such power. Equally significant, however, is that the Court has redefined the boundaries of federalism several times, depending upon emerging issues, changing values of society, and the jurists' interpretations of how those issues and values mesh with the Constitution. These eras are described below.

1803 to Late 1830s

Between 1787 and 1803, the Supreme Court maintained a low profile, restricting its decisions to narrow matters largely relating to the encroachment of state legislative acts on the national Constitution.[9] In *Marbury v. Madison*, under the leadership of Chief Justice John Marshall (who served from 1801 to 1835), however, the Court clearly established its role as the interpreter of constitutional questions. This in itself represented a remarkable recalibration of the **separation of powers doctrine**, yet even more fertile ground was covered over the next thirty years.

In the period immediately following *Marbury*, the Court continued to reinforce its role as national arbiter. In 1819, the justices discussed the question of national government preeminence in *McCulloch v. Maryland*, which centered on whether a state could tax a branch of the United States Bank. In this early defining moment of federalism, Marshall and his colleagues unanimously found that the Congress did have the power to create a national bank. In addition, the Court held that while states and the national government had their own spheres of sovereignty, national sovereignty is supreme over state sovereignty. As a result, Maryland had no power to tax an instrument of the national government. With this and other decisions soon to follow, the Court embraced the **doctrine of implied powers**, holding that many of the national government's powers were implied by the language in Article I, Section 8, and Article VI, Section 2, of the Constitution.

To be sure, the Court's decisions during the Marshall years offended Anti-Federalists, particularly Southerners, who argued that they violated the delicate compromises on power that had been secured in Philadelphia and intruded unnecessarily upon the will of the people. In summarizing the Anti-Federalist argument of the day, Saul Cornell writes, "The states were the only true guardians of the people's rights, and it was essential that they retain the ability to judge infractions that violated the Constitution."[10] As protectors of individual rights, states, Anti-Federalists argued, were jeopardized by overtly nationalist policies handed down by an unresponsive Court. Nevertheless, the Marshall Court set two unmistakable standards in the early years of the Republic: judicial power and a strong national government.

Late 1830s to 1937

Beginning in the late 1830s, the Court changed course on the delineation of national and state powers, while maintaining its authority to make such determinations. Once again, with Roger Taney serving as Chief Justice between 1836 and 1864, the Court was assured a steady voice. Thanks to numerous vacancies, President Andrew Jackson had the ability to appoint seven justices during his eight years in office, assuring a Court that would closely mirror his suspicions of excessive government and concern for popular sovereignty.

The Taney Court embraced citizen participation as a guarantor of democracy. A slave owner and native of Maryland, however, Taney defined "citizen participation" as the involvement of all white males, irrespective of property. At the same time, Taney and his colleagues distrusted government power, particularly at the national level. "If government action were required [to manage an issue], it was both democratic and practical to let the states take the initiative."[11] Whatever the limitations by twenty-first-century standards, the change from the Marshall Court was palpable. Whereas the Marshall Court stretched the Constitution through sweeping interpretations of the interstate commerce clause and references to the general welfare, the Taney Court offered narrow approaches. Seizing upon the development of nineteenth-century capitalism, the Court "modified constitutional federalism to accommodate the new responsibilities which fell to the states in banking, internal improvements, and economic promotion and regulation."[12] Decisions were predicated upon the value that the states were the political vehicles best able to drive the nation's economy.

The economic dispositions of the Taney Court guided decisions regarding social issues as well. Nowhere was the philosophy better displayed than in *Dred Scott v. Sandford* (1857), which dealt with the slavery issue. Although the Framers largely had dodged the question, economics and social values clashed increasingly to the point where slavery emerged as a burning national political debate. The matter came to a head when Dred Scott, a slave, sued for his freedom after his master's death in Illinois, a "free" state. By a 7–2 vote, the Taney Court responded that whatever Scott's rights in Illinois, there was also the question of national citizenship. Negroes were not citizens but property and, as such, had no rights to sue anywhere. The majority went on to say that Congress could not deny the right of property, and declared unconstitutional the Missouri Compromise of 1850, which had stipulated where slavery would and would not be permitted. That being the case, the earlier decision by the Missouri State Supreme Court spurning Scott's claim would stand. This decision added to the furor that would soon manifest as the Civil War.

Whatever the Civil War determined regarding slavery, its outcome had little impact upon the Court for another seventy years, long after the departure of Roger Taney, as the jurists continued to approach equality on very narrow terms. In *Plessy v. Ferguson* (1896), the issue revolved around an African American in Louisiana who was denied access to a "white" railroad car, so designated because of a law passed by the state legislature in 1880 that provided "equal but separate" railroad cars for African Americans. Plessy sued, claiming that the "equal protection" of the post–Civil War Fourteenth Amendment ratified in 1868 prohibited separation by race. Voting 7–1, the justices ruled that the separation of people by race did not violate the Fourteenth Amendment because Plessy was able to travel to the same place at the same time as whites.

The political basis for independent state authority was sharply affirmed just after the Civil War in *Texas v. White* (1869). The state of Texas attempted to collect a debt that had accrued during the Civil War, but the defendant countered that the claim was groundless inasmuch as Texas ceased to exist as a state during the period. A 6–3 vote of the Court concluded that the union of Texas and the other states was indivisible; as such, Texas had the right as a state to collect on its debt. The significance here is that the Court expressly acknowledged the significance of states as independent agents in the federal system.

Cases other than race were decided on similarly narrow grounds. In 1908, the Court considered whether a state could have different working conditions for men and women. The justices unanimously agreed in *Muller v. Oregon* that the state's rules did not violate the "equal protection" guarantees of the Fourteenth Amendment. Such an approach continued to underscore the power of the Tenth Amendment, which left those matters not assigned to the national government in the hands of the states.

The Court's narrow view persisted into the Great Depression. After Democrat Franklin D. Roosevelt became president in 1933, Congress passed the National Industrial Recovery Act (NIRA), which authorized the executive branch to manage the nation's economic crisis in new expansive ways. Roosevelt then approved via executive order new rules for the poultry industry on everything from slaughter to sales. A poultry company sued, arguing that Roosevelt and the national government exceeded their authority. In *A.L.A. Schechter Poultry Corp. v. United States*, the Court unanimously agreed that the national government had overzealously used the interstate commerce clause, the basis for the executive order.

None of the discussion above is intended to suggest that the Supreme Court always undermined the national government in favor of the states. In many instances, the Court restrained both governments, particularly to the extent that they hampered the growth of business.[13] However, more times than not, on questions relating to equality, commerce, police powers, family and criminal law, the state views were upheld, particularly in clashes with national government claims. To this end, the Court narrowed the role of the federal government.

1937 to mid-1980s

The thinking of the Court's majority took a sharp turn yet again in 1937. For four years between 1933 and 1936, an ambitious Roosevelt and Democratic Congress enacted countless legislative changes designed to use the power of the national government to leverage the nation out of economic calamity. Virtually every effort attracted a lawsuit, followed by a Supreme Court decision overturning the law as unconstitutional. Then with his overwhelming reelection victory in 1936, Roosevelt proposed to restructure the Supreme Court. For every justice beyond the age of seventy, another justice would be added, with the total membership not to exceed fifteen. The potential of six new justices offered the possibility for Roosevelt to mold a Court majority favorable to his policies.[14] Passage of a new statute by the Democratic Congress could legalize such a change, although tampering with tradition would no doubt present a political risk. Nevertheless, with the Roosevelt proposal under consideration, several justices seemed to change course.

The first result was seen as early as 1937, just months after the Roosevelt proposal, beginning with the Court's opinion in *National Relations Labor Board v. Jones and Laughlin Steel Corporation*. Created by Congress in 1935, the NLRB was empowered to investigate charges of employer interference with union activity under the auspices of the interstate commerce clause. Attorneys for the steel company argued that the legislation actually interfered with commerce, but a narrow 5–4 vote defined labor conditions as part of commerce, thereby upholding the law and creating a strong position for the national government. The New Deal justices ruled again shortly thereafter in *Helvering v. Davis*, a case that tested the constitutionality of the Social Security system enacted by Congress in 1935. The plaintiff claimed that the Congress had violated the Tenth Amendment by taxing individuals and companies. This time, a solid majority (7–2) replied that Congress simply had addressed the old age security issue in the context of the "general welfare" as provided in Article I, Section 8.

The sharp about-face of the Supreme Court after the Roosevelt gambit signaled a dramatic shift in the assignment of powers and responsibilities. So radical was this change that Michael Reagan and John Sanzone refer to it as the "constitutional revolution of 1937."[15]

As with the previous era, many of the first decisions regarding federalism during the New Deal focused on economic questions critical to the well-being of the nation. But there were social issues, too. Several such decisions occurred during the stewardship of Chief Justice Earl Warren (1953–69). In the 1954 landmark *Brown v. Board of Education* case, the Court reversed *Plessy v. Ferguson* by a 9–0 vote, declaring that "separate but equal" is inherently unequal and therefore violated the equal protection clause of the Fourteenth Amendment. With this decision, the Court denied states the right to segregate public education and eventually all forms of public accommodations. Regarding the issue of representation, the Court took on the rights of states to redistrict in a series of cases, beginning with *Baker v. Carr* in 1962, forcing the state of Tennessee to apportion its lower house legislative districts so that they reflected "one man, one vote" as guaranteed under the equal protection clause. That decision was followed by others that required similar compositions for state upper houses and congressional districts.[16]

With respect to individual liberties, the Warren Court issued numerous rulings based upon interpretations of the Bill of Rights. Many decisions denied various police powers to the state governments that had been part of their arsenal for the better part of two centuries. Particularly during the 1960s, the Court addressed search and seizures, the right to counsel, and a fair trial and privacy, usually limiting the scope of state clout vis-à-vis the individual.[17]

Warren retired in 1968, and several colleagues on the Court stepped down or passed away shortly thereafter. As a result, President Richard Nixon was able to appoint four justices, including Chief Justice Warren Burger, within the first three years of office. The role of the Court in defining federalism was a critical political element to Nixon. During his presidential campaign, Nixon promised to restore "law and order" through appointing judges who would view the Constitution through the lens of "strict constructionism," thereby reversing many activist decisions of the Warren Court.[18] The lynchpin of the strategy was to turn back to the states responsibilities for management of criminal issues. Yet the shift was not as abrupt as some had hoped.

Although more conservative than its predecessor, the Burger Court perpetuated the concept of judicial activism. True, in criminal cases, the Court curbed earlier decisions. For example, after temporarily banning the death penalty because of Eighth Amendment concerns for "cruel and unusual punishment," a 7–2 vote in *Gregg v. Georgia* (1976) ruled that states could impose capital punishment under strict guidelines. Other national guarantees were also trimmed. In *Bakke v. Regents of the University of California* (1978), a bitterly divided Burger Court upheld the concept of affirmative action in principle, but denied the use of quotas as a mechanism for achieving affirmative action. In *Harris v. New York* (1971), the Court eased the requirements for obtaining confessions without clear opportunities for counsel; in *United States v. Leon* (1984), the justices voted to ease the tests for search warrants. In at least one early case, *Roe v. Wade* (1973), the Burger Court bucked the trend and paved new ground regarding a woman's right to choose an abortion. Nevertheless, for the most part, the Court muted numerous Warren Court decisions. A study of the Burger era found that support for civil liberties, particularly those applying to criminal cases, fell from 80 percent in 1968 to 34 percent in 1985, a powerful indication of the shift of the Court's majority.[19]

On other matters, the Burger Court swung to the states, although not always with great clarity. In *National League of Cities v. Usery* (1976), a divided Court ruled 5–4 that Congress had exceeded its powers by requiring local governments to abide by the federal minimum wage. But a decade later, in *Garcia v. San Antonio Metropolitan Transit Authority* (1985), the Court went the other way by a 5–4 vote, declaring the *National League of Cities* decision unworkable. Whatever the confusion, for the most part the Court seemed ready to once again embrace the merits of state authority. In the case of *Silkwood v. Kerr-McGee* (1984), the justices allowed the state of Oklahoma to establish the financial remedy for corporate mismanagement of a nuclear power plant even though Congress has authority over safety at such facilities. Writing about the Burger Court, David Walker finds that it upheld state levies on imports, was more willing to allow states to determine the conditions of legislative redistricting, and accepted state property tax methods even though they might not apply equally to all populations.[20]

The Burger Court remained activist, despite moderating twenty years of decisions protecting the rights of criminals. "On balance," conclude David Neubauer and Stephen Meinhold, the Burger Court "was more conservative than its predecessor, but there was no constitutional revolution, only modest adjustments."[21] The direction of the Court may have shifted toward the end of this period, but the fact remains that the justices were not shy about wielding authority.

Mid-1980s to the Present

The somewhat inconsistent decisions of the Burger Court yielded to a period of renewed energy for more states' rights and restrictions on the national government. This approach was led by Chief Justice William Rehnquist, who was elevated to his post from his position as associate justice by President Ronald Reagan in 1986.

More than any other Court in recent memory, the Rehnquist Court underscored the value of states in the federal arrangement. In a series of cases, the Rehnquist Court renewed the dual federalism arguments so clearly expressed in the *Texas v. White* case more than one hundred years earlier. One such decision occurred in 1992, when the Environmental Protection Agency, an agency of the national government, attempted to force the state of New York to dispose of radioactive waste. By a 6–3 vote, the Court in *New York v. the United States* held that any such effort violated the Tenth Amendment.

Similarly, in *Printz v. the United States* (1997) the Court struck down the Brady Act requiring mandatory state and local background checks of prospective gun buyers by ruling that the law violated state sovereignty.

The Rehnquist Court relied upon justifications other than the Tenth Amendment to defend state sovereignty. Protection of the states against lawsuits from the federal government was affirmed in a narrow 5–4 vote in a 1996 case, *Seminole Tribe v. Florida*, where the justices ruled that states cannot be sued by Indians in federal courts. Similarly, in 2002 the Court decided also by a one-vote margin (5–4) in *Federal Maritime Commission v. South Carolina Ports Authority* that states could not be sued by companies in federal courts. The long-term significance of the last two cases remains to be seen, not only because of their narrow margins but because they were based on the Eleventh Amendment, rather than the Tenth.[22] Still, as a state attorney general noted, "there are five justices who care deeply about the states having a strong independent role."[23]

On matters relating to civil liberties, the Rehnquist Court reinvigorated the power of the states in several areas. With respect to abortion, on several occasions the Court allowed states to regulate the conditions under which women choose abortion while upholding a woman's right to choose. In *Planned Parenthood of Southeastern Pennsylvania v. Casey* (1992), the Court agreed that the state could require a twenty-four-hour waiting period before permitting an abortion. Five years later, the Court redefined the separation between religion and the state in *Agostini v. Felton* (1997) when a narrow majority approved state-funded public school teachers' working in parochial schools.

Not all Rehnquist Court decisions supported the states. Decisions limiting the use of the death penalty against retarded individuals and minors are two such examples.[24] Additionally, the Court found repeatedly for the national government with respect to the unconstitutionality of state laws that permit the sale of medical marijuana, such as the 8–0 decision in *United States v. Oakland Cannabis Buyers' Cooperative* (2001).

In a particularly ironic twist, the conservative five-vote bloc of the Court defied its growing states' rights reputation when ruling on *Bush v. Gore* in 2001. Due to an incredibly tight presidential election vote, Florida officials had begun a recount to determine the outcome of the 2000 race there, with the national outcome hinging on the Florida result. The campaign organization of Democratic presidential candidate Al Gore asked the U.S. Supreme Court to uphold a process established by the Florida State Supreme Court, a Tenth Amendment argument to be sure. Meanwhile, the legal team of Republican opponent George W. Bush requested that the Court overrule the Florida decision on Fourteenth Amendment grounds. The High Court held that the Florida recount system was so flawed that voters could not possibly receive "equal protection under the laws," a Fourteenth Amendment argument, and that the recount should cease with Bush holding a 533-vote lead in the race.

The *Bush v. Gore* decision based upon Fourth Amendment grounds represented a radical departure of the behavior of the Rehnquist Court, leading some people to wonder whether the Court had become unduly politicized.[25] Nevertheless, more times than not, the Rehnquist Court moved aggressively toward the states on matters relating to commerce, civil rights, gun control, and environmental protection.[26] As with the other eras, the justices were not reluctant to push the judicial activist envelope.

With the appointment of new Chief Justice John Roberts, Jr., in 2005 and new Justice Samuel Alito in 2006—both viewed as conservatives—observers expect the Court will continue on its current path on federalism-related issues well into the future. An early indication of the Court's comfort with states' rights may be with its response to *Gonzales v. Oregon*, a case that sought to overturn Oregon's Death with Dignity Act, which allows terminally ill individuals to request lethal prescriptions from physicians under strict conditions. U.S. attorney general John Ashcroft had attempted to neutralize the decision by contending that the lethal drug prescriptions were under jurisdiction of the federal government's Controlled Substances Act. However, by a vote of 6–3, the majority wrote that to accept Ashcroft's interpretation would allow the attorney general "to effect a radical shift of authority from the states to the federal government to define general standards of medical practice in any locality."[27] Chief Justice Roberts, as it turns out, was in the minority; Justice Alito joined the Court too late to participate in the case.

The Supreme Court as a Coequal Branch

When the Framers created Article III and the Supreme Court in Philadelphia, no one forecast that the judiciary would emerge as a powerful institution. But it has become a great balancer of political power, bringing joy to some and hand-wringing to others, depending upon its management of countless issues. Whatever else, the Court has emerged as a major player in defining and redefining federalism—a role that few people initially anticipated.

The President as a Change Agent

If the organization of the federal judiciary initially was something of an enigma to the Framers, the presidency was not. There was no easy solution to bridging the concerns of those who feared an American monarchy and those who were just as concerned about reprising the rudderless Articles of Confederation. Out of this tension emerged the design of the presidency. Whatever the preliminary blueprint of the office, however, the presidency has become a major institution in defining federalism. We will examine the office in two respects—the growth of the executive order and creation of the Office of Management and Budget.

The Executive Order

Nowhere in the U.S. Constitution is there precise language allowing the president to write executive orders. Just as with judicial review, however, presidents have assumed the power to issue decrees that are considered legally binding except where they conflict with a law passed by Congress or a decision of the federal courts. Absent those conditions, executive orders remain as policy until they are removed or replaced by the chief executive. Presidents have issued more than 13,000 executive orders since the administration of George Washington, each of which is published in the *Federal Register* unless it has national security implications. Through use of this tool, presidents have added to the power of the national government often at the expense of the states.

For the first hundred and forty years or so, presidential executive orders tended to be narrow in scope, often providing technical instructions to federal agencies about existing legislation. Occasionally, these directives would take on particular significance, such as when President Abraham Lincoln wrote the Emancipation Proclamation as an executive order in 1862. But until the 1930s, an executive order such as that written by Lincoln was very much the exception, although Theodore Roosevelt argued passionately for strong "presidential stewardship" during his presidency in the early years of the twentieth century.[28]

The U.S. Supreme Court provided a framework for defining the limits of executive orders in 1952. At that time, the justices ruled that an executive order issued by President Harry Truman temporarily seizing the nation's steel mills during the Korean War was a legislative act, and therefore a violation of the separation of powers doctrine.[29] Thus, as long as presidents do not overtly legislate, they may issue executive orders. Such admonitions have had little influence on the nation's chief executives. Kenneth Mayer writes that the Court's occasional restrictions notwithstanding, executive orders have become "presidential edicts, legal instruments that create or modify laws, procedures and policy by fiat."[30]

Through executive orders, presidents have affected the relationship between the national and state governments. Among the many executive orders issued by President Franklin D. Roosevelt were those providing federal protection of the civil rights of African Americans. In 1943, Roosevelt issued Executive Order 8802, creating the Fair Employment Practice Commission, a federal agency to investigate complaints of discrimination. President Harry Truman added to the federal government's role in civil rights when he desegregated the military with Executive Order 9981 in 1948. Similarly President John F. Kennedy issued a series of executive orders on housing, employment, and other issues related to civil rights. Lyndon Johnson advanced the equality question further by establishing affirmative action through Executive Order 11246 in 1965. In each case, presidents moved the power to desegregate from the states to an expanding national government.

Presidents also have affected state economies through executive orders. Shortly after the passage of the National Environmental Policy Act in 1969, President Richard Nixon signed an executive order creating the Environmental Protection Agency. The new organization assumed responsibility for air, water, and land pollution standards, enabling centralized administration.[31] Later, President Ronald Reagan signed another executive order, 12291, which stripped from the EPA a good deal of its rulemaking independence, sending such proposals first through the Office of Management and Budget. EO 12291 also mandated a regulatory impact analysis on any future rule that would cost the economy $100 million or more, a change described by one political scientist as "arguably the most significant incursion by any president into the core processes of rulemaking."[32] This order returned control of many environmental protection issues to the states.[33]

Some executive orders have spoken directly to the issue of state power. In 1987, Reagan issued Executive Order 12612, which deferred to the states interpretations of "national standards." This order became a "states' rights" signature piece of the Reagan administration. However, it was replaced by President Bill Clinton's Executive Order 13083 in 1993, allowing federal agencies to limit the policymaking capabilities of states and local governments. In 2002, President George W. Bush superseded Clinton's action with Executive Order 13274, which made transportation planning dependent upon the comments and feedback of representatives at all levels, including state and local. These examples show the extent to which chief executives have widened and narrowed federal and state policymaking opportunities through use of this tool.

As with judicial review, executive orders can move the nation in a variety of directions. Fundamentally, however, their contents and emphasis often alter the delicate power relationship between governmental units.

Office of Management and Budget (OMB)

One of the most significant executive orders signed by Richard Nixon, 11541, added yet more strength to the executive branch. Written in 1970, this order folded control of proposed regulatory changes into the newly created Office of Management and Budget (OMB), a beefed-up version of the Bureau of the Budget (BOB). The BOB had been created by Congress in 1921 as part of the Treasury Department, and then moved to the Executive Office of the President in 1939, to assist the president with the budgetary process. Now, through the OMB, all decisions regarding federal regulations would have to pass the "smell test" at the White House. Successive presidential administrations have put their own spin on the new and more powerful OMB.

The Nixon administration had a rather benign view of the OMB, using the new agency as a giant net to manage any and all regulatory concerns. Other administrations have put their own imprints on the rulemaking capabilities of the OMB. During the Carter administration, for example, the OMB emphasized rational decision making as the basis for determining whether proposed rules made sense. The OMB became somewhat more politicized under the Ronald Reagan and George H.W. Bush administrations. During this twelve-year period, the White House was much less likely to intervene in state or local affairs. Particularly during the Reagan presidency, the OMB "gave up its role as protector of [federal] agencies against sudden and unreasonable reductions,"[34] thereby shifting more control to the states on a variety of issues ranging from mass transit to welfare.[35] The Clinton administration utilized the OMB only for "economically significant" decisions, leaving minor questions to the various agencies in place. Most recently, the George W. Bush team has been very slow to adopt new rules.[36] In fact, the Bush administration began in 2001 with a six-month moratorium on all proposed regulations.

Among these various interpretations of executive authority, one fact is clear: the OMB has moved from a politically passive "bean counting," numbers-crunching administrative office to a policymaking entity of great reach. To the extent that the agency promotes or discourages federal regulations of the economy, environment, workplace, or any other policy area, state powers are affected.

Of the recent presidents, Ronald Reagan and Bill Clinton both came to the White House after serving as the governors of their states. As such, they were familiar with the love/hate relationship that often occurs in federal/state entanglements. Their common political backgrounds notwithstanding, each used the OMB in different ways to change federal/state government regulations. Their efforts showed the extent to which the OMB can be a powerful force in molding federalism.

As a critic of overly complex governmental relationships, Reagan pledged to deregulate the federal government's involvement in state and local affairs wherever possible. Nowhere were his administrative changes more telling than in environmental policies, where for years new regulations associated with the Clean Air Act had compelled the states to submit State Implementation Plans (SIPs) for complying with various federal environmental rules and regulations. Instead, rather than review SIPs for content and follow through, the OMB accepted state approaches as valid, regardless of the extent they varied from federal law.[37] The number of regulations put into place during the Reagan administration fell markedly, while countless others were rolled back. Although the impact of the national government clearly diminished, some critics viewed the changes as more helpful to big business than state and local governments.[38]

Bill Clinton shared Reagan's concern for excessive rulemaking. The major distinction between the two, however, lay in Clinton's willingness to use the OMB for important, broad-based changes. During the Clinton administration, the annual number of regulations promulgated by OMB declined. However, new rules proposed by agencies were vetted thoroughly and often changed by OMB personnel.[39] Ultimately, many of the rules adopted by the OMB during Clinton's administration moved toward additional economic and environmental regulation. The result was more centralized government.

George W. Bush, also a former governor, has left his own stamp on the OMB. Concerned about business being stifled by the federal government, Bush has consistently relied upon the OMB to prevent federal regulations that might be harmful to commerce.[40] By using his office to limit federal authority over economic matters, Bush has provided cover for state rulemaking.

The Power of Executive Authority

Executive orders and the OMB represent two tools for presidential influence on federal/state relations. Clearly, presidents use these tools for other purposes as well, such as extending the boundaries of presidential authority. Presidents also have indirect opportunities to impact federalism, such as their appointees to the U.S. Supreme Court and other judicial posts. Ronald Reagan, for example, was able to appoint four Supreme Court justices during his presidency, helping to forge a states' rights–tilting judiciary.[41] During the first five years of his presidency, George W. Bush had appointed one-quarter of the federal appeals court judges. With respect to immediate impacts, however, the ability of presidents to issue executive orders and OMB regulations gives them capabilities that others do not enjoy. [42]

Congress as a Change Agent

Unlike the courts or executive branch, Congress works in ways that require no explanation or interpretation. It has explicit constitutional expectations to legislate, or make laws, for the public good. Further, the impact of the work of Congress upon federalism has been most observable through the passage of national legislation and the development of grants-in-aid. Less clear has been any single direction of whether Congress has assumed more national power or protected the rights of states to address their own unique needs. The answer to that question seems to change with the times and the values of those in power. Nevertheless, as with the Courts and the executive branch, Congress is a player in defining and redefining American federalism.

National Legislation

The chief task of Congress is to legislate; clearly, the Framers were comfortable with representatives of the people having this role. In assessing the latitude accorded Congress in Article I of the Constitution, Roger Davidson and Walter Oleszek observe that "no one reading this portion of the Constitution can fail to be impressed with the Founders' vision of a vigorous legislature as a keystone of energetic government."[43] Early on after the ratification of the Constitution, Congress emerged as the dominant policymaking authority of the three branches. Historian Jack Rakove notes that "not only did it [Congress] enjoy the political advantages that flowed from popular election, it could also exploit its formal rule-making authority to circumscribe the discretion of the other branches, override particular decisions to which it objected, or use its power of the purse to make other departments bend to its will."[44] What may raise an eyebrow or two is the extent to which national legislation has molded federal/state relations.

During the nation's two-hundred-and-thirty-one-year history, Congress has participated in the national/state balance. Early in the 1800s, when Congress created the Bank of the United States, it assumed control of the monetary notes handled by state banks. After the Civil War, Congress was vigilant in enforcing its Reconstruction Acts in the South over the objections and interference of President Andrew Jackson. And during the early 1900s, Congress exerted its influence on interstate commerce by passing several laws that subjected the states to national regulation.

The activism of Congress vis-à-vis the states increased considerably with Franklin D. Roosevelt's New Deal, beginning in 1933. Among the many changes enacted during this period were the establishment of a federal power agency in Appalachia, a national unemployment program, and a law allowing the formation of workers' unions. These and other enactments shifted control of the economy and social programs from the bankrupt states to the national government. Similar federal activity occurred during the Great Society era of President Lyndon Johnson, when Congress passed a series of laws empowering officials of the national government to go into the states to register voters, thereby countering state segregationist policies that had left African Americans without the franchise.[45] So controversial were congressional efforts that a number of states rebelled, first through ignoring federal laws and later through large numbers of white voters supporting Republican Party candidates who called for the states to manage these issues.[46]

In recent years, Congress has continued its activism regarding the states. The most significant flashpoints have been social values and economic issues. Regarding social questions, Congress has enacted legislation requiring states to pass seat belt laws and minimum ages for the purchase of alcohol. In each of these cases, Congress has used the threat of withholding financial support from state projects, commonly highways, as the inducement for state cooperation.

Congress has also attempted to mold behavior of the states on the availability and control of firearms, although not with particular success nor any consistency. In 1990, Congress attempted to keep guns at least 1,000 feet from public schools through passage of the Gun-Free Zones Act, but the Supreme Court declared the legislation an unconstitutional use of the interstate commerce clause when it decided *U.S. v. Lopez* in 1995. In 1994, Congress, controlled by Democrats, turned to the issue of semi-automatic firearms and other military-style weapons. After a heated debate, national legislators passed the Violent Crime Control and Enforcement Act, commonly known as the Assault Weapons ban, a law with a ten-year life. The new law prevented the sale of weapons listed as "dangerous," thus taking the matter out of state hands. In 2004, with Republicans in charge and pressure from gun owner groups, Congress allowed the law to "sunset," or expire. As a result, states were once again allowed to regulate the conditions of sale of these weapons.

With respect to economic policies, the national legislative branch has been active in restraining state activities. A current issue is the question of Internet taxation. Consumer purchases "on-line" amounted to $65 billion in 2004, and were forecast to reach \$117 billion by 2008, according to a private survey.[47] Such purchases could amount to billions of dollars of sales taxes to the states, whose treasuries have been denied revenues as consumers switch from traditional sales-tax-collecting retailers to Internet sources. Meanwhile, in 1998, Congress enacted the Internet Tax Freedom Act, declaring a moratorium on any state or federal tax levies on Internet purchases. The moratorium has been continued in various forms ever since. In 2005, Congress addressed the issue of tort reform. Reacting to large awards in class-action suits tried in state courts, Congress passed the Class Action Fairness Act. The new legislation requires major class-action suits to be filed in federal courts, where sponsors believe that as a result of consolidation to a single trial court, the financial awards will be lower than at state levels.

Fiscal Federalism

That Congress has the right to legislate for the nation is clear in areas listed in Article I of the Constitution and elsewhere. In many cases, however, the limits of congressional primacy are blurry, creating both uncertainty and the possibility of lengthy court battles. Rather than subject its authority to challenge, Congress upon occasion has cemented its policies through financial carrots and sticks in the form of extra funding or the withholding of funding to the states for various programs established through national legislation.

The ability of Congress to assert financial control stems largely from the adoption of the national income tax, courtesy of the Sixteenth Amendment. Ratified by the requisite number of states in 1913, this amendment paved the way for the national government to reach new levels of fiscal clout with respect to funding the nation's infrastructure. The impact has been profound. Michael Reagan and John Sanzone write that as the result of the Sixteenth Amendment, "there has been a drastic centralization in American federalism,"[48] giving the federal government a huge tool in its ability to leverage national policymaking and set national priorities.

Grants-in-Aid

Throughout the twentieth century, Congress flexed its political muscles in redesigning the relationship between the national government and the states. Much of its success was due to the proliferation of **grants-in-aid**, payments from the national government to the states, and later to local and other governments, as a means of assuring the implementation of objectives determined in national legislation. Political scientists have dedicated reams of paper to classifying various forms of grants-in-aid.[49] Such efforts notwithstanding, there are basically two forms today. **Categorical grants** are allocations where Congress is very specific in the use of the federal money by the states or other lower levels of government; such programs commonly include "strings" or specific conditions. **Block grants** are funds that Congress provides for general use with few conditions, often on a per capita basis; these dollars are very fungible, meaning that they can be used by state or local governments for a wide variety of purpose. Either way, Congress requires recipient state or local governments to pony up a percentage of the program cost, with the percentage varying according to the terms of the grant.

Consider the following example as a way of understanding the difference between categorical and block grants. If Congress designates transportation funds for something specific like airport runway repairs, the applicant governments may use the funds for runway repairs and nothing else, a classic example of a categorical grant. And if Congress designates transportation funds for any use related to the movement of people from one location to another, the applicant governments may apply to use these federal block grant funds for anything from runway repairs to local waterways to bicycle paths.

Grants-in-aid are part of the fabric of American history, although their numbers and dollar amounts were limited during their originating years in the nineteenth century. Some examples: In the early 1800s, states completed the Erie Canal, a critical transportation corridor from the Midwest to the East Coast, through the assistance of congressional grants-in-aid. Later, Congress enacted grant-in-aid programs for states to establish agricultural and mechanical arts colleges (1887) and state irrigation programs (1890). As the twentieth century unfolded, Congress made a few more grants in very specific areas, among them state forestry assistance (1911) and highway construction (1916). By 1927, annual federal grants amounted to a little more than $500 million, or 2 percent of all state revenues.[50]

Total federal grants-in-aid increased to $1.8 billion just after World War II. But grants-in-aid have become even more important ever since. Commencing with the 1960s, Congress began extending grant-in-aid opportunities to local governments, bypassing states as the distributing entities of funds. Today there are more than 600 grant-in-aid programs available for state and local governments, amounting to more than $400 billion in annual federal expenditures for fiscal year 2006—an extensive commitment, given that the entire national budget for fiscal year 2006 was $2.57 trillion. Moreover, dollars from these programs account for more than 20 percent of the typical state budget, or ten times the amount before the Great Depression.

Most grant-in-aid programs are passed by or reauthorized by Congress every few years. Nearly 90 percent are of the categorical variety, simply because most members of Congress like to know exactly how the money is used, something that simultaneously provides credibility and allows congressional members to take credit. The remaining programs are block, a variety preferred by some political conservatives because the programs do not require state and local governments to jump through so many political hoops to get and keep the money. But here is perhaps the most fundamental point of all—although the legislative and executive branches have reduced the amount of grants-in-aid from time to time, the expenditure line has gone up irrespective of political party or philosophy in decision-making positions of authority. Simply put, grants-in-aid have emerged as a key device for Congress to determine the nation's priorities, and states have become very dependent on the funds.

Unfunded Mandates

Although Congress often has taken the lead in repositioning the relationship between the states and the federal government, the national legislative branch has not always provided the funds for states to carry out the national will. Beginning in the 1960s, Congress began passing legislation that required national standards for various policies. Congress tended to assign the implementation of these requirements, known as "mandates," to the states. Ironically, this new use of federal power increased dramatically during the Ronald Reagan administration, an era often described as anti–federal government,[51] but one in which Congress more accurately reassigned more and more tasks of the national government to the states. In the process, Congress and the president continued the theme of assuming responsibility for national policymaking, with implementation directed to lower levels of government. During the Reagan years (1981–89) alone, Congress created new federal standards for the minimum age for consuming alcohol, underground storage tanks, trucking capabilities, asbestos in local schools, and water pollution.

By the end of the 1980s, the annual number of congressionally passed mandates exceeded that of any previous period, including the 1960s. Environmental mandates alone cost state and local governments $19 billion annually by 1987.[52] Local governments were not exempt, as attested by a study in 1993 that showed mandate requirements costing cities and counties more than $11 billion annually in addition to burdensome state costs.[53] These policies continued through the presidential administration of George H.W. Bush and the 102nd Congress.

The mandate issue came to a head in 1995, with the election of a Republican majority to the House of Representatives. Inspired by the value of making the national government less demanding on the states, Congress enacted the Unfunded Mandates Reform Act of 1995. Ostensibly, the law was written with the idea that Congress would have to know ahead of passage the impact of mandates upon the states, with the exception of a few policy areas.[54] In addition, Congress was not required to conduct cost estimates on bills with annual state implementation costs of less than $50 million. The result has been something considerably less than a comprehensive overhaul of federal/state responsibilities. In fact, a study published in 2005 revealed that states were still left with annual costs of $30 billion due exclusively to unfunded mandate requirements legislated by Congress.[55]

Observers still disagree over the extent to which the federal government continues to saddle the states with funding responsibilities for the implementation of national programs. Consider the No Child Left Behind Act (NCLB), legislation passed by Congress and signed by President George W. Bush in 2002. Under this legislation, Congress required states to establish "accountability plans" to assure that public school children would achieve national standards by 2008. The plans would be implemented through annual test results that, if below expectations, would trigger a series of options including allowing children to change schools and denial of federal funds to schools that underperform. Critics dispute whether this law is an unfunded mandate. According to John Boehner, then chairman of the House Education and the Workforce Committee, NCLB requires Congress to spend the necessary funds to implement the education reforms contained in the legislation. As such, Boehner wrote in 2003, "states are receiving more than enough money from the federal government to pay for all of NCLB's testing requirements."[56] Yet a study published in *Education News* found that schools were not given sufficient funds to prepare children for testing to the tune of $26 billion for the first three years of the law's existence.[57]

Whether NCLB is an unfunded mandate may be a difficult question to answer. Clearly, however, Congress continues to assign some implementation requirements to state and local governments without the necessary funds required to carry out the assigned tasks. To this extent, the Unfunded Mandates Reform Act may provide more symbolic than substantive relief for state and local governments.

The Role of the Legislative Branch in Defining Federalism

Like the decisions brought forth by the judicial and executive branches, the activities of Congress have contributed significantly to defining and refining the boundaries of federalism. And like the courts and president, Congress has not been stagnant on this issue. As David Walker writes, "To overlook Congress [during this long period] is to ignore one of the key forces for the recent centralization of the entire system."[58] And to the extent that congressional action diverges from one or both of the other branches, opportunities for clashes exist.

National Institutions on the March

This chapter began with the claim that the three branches of national government have had profound impacts on framing federalism. Not to be lost in the discussion, however, is that singularly and collectively, gradually, if haltingly, they have moved the political power relationship to one in which the national government has assumed greater dominance in the twenty-first century than it did in 1787. That said, the three branches have not always marched in lock step, as demonstrated through the *Marbury v. Madison* case and presidential executive orders.

To be sure, the road to redefining federalism has been neither straight nor without bumps, but the power of the national government has grown, and often at the expense of the states. And lest the leaders of one branch point to the others as culprits, the record shows that all branches have participated in this power shift over time.

5

✩ ✩ ✩ ✩

Informal Pressures on the Power Flow

Power is a most unusual commodity. At its root, it is a means of domination exercised by an individual or collection of individuals over others in ways that the dominated would not necessarily choose if left alone without any pressure to submit. Talcott Parsons describes power as "relational," where the ability of one to succeed vis-à-vis another "is dependent upon his relations to other actors."[1] Thus, power has two important elements: control and involuntary submission. Power relationships can be found at all levels of human behavior, ranging from the struggles between individuals at home or in the workplace to the titanic clashes between nations. In short, power relationships are all around us. Perhaps that it is why the operation of power is fairly easy to identify, if not always understood.

The attributes of power commonly include physical command, although more mature relationships may depend upon other ingredients such as logic, voluntary agreement to a set of rules, or emotional underpinnings. Some power relationships are much easier to understand than others. A parent has supremacy over a young child both in physical and intellectual dimensions. A nation may prevail over others because of military advantage such as the possession of superior weaponry, but also because of economic prowess, historical factors, or cultural circumstances. In any case, these hierarchies help explain power flow interactions, whether between people or governments.

Within societies, power relationships depend upon their political composition and levels of maturity. In countries with undeveloped political institutions, power is often arbitrary and assigned by tradition or held by physical strength; accordingly, it is unpredictable, unevenly distributed, and often changes hands through volatile events such as revolution or civil war.[2] In more developed societies, power is determined by widely understood rules such as a constitutional framework or similar set of standards. Under these circumstances, distribution of authority and accountability of leaders are more likely to be in place. As Samuel P. Huntington notes, modernized societies tend to be more complex, with greater capacity for complex political relationships than less developed societies. These conditions allow for the possibility of diffuse distributions of power among many social forces within the same nation.[3] Some power relationships are observed through the arrangements of established political institutions, while others appear as almost tangential forces. Power, therefore, operates in different ways, depending upon the actors, issues, and conditions.

What do these broad-brush descriptions of political conditions have in common with American federalism? More than you might think. As discussed in Chapter 2, for more than one hundred years prior to the Philadelphia meeting in 1787, the earliest leaders of the American nation struggled to define relationships between levels of governance as well as individuals and their governments. They lunged ahead over the pre-Philadelphia period bearing an odd combination of disdain for the present and blurry vision of the future. The written product that emerged was anything but complete, yet it was a start beyond the wildest dreams of most Framers. As Jack Rakove writes, "no single vector neatly charted the course the framers took in allocating power between the Union and the states."[4] Rather, the Constitution created a new political arrangement that allowed for future influences from unanticipated directions.

This chapter focuses upon the many sources of informal pressure for organization and control of power in the federal arrangement. These include political parties, interest groups, bureaucracies, and the elusive, yet everchanging element of public opinion. Over the years, they have coexisted, at times independently of one another and at other times as part of ad hoc alliances of influence. Most significant, the efforts of groups outside of the government boundaries have often led to the reassignment of responsibilities among governments, helping to assure an ever-changing distribution of power and continuously evolving definition of American federalism.

Political Parties

Political parties are unconventional sources of political power, particularly in American society. Parties operate as political communication channels that link citizens, organizational leaders, and governmental officials in ways that they can move forward with sets of ideas to govern the polity.[5] Although they are not part of the official governmental arrangement, political parties nonetheless contribute to the makeup and direction of governments at all levels of authority. They are different from interest groups because the leaders of parties seek to govern within the framework of their own specific ideas, whereas interest groups want only to influence those who govern, regardless of their party.

American political parties are somewhat different from their counterparts elsewhere because of the unique electoral system in which they operate. In most other countries, parties are ideological organizations whose elected members adhere closely to the same set of values, thereby assuring cohesion.[6] To act independently on votes often leads to removal of the member from the party ticket at the next election. In the United States, political party organizations are looser coalitions, with few penalties for individual departures from leadership objectives and greater tendencies for defections on different issues.

Another difference: Most democratic countries operate with proportional representation systems that allocate the numbers of legislative seats as percentages of the votes captured by the various parties at elections. With the possibility of gaining some seats, many parties form, usually leading to an election outcome where no single party wins a majority of seats. As a result, several parties often are required to create a functioning majority coalition. However, multiparty coalitions are potentially unstable arrangements because of the ability of any party to withdraw over policy differences at any time, thereby destroying the majority and bringing about the need for a new election. This is not the case in the United States, where the organization of the electoral system encourages two major parties, because whichever candidate wins the most votes in a given race captures the office. As such, loose coalitions or factions often develop within the two major parties, with minor parties rarely affecting an election outcome.

So diffuse are American political parties that even activists of the same persuasion may simultaneously work with and against one another at the national and state levels of power, depending upon the issue or values behind the issue. Thus, offshore oil drilling may be favored by Republicans leaders in Alaska, yet opposed by Republican leaders in California. Likewise, public education voucher programs may be supported by Democratic leaders in Ohio, but disputed by Democratic leaders in New York. Acting as large philosophical tents, parties accommodate individuals of varying views on the same issues, often making it difficult for people to know what the parties "stand for." Because of so many uncertainties relating to their abilities to influence the political process, political parties are "wild cards" when it comes to federalism. Nevertheless, they should not be dismissed as participants.

Party Pressures at the National Level

A fundamental goal of political parties is to govern.[7] Yet, in the United States, party organizations are anything but unified. Therein lies some of the novelty and frustration of American politics. On a philosophical level, people in or out of government adhere to rigid ideological conditions; on a practical level, party operatives can be almost chameleon-like to attain their goals. To that end, the most liberal Democrat in Congress may vote for a conservative Republican proposal because of his or her own personal values or the values of his or her district or state. The same goes for conservative Republicans who, on occasion, may cross the party line to join Democrats. Studies show that in recent years, the divisions between the parties in Congress have actually increased, suggesting that there are some significant differences between them on how government should function.[8] So, how does this play out on the national stage?

As a general rule, Democrats at the national level believe that the national government should have a powerful role in our lives except, perhaps, in personal choice issues. Much of this approach is based upon the value of equality promoted by the national government, as found in Article I, Section 8, of the Constitution. Thus, they tend to support higher minimum wages, regulation of businesses, affirmative action, affordable health insurance, more public lands, and social programs for the elderly that tend to offer widespread benefits to as many people as possible. Even on issues such as abortion, the "right" to die, and other individual public policy questions, most Democrats like to see the national government operate as a guarantor against intrusions into the management of personal issues. This collection of activities comes at a cost, of course, and for that reason, most Democrats support higher levels of taxation, particularly among the wealthier segments of society.

What about Republicans? Here, too, generalizations dominate the discussion, and, as with Democrats, they tend to be true more times than not. Republicans at the national level lean toward minimal amounts of government involvement in most policy areas. When considering the list of economic issues mentioned above, Republicans would rather see most of them solved in the private sector or, if by government, at the state level. The thinking here is that individuals ought to be responsible for their own well-being, and that state governments are closer to the needs of their populations than the sprawling national government. Only on social issues such as abortion, religion in the schools, and the right to die, or assisted suicide, according to opponents, do some Republicans argue that the national government should direct policy. Otherwise, they opt for the states' rights approach to federalism spelled out most clearly in the Tenth Amendment of the Constitution.

The differences between the two parties are reflected in countless policy areas. Consider a case in point, such as mining regulations or the management of national forests. Most Democrats at the national level would prefer national rules for mining safety that offer the same protection to all, regardless of their state. Similarly, they would prefer to see federal management of national forests, lest the states allow private interests to cut down timber indiscriminately or overgraze the land. On the other side, most Republicans would rather see states determine their own mining rules, even though some state governments have cozy relationships with mining interests. Likewise, most Republicans believe that the costs of maintaining national forests could be offset by leasing out land or turning over some of it to states or private interests for more efficient management. The bottom line is this: The leaders of political parties at the national level pursue more or less national dominance depending upon their political values.

Party Pressures at the State Level

If the American political system is organized in terms of two broad major political cal parties, the states are characterized by fifty different political party systems. Some states are well organized, with strong party organizations, while others are little more than extensions of elected officeholders. These differences notwithstanding, state parties are heavily invested in national elections, whether for Congress or the presidency. State involvement ranges from fund-raising to nominee selection. To the extent that the leaders from a state political party help deliver winners at the national level, their hopes for a close relationship with Washington rise; to the extent that they fail to generate a close connection, their concerns about being on the periphery of policymaking grow.

As national parties have strengthened their abilities to conduct comprehensive campaigns, so have the states. At election time, leaders at the two levels often coordinate scarce resources such as personnel and money to maximize opportunities for success. Still, Malcolm Jewel and Sarah Morehouse note, activists associated with different levels of government do not always see eye to eye. "Sometimes ideological or other divisions in a state result . . . where the leadership of the state party is out of step with the national party. Sometimes state-national party linkages break down simply because of personality differences."[9] Simply put, weak connections exist between levels of parties, often allowing fissures in the framework that contribute to electoral defeat.

Whatever the coordination, party organizations and their elected officials operate at state and local levels, and often behave independently from their counterparts in Washington, D.C. This lack of linkage is a hallmark of American federalism, which offers multiple sources of power. L. Sandy Maisel notes: "American politics is most notably characterized by its decentralization; local and state politics are *not* totally controlled by national forces."[10] With different resources available at different levels of government, the desire to push for or against federal involvement often depends upon what the states will get in return for their support. And considering that the states have radically different agendas and needs, it is not surprising that the relationships between state and national party organizations are also different.

Unlike their national counterparts that wage deeply partisan battles, parties at the state level are less concerned with ideological concerns than the economic realities of trying to balance budgets. Alan Rosenthal notes that although the two parties occasionally take opposite sides on issues, nowadays agreements on major decisions arise "more out of common need than feelings of party loyalty."[11] In other words, practical considerations govern the decisions of party leaders in state legislatures. That said, the states are very different from one another in their needs and abilities to meet those needs. Some may cry for federal assistance in a given area, while others have no interest and view federal involvement as an unnecessary intrusion.

Clearly, the actions of political parties with respect to federalism are significant at both the national and state levels of authority. Ideological differences are most distinct at the national level, where the wielding of power and money go hand in hand, and can have tremendous impact on national/state relationships. While the leaders of state party organizations often lobby the federal government for special treatment or concessions, their concerns are often based on managing day-to-day issues like local water quality or seat belt compliance laws, rather than broad philosophical questions. Getting a federal waiver on state fulfillment of these kinds of obligations will mean a lot more to a state than whether Congress balances the budget or saves Social Security.

Interest Groups

Whereas the different levels of authority and types of power often dictate the approaches of party leaders to a given question, interest groups generally have no such concerns. Rather, interest groups operate with narrow objectives. Which level of government has responsibility for policies relevant to their concerns is less important to interest groups than the way their concerns are managed by whoever has responsibility. Thus, many interest groups are rarely attached to a level of government as much as they are attached to results that benefit the members of their organizations. In other words, they tend to "shop" the level of policymaking authority that will be most responsive to their needs.

In Pursuit of National Management

Some interest groups prefer the national government to address their concerns because of the nature of their interests and the needs of their constituencies. National applications result in fairly uniform treatment, thus reinforcing the equality theme. Citizen groups such as the Sierra Club, the National Rifle Association, and the American Association of Retired Persons (AARP) are collections of individuals that cut across the economic and social fabric of society, while holding a key value in common.[12] Typically, these organizations attempt to exert pressure at the national level because they have limited resources and their members are scattered throughout the nation. In addition, these groups tend to seek consistent, across-the-board outcomes. Thus, the AARP attempts to influence policy at the national level because its members (ages fifty and over) will benefit from federal policies wherever they are. Pressure at the state level could result in inconsistent policies from state to state and confusion for members.

Like citizens groups, labor unions are much more comfortable with national rules rather than state rules because laws and regulations enacted in Washington affect everyone the same way. Thus, the national minimum wage and rules on workplace conditions are applied everywhere, although some states enact minimums higher than the federal standard. This situation also allows unions for the most part to concentrate their limited political capital in one location, rather than fight battles in several jurisdictions.[13] The American Federation of Labor and Congress of Industrial Organizations (commonly referred to as the AFL-CIO) is the largest and most effective of the labor organizations. Although the umbrella group has several unions and chapters of individual unions in many states, the AFL-CIO is "the dominant national voice of the American labor movement."[14] More often than not, the AFL-CIO is viewed as the voice of working people. Internal divisions over strategies and tactics led several unions to separate from the AFL-CIO in 2005.[15] Still, combined organized labor accounts for more than 13 million members.

Just because organized labor commands substantial numbers does not assure success, however. Two recent examples of failure occurred with the battles over the North American Free Trade Agreement (NAFTA) in 1994 and Central American Free Trade Agreement (CAFTA) in 2005. In each case, the AFL-CIO lobbied hard against the agreements on the grounds that they would cost American jobs and hold down wages. In each case, the president and Congress were more persuaded by business interests that argued adoption of the agreements would make the United States more competitive with the rest of the world. Whether these trade pacts are good for workers and businesses alike remains a point of controversy and continued debate.[16]

On the other hand, sometimes numbers can be powerful. Consider Social Security reform, a cause championed by Republican President George W. Bush. In 2005, the president publicly declared this program as the centerpiece of his domestic agenda. He argued for reduced government-provided benefits and the creation of individual retirement accounts as a new framework to control the increasing costs of the program. The 35.6-million-member AARP provided Congress with staunch and persistent opposition to making radical changes in the Social Security system. Not only did the group dissuade congressional Democrats commonly close to AARP values, but also large numbers of congressional Republicans, who typically favor fewer government services—all this in the face of pressure from more than one hundred business associations that sided with the president.[17] In this case, the numbers were too powerful for national policymakers to ignore.

In Pursuit of State Management

Some interest groups seek policy influence at the state level rather than the national level because their organizations believe they will benefit from state oversight of their activities. In most cases, the rise of interest group efforts in states has occurred in tandem with activities such as taxation or regulations.[18] Particularly active at the state level are professional groups, educators, agriculture, health-care groups, insurance interests, lawyers, utilities, various manufacturing associations, and local governments.

By participating in state politics, groups can help shape the policies that will affect their members. At the same time, the results of their activities may differ substantially from state to state, setting up networks of conflicting policies. Nowhere is this more evident than in the implementation of the $246 billion settlement in 1998 between the states and the tobacco industry as compensation for tobacco-caused illnesses and social problems. As funds began to roll in, North Carolina used much of its allocation to help tobacco farmers shift to other crops,[19] while local governments in California considered using their funds to build sidewalks in compliance with the Americans With Disabilities Act.[20] In fact, only a few states have used tobacco settlement funds to promote anti-smoking programs in accordance with the framework proposed by the federal government's Centers for Disease Control.[21]

The most successful groups at the state level operate on the principle that doing less is best. That is because many powerful groups appreciate the predictability that comes with the status quo. Particularly, business organizations lobby state legislatures and executives to preserve advantages in taxes, workers' compensation programs, health care, and other elements that will leave them at a competitive advantage with other states. A recent study shows that business and development interests have actually increased their influence in state politics since 1994, when Republicans swept congressional as well as a large number of state elections. Other groups, such as public education and environmental organizations, have enjoyed much less consistent influence.[22] Their successes and failures often correlate with the political party in power and temporary condition of the state treasury. Thus, when Democrats prevail and the economy is healthy, these groups do well; when Republicans rule or the economy flags, they do not.

For the most part, gun owner groups have lobbied both the national and state governments against legislating rules regarding the conditions of gun ownership or types of firearms available for purchase. Although they argued that the Second Amendment of the U.S. Constitution prohibits any constraints whatsoever, decisions by the United States Supreme Court since the 1870s to the present day consistently have found otherwise.[23] Still, gun owner groups despised the national assault weapons ban enacted in 1994. With states rights allies, the National Rifle Association (NRA) not only blocked extension of the ban in 2004, but set the tone for other efforts to whittle away at regulation. Fresh off its victory, the NRA has lobbied several states for legislation allowing concealed weapons in automobiles and lowered ages of gun ownership. In other instances, the reenergized NRA has worked hard to block legislation that would ban assault gun ownership at the state level.[24]

Native American tribes are among the newest interest groups that have turned their attention to influencing state policies. In 1988, Congress passed the Indian Gaming Regulatory Act, a law that allows federally recognized tribes to negotiate gaming agreements with the states. Over the next fifteen years, seven states negotiated operating deals with tribes, with state revenues ranging from 1 to 25 percent, depending upon the agreement. Another thirty states developed less formal agreements with Indian tribes. Inasmuch as many states have flagging economies, the amount of money at stake is staggering. Between 1995 and 2003 alone, revenues from Indian gaming jumped from $5.4 billion to $16.7 billion. With these kinds of stakes, Indian tribes and state governments often have formed mutually dependent relationships.[25] Nevertheless, the new opportunities for states to manage Indian affairs sometimes have produced inconsistent, undesirable results. In Texas, for example, the state attorney general actually used the 1991 federal law to shut down Indian casinos, even though Indian tribes had won federal recognition to have them, pursuant to agreements with the state of Texas.[26]

Changing Horses

Interest groups have loyalties to their members, not particular governments. For this reason, interest group lobbyists sometimes change influence strategies if they find that one level of government may be more responsive to their needs than another.

From State to Federal Pressure

In recent years, some interest groups have switched their emphasis from pressure on the states to pressure on the federal government. The primary reason for the change in strategy centers on states' rights conservatives enjoying substantial power both in the executive and legislative branches, giving those of similar persuasion in the private sector the hope of obtaining national legislation favorable to their issues and causes.

The issue of tort reform recently has drawn considerable attention. Business groups have turned to the national government to streamline the flow of several state cases into a single federal court, rather than suffer defeats on the same issue in several state courts. After seeing trial lawyers win huge verdicts on cases relating to drugs with unanticipated side effects, poorly constructed medical instruments, deficient tires, and faulty automobile design, business groups descended upon Washington with demands for the federal courts to receive these and other cases. Congress responded with the Class Action Fairness Act in 2005. Advocates described the new law as necessary tort reform that reined in greedy lawyers; opponents, particularly consumer groups, viewed the law as the newest way of letting irresponsible corporations off the hook.[27] Either way, the new legislation has reduced the role of states and enhanced the role of the federal government in consumer protection, antitrust, environmental protection, and securities law.

Similarly, lending institution organizations have changed course regarding the level of government best able to meet their needs. Historically, banks have always had the choice of operating under state or federal laws. Federal laws provided much more security for depositors than state laws and greater safety for the lending institutions, along with more rigorous compliance rules for member banks. The loose nature of many state laws, aided by federal deregulation during the 1980s,[28] allowed savings and loans to operate with sloppy bookkeeping practices, and ultimately sent many into bankruptcy. In all, during the 1980s, state savings and loan bankruptcies cost taxpayers more than $160 billion.[29] Seeing the need for more stability in their industry, lobbyists for the savings and loans sought new protection from Congress. In 1989, President George H.W. Bush and the Congress responded to the problem with a massive industry bailout. As part of the effort to salvage the remaining S&Ls, the new legislation allowed the institutions to abandon their state charters and become part of the federal system of financial regulation. By assuming financial responsibility for the ailing institutions in the financial industry, Congress and the president altered the relationship between the federal government and the states.

From Federal to State Pressure

Another variation of the "changing horses" theme has been for private interests, once protected by the federal government, to pursue policies that leave them under the jurisdiction of states. As with the cases above, the reasons seem to be strategic, rather than philosophical, but nevertheless providing the interest a better deal.

Few issues in recent years have received as much attention as management of public lands. For more than twenty years, timber interests and the federal government have sparred over the headwaters forest area in northern California. Because of endangered species, water impurities associated with logging, and other concerns, numerous pieces of environmental legislation passed by Congress kept the area under federal control. As a result, lumber companies were unable to harvest some of the most valuable redwood anywhere. In 1999, U.S. senator Dianne Feinstein (D-CA) brokered a deal that included deferral purchase of 10,000 privately held acres and new terms for logging more than 220,000 acres in the region.[30] To the consternation of environmental groups, state and local agencies emerged largely in control over the implementation of the deal. With a new governmental arrangement in place, a major lumber company began harvesting lumber on what it perceived to be much more favorable terms than before the deal. State and local authorities objected, but the logging continued.[31] At least for the moment, a different set of controls seemed more beneficial to the lumber interest group.

Blending Institutions and Values

The simple fact is that governments and those who preside over them are not neutral. Institutions are designed in terms of political capabilities and are operated by people with their own political values. Moreover, depending upon the outcomes of elections the values of the people who control public institutions may change greatly over time. These changes do not escape the attention of savvy interest groups. To the extent that interest groups may perceive one level of government as being more responsive to their needs than another, they will attempt to alter their political courses accordingly. To the extent that different levels of government assume powers they may not have assumed previously, they may redefine the meaning of federalism. Even at that, in many cases a group that cozies up to one level of government for assistance today may well turn to another tomorrow.

Bureaucracy: Pushing from the Periphery of Power

People often think of the bureaucracy as a faceless collection of civil service employees who operate in gray cubicles with the sole task of carrying out the will of others in official positions of power. By "civil service" we mean the collection of individuals who gain their government jobs via competitive examinations or unusual skill-sets. Most of the time, these individuals work without partisan attachments via appointment and pursue their responsibilities within a "neutral" implementation environment; the period of their work spans decades, rather than two- or four-year terms of office. In this classical context, Anthony Downs points out, the bureaucrat does not come to his or her job via election, "nor is his continuance in office tied directly to the continuance in office of some other person who is periodically elected."[32] Instead, bureaucrats function in government offices to carry out the policies prescribed by others. Whatever bureaucrats' personal political values, their obligations are tied to their offices or agencies, rather than the coattails of a particular elected official.

With the growth of governments at all levels, bureaucracies have assumed major roles in carrying out the wills of those elected or chosen to govern. As of 2005, nearly 3 million bureaucrats worked for the federal government in jobs ranging from letter carriers to immigration officials to coal mine inspectors to airport security screeners. The numbers at state and local levels are much larger, amounting to about 5 million and 13 million respectively. Here, too, are a wide variety of jobs, including teachers, police officers and firefighters, welfare workers, public hospital personnel, construction personnel, prison guards, tollbooth operators, janitors, and department of motor vehicle employees, just to name a few.

As with elected officials, bureaucrats tend to perceive the limits of their responsibilities within the constraints defined by the Constitution and elaborated through the policies created by actors in the traditional three branches at the national and state levels of government. But they also consider their responsibilities in the context of the mandates of their jobs, seeking to fulfill their duties in the most thorough fashion possible. That said, bureaucrats, like elected officials, have constituencies that can be as broad as the general public or as narrow as groups such as farmers, insurance agents, or safety engineers. As they attempt to carry out their tasks affecting their constituencies, bureaucrats often test the boundaries of their implementation roles, often seeking to expand or redefine their powers.

The most commonly observed bureaucratic relationships occur among the struggles for primacy between the national and state levels of government. Here federal and state counterparts in various policy areas attempt to exert influence over the other. The "nation-centered" approach focuses on bureaucratic reign from the national government down, relying upon broad-based national interpretations to guide all other levels of authority, including the states. Conversely, under the "state-centered" model, state bureaucracies exercise more independence, often leading to different approaches to the same policy area.[33] The results is "turf" wars, which create their own special tension in the federal arrangement.

Nation-Centered Battles

Top-down relationships occur at one end of the bureaucratic continuum. In this situation, the federal agency attempts to carry out the mandate prescribed by national authority. With power distributed in a top-down fashion, states and local government bureaucracies are required to comply.

The Environmental Protection Agency (EPA) stands out as a federal bureaucracy that has attempted repeatedly to set standards for all levels of government since its creation in 1970. Since that time, the agency has been charged with implementing more than 150 federal laws on subjects ranging from the regulation of business and the economy to health and safety. Often, the EPA's actions have led opponents to rush to the courts in hopes of slowing down or reversing federal rules. One study sees these never-ending tests as the consequence of an agency that, although funded by Congress, "has no clearly mandated priorities."[34] This lack of clarity has led various EPA administrators to enlarge or constrict the federal role from time to time, although the ability of the agency to have its way is rarely thwarted.

State-Centered Management

At the other end of the federal hierarchy are state bureaucracies, which sometimes carve out their own unique paths on public policy issues in the absence of national activity. In these instances, management of the same issue may vary greatly from state to state, depending on the rules, values, and interpretations of the bureaucracies in the states. More significantly, such interpretations often become the springboard for national policies down the road.

The idea of vouchers for public education began and has continued as state initiatives. In 1990, the school district in Milwaukee, Wisconsin, created the first program that dedicated state and local funds to private schools as a replacement for public school instruction. Since then districts in Ohio, Colorado, Utah, and Florida have also set up voucher systems that allow students to transfer from poorly performing or inadequate schools. Although Congress shied away from the idea, the U.S. Supreme Court ultimately endorsed vouchers in 2002 by a narrow 5–4 vote over the objections of those who feared that privately run voucher schools would obliterate the line between religion and public education.[35] With its decision, the Court left it to state courts to determine the merits of local voucher programs. The decision opened the door to more confusion than clarity. In 2006, the Florida State Supreme Court overturned the state's voucher program by a vote of 5–2 because it violated the state's constitution.[36]

Changing Direction

Sometimes the roles of bureaucracy change because of the action of other public policy authorities. Along with the federal courts, leaders of the executive and legislative branches can alter bureaucratic roles dramatically. For example, when President Ronald Reagan, an outspoken opponent of "big government," signed Executive Order 12291 shortly after assuming office in 1981, he stipulated that any future regulations under the auspices of the national government be submitted first to the Office of Management and Budget (OMB) to ascertain the full fiscal impact of their costs. The thinking behind Reagan's move was to reduce the flow of bureaucratic power at the national level in favor of greater state-level activities. Ironically, by adding new powers to the OMB within the executive branch, Reagan actually set the tone for a more powerful national authority, an opportunity that was seized during the Clinton years.[37]

Recently, under the direction of the little-known Office of Information and Regulatory Affairs, a unit housed within the better known Office of Management and Budget, the George W. Bush administration rolled back several previous regulations and rejected new ones on topics from aircraft repair rules to health and safety guidelines. In most cases, the new rules once again have lessened the role of the federal government, to the delight of corporate interests.[38] A byproduct of this shift is more attention to such issues by bureaucracies at the state levels, where widely differing interpretations may take place. Moreover, such interpretations may shift over time, depending upon those in the highest leadership positions.

Intergovernmental Bureaucratic Relationships

Along with the endless struggles to protect political turf, bureaucracies at the national and state levels at times work together on issues of common interest. The ability for different levels to converge on the same policy area has been described as **picket fence federalism**, a network where program specialists from various levels of governments set aside their turf interests in the name of satisfying mutual objectives.[39] One area of joint interest is Medicaid, the national state program that provides health care for the poor, disabled, and elderly. In all, Medicaid covers about 50 million Americans. As of 2005, Medicaid accounted for about 22 percent of all state budgets. The Bush administration sought to curtail federal spending on Medicaid by $40 billion over the next ten years. The answer to the excesses was provided, in part, by states and the federal government working to cut out abuses while providing the necessary care for those in need.[40]

State and federal bureaucracies have also worked cooperatively on protecting the United States against illegal immigration. Since the terrorist attacks of September 11, 2001, agencies from both levels have collaborated on a number of initiatives to thwart illegal border crossings. Particular cooperation has occurred between the Federal Bureau of Investigation and U.S. Border Patrol and state and local police in myriad contexts ranging from joint training to apprehension.[41] Policy implementation notwithstanding, considerable conflict remains, however, over the funding of these programs. Although state and local law enforcement agencies now contribute vast resources to border protection, many maintain that the federal government should pay for their contributions, inasmuch as protection of the borders is a federal responsibility.[42]

How is it that bureaucracies have become pivotal to federalism? The answer lies with the latitude that they are given by policymakers at all levels of government. As society has become more complex, elected officials have assumed the role of framing the major decisions, leaving it to the bureaucracies and their experts to "make things work."[43] In the process, the actions of bureaucracies sometimes impact the national/state relationship. As a result, these agencies sometimes frame policy as much as they carry it out. Still, bureaucracies do not act completely without guidance, as demonstrated by the dramatic swings in the use of federal authority over the past two decades.

Public Opinion

The connection between public opinion and federalism sometimes seems very indirect; after all, under the American style of government, people do not directly make policies (except in the instances of state initiatives and referenda). Nevertheless, the voices of the public occasionally may influence the distribution of power, especially if those voices are loud.

Generally, the public does not say much one way or the other on issues relating to federalism. The fact is that most people go through their daily routines with an "if it ain't broke, don't fix it" approach. Many are unaware of which level historically has or currently does wield power, and tend not to care as long as things work well. When something is amiss, however, the public may become involved. Even then, constitutional prescriptions may keep the public from having its way. On those issues of great intensity or lopsided support, the public may sway federalism one way or another, especially when public policy responsibilities are not clearly constitutionally defined.

Consider the question of government-funded stem cell research, which touches on a wide range of issues ranging from the philosophical meaning of life to the practicalities of expensive health care. Because of their ability to generate any type of human tissue, stem cells have been heralded by some as the twenty-first-century answer to crippling medical maladies such as Parkinson's disease, Alzheimer's disease, diabetes, various cancers, and as many as 700 other diseases. Others view stem cells as an accomplice to the denial of life, particularly if they are harvested from embryos or fetuses associated with late-term abortions. In 2001, President George W. Bush joined the second group, and decided to allow federal research only on those stem cells already in existence, a very small number that would provide relatively few opportunities for the scientific community.[44] Meanwhile, scientists in several other nations without such research limitations proceeded with their own aggressive research programs, attracting the world's most talented scientists, including many from the United States.

Public opinion has strongly supported government-funded stem cell research. A national survey conducted in 2005 found that only 20 percent agreed with President Bush's decision to limit stem cell investigations. In addition, the survey respondents endorsed states undertaking the research effort by a ratio of three to two.[45] These feelings fueled attention at the state level.

In 2004, California became the first state to break from the president when the voters passed an initiative for a $3 billion bond to sponsor stem cell research. Other states followed. In 2005 alone, a half dozen states established stem cell research funds. A particularly compelling drama occurred in Massachusetts, where, guided by a statewide poll showing 81 percent public support, the state legislature overturned the veto of a stem cell research bill by Governor Mitt Romney. Thus, in a very real way, and on very practical grounds, public opinion moved the states to do what the federal government chose not to do.

We should not overstate the connection between public opinion and federalism. In fact, opportunities for direct public influence may often be limited because of the rules prescribed in the Constitution and applied by government leaders. Staggered elections, separation of powers, and divisions of authority between the two major levels of government all minimize links between public opinion of the moment and public policies; in fact, they tend to serve as filtering mechanisms against radical and abrupt change. Still, there is room for public input, sometimes leading to cautious responses by those in positions of authority. As John Kingdon concludes, "Public opinion may sometimes direct government *to* do something, but it more often constrains government *from* doing something."[46] Further, in those instances where policy responsibilities are not firmly established, public opinion may push leaders of state government to innovate solutions to pressing issues.[47]

Recently, public opinion has been quite vocal on the issue of immigration. During spring 2006, hundreds of thousands of people took to the streets in organized marches. Most of the protests demanded favorable congressional action toward immigrants, particularly on the question of legal status for the 12 million undocumented residents already in the United States; a few marches were organized in protest of the illegal immigrants already in the United States as well as the estimated 500,000 who enter the United States every year.

The public's confusion over immigration is revealed through the findings of national surveys. In a recent poll, 67 percent of those interviewed say that anti-immigrant sentiment is growing in the United States. In the same survey, however, 81 percent agree that illegal immigrants take jobs that no one else wants; 73 percent agree that illegal immigrants help the U.S. economy by providing low-cost labor.[48] Meanwhile, conflicting public sentiment on immigration became a central theme of the 2006 midterm congressional and state elections. A nonpartisan political analyst observed, "It's [the immigration issue] coming up everywhere and at the very least, there won't be a debate where this is not a big question."[49] In the end, several congressional and a few Senate races were decided as the result of the public's collective opinions of candidates and their positions on this controversial topic.

Informal Pressures: Ambiguous but Real

Social scientists often struggle to explain their relevance by using scientific techniques and various benchmarking tools to measure change and direction. We look at something at one point, examine it at another, and then attempt to explain the basis of any variation. Sounds good in theory, but it often does not work that way in the real world. Nowhere is this more apparent than in attempting to account for informal pressures on the federal arrangement.

Clearly, elements such as political parties, interest groups, bureaucracies, and public opinion contribute to defining and redefining federalism, but the linkages are often obscure and may occur in changing environments that make it difficult to explain anything but a case-by-case basis. That is because rarely do we see a simple "cause" and "effect" when it comes to political activity. Instead, numerous factors are involved, often combining to influence political actors. The confusion of informal pressures notwithstanding, they are real and they play meaningful roles in explaining the influences associated with defining and redefining federalism.

Part III

The Dimensions of Modern Federalism

6

✩ ✩ ✩ ✩

Vertical Federalism

Of the many definitions of federalism, none attracts more attention than the relationship among the national, state, and local governments. "A federal system," Jeffrey Henig writes, "is one in which power and authority are shared between a central government and one or more levels of subgovernments."[1] Similarly, Joseph Zimmerman observes that "in a federal system, all exercisable governmental powers are divided between a national government and several state (province, canton, land, etc.) governments with the exception of the concurrent powers exercisable by either plane of government."[2] For many students of the subject, the designation of powers to the various levels of public authority is the centerpiece of dividing the responsibilities for collective governance. Because federalism defines limits of authority as much as the assignment of authority, it can be a means of preserving representative democracy.[3] It also blends the best of centralized and decentralized political systems.[4]

So much for the broad brush. Beyond the areas of general assignment outlined in the U.S. Constitution, the real struggles occur over specific application in the numerous and multifacted public policy making arenas. Even the most defined constitutional missions often seem to invite more questions than provide answers. Thus, if Congress is to provide for the "general welfare," as outlined in Article I, Section 8, of the Constitution, does that power preclude the states from creating public education systems that treat illegal immigrants differently from legal residents? Conversely, if the states are entitled to those powers not specifically granted to the federal government as discussed in the Tenth Amendment, why should Nevada not have the right to prevent the federal government from storing spent nuclear materials within its borders? Or, why should the U.S. Food and Drug Administration be able to stop the state of California from requiring the tuna industry to place mercury warnings on labels? Or, on what grounds can the U.S. Department of Interior allow energy companies to drill for oil and gas if the state governments of Colorado and Montana argue otherwise?

The answer, Aaron Wildavsky concludes, has to do with all the uncertainties of application as participants in the policymaking process move from the abstract to the concrete. Whatever the attempt to balance responsibilities of the national, state, and local governments, "the operational meaning of federalism is found in the degree to which the constituent units disagree about what should be done, who should do it, and how it should be carried out. In a word, federalism is about conflict."[5] And conflict manifests itself in all kinds of issues ranging from social values to natural resources to financial responsibilities.

Clearly, over the long term, the national level has assumed more power on myriad matters, leaving the states and local governments in less powerful positions. Yet developments since the beginning of the twenty-first century suggest renewed support for the reallocation of some acquired federal authority back to the states and smaller units. This most recent movement is referred to by some as "devolution."[6]

This chapter focuses on the vertical tensions over the distribution of authority at the various levels of power. Most often, struggles have occurred between representatives of the national and state governments. Beyond the national/state disputes, there are issues between the national and local levels of government as well as between state and local governments. In addition, increasingly, power questions have emerged over relations between governments and elements of the private sector. Many of these relationships were well beyond the sights of the visionary Framers, yet they are part of the federalism framework today.

National/State Relations

We begin with the most observable area of debate, the arrangement of responsibilities between the national and state governments. There is little doubt that today the national government flexes its muscles over the states in most substantive areas of public authority. That said, the domination does not always take place in a way that extracts power from the states.

Policy from the Top

Earlier we discussed the evolution of the national government as a key policymaking entity (see Chapter 4). The examples below chronicle recent behavior of major national institutions as they pertain to refining federalism in the twenty-first century.

Congressional Activity

Congress passes relatively few laws each year, but they almost always reverberate throughout the states. Cornelius Kerwin notes: "If we examine the body of laws enacted by Congress, it is immediately apparent that those laws touch virtually every aspect of human life."[7] From minimum wage laws to maximum speed limits, Congress sets policies for the entire nation, including its subgovernment units. In recent years, congressional activity has changed markedly, with the political party leaderships often favoring different approaches to federalism issues.

From the days of the New Deal until the end of the twentieth century, most congressional Democrats strived for uniform national responses particularly in social policy. Thus, beginning with the days of the New Deal in the 1930s and 1940s through the civil rights years of the 1960s, and even the post-Watergate period of the late 1970s, 1980s, and early 1990s, Congress enacted a series of laws that emphasized national standards and state compliance. Civil rights, affirmative action, employment conditions, and environmental protection were among the many areas where a generally Democratic Congress embraced national guarantees over states' rights.[8] In most instances, Republicans philosophically were opposed to requiring states to conform with national objectives for these policy areas on the grounds that the individual needs and circumstances of the states took precedence over blanket national requirements.

Liberal Democratic dominance gave way in 1994, after conservative Republicans won control of the Congress, thereby setting the stage for new interpretations of federalism through management of the public policy process.[9] Led by the new speaker of the House, Newt Gingrich, and his "Contract with America," the majority pledged fiscal conservatism and other reforms dedicated to reducing the size of government. The most obvious manifestations of the new spirit emerged with the Unfunded Mandates Reform Act of 1995 (see Chapter 4) and Personal Responsibility and Work Opportunity Reconciliation Act of 1996, in which Congress transferred to the states responsibility for welfare reform and management. As a result, shortly after enactment, some states paid three or four times as much as other states for temporary welfare assistance.[10] Nevertheless, states were given enhanced authority in this policy area.

Republican majorities continued into the twenty-first century. Emboldened with the election to the presidency of conservative Republican George W. Bush in 2000 and his reelection in 2004, Congress enacted two major tax cuts totaling $1.5 trillion over ten years, thereby providing fewer resources for the federal government. This commitment, in turn, served as a strong check on spending for most domestic programs.[11] Less money for domestic needs led several states to raise taxes, resulting more in a shift of responsibilities than the economic stimulus sought by congressional reformers.[12]

On rare occasion, the Republican Congress has strengthened the role of the national government, although usually with the idea of addressing a conservative value. One example occurred in 2005, with the passage of the Class Action Fairness Act, legislation that required the class action suits on the same complaint to be filed as a single case in federal court, rather than dozens of state courts.[13] Fewer lawsuits resulted, meaning less exposure of business interests to citizen claims. "The bottom line," an observer has written, "is that much of organized business now prefers to deal with a single 800-pound gorilla, rather than 50 monkeys."[14] Such changes have strengthened the role of the federal government over the states. At the same time, they have reframed the litigation environment in a manner that has aided private interests over public concerns.

In other public policy areas, Congress has transferred responsibility for public policy issues to the states. For example, an omnibus spending bill in 2004 contained a section on abortion counseling that freed hospitals from performing abortions, essentially turning over such responsibilities to state governments.[15] Similarly, in 2005, when Congress reduced federal Medicaid expenditures by $10 billion over five years, the national government "gave" to the states new abilities to craft their own health-care policies for the poor and infirm, although many states looked at the "opportunity" as a liability.[16]

In summary, the following can be said: On social issues, the Republican Congress in the first years of the twenty-first century has shifted many policy responsibilities to the states, leading to distinctly different applications. On economic matters, Congress has shown less consistency.

Presidential Activity

Along with Congress, presidents impact states and other governments with their actions. President Franklin D. Roosevelt showed the changing dimensions of presidential power when he expanded federal authority with a series of executive orders during the Great Depression, many of which were enabled by passage of the National Industrial Recovery Act in 1933. His successors have done so as well, particularly with respect to management of domestic issues. Presidents Dwight D. Eisenhower and John F. Kennedy, for example, ordered troops to Southern states to assist with court-ordered desegregation. During his presidency, Richard Nixon signed an executive order creating the Environmental Protection Agency, thereby establishing federal hegemony over the states.[17] President George W. Bush, however, used the executive order several times in response to the terrorist attacks of September 11, 2001. In 2005, after the devastating Hurricane Katrina caused thousands of deaths and $125 billion in damage to the Gulf states, Bush ordered troops and badly needed supplies to the region.

In addition to their ability to act, presidents set the tone for other public policy making authorities. Richard Neustadt describes this important quality as the "power to persuade."[18] George W. Bush has actively used his presidency as a bully pulpit for persuading various authorities to act, sometimes successfully, sometimes not. Affirmative action serves as a case in point. In 2003, as an affirmative action case worked its way up to the U.S. Supreme Court, Bush argued that affirmative action programs were "divisive, unfair and impossible to square with the Constitution."[19] Ultimately, the Court narrowly voted to uphold application of the concept.[20] However, Bush argued successfully for the No Child Left Behind Act that requires states to meet federal standards on education tests. On a related topic, Bush has called upon Congress and the states to pass a constitutional amendment that would prevent states from recognizing gay marriages. In each of these cases, the president did not create policy; however, he participated decisively as a moral force, exhorting Congress or the courts to act.

Often, presidents invoke their will regarding federalism through the actions of the regulatory agencies at their disposal. The outcomes of these efforts are sometimes hard to see, particularly because they take place as changed rules and in incremental fashion, but the activities of regulatory agencies housed within the executive branch can change mightily the flow of federalism.[21] Consider changes in environmental policy. During the administration of President Bill Clinton, the Environmental Protection Agency developed several national rules on energy efficiency, water purity, and land use. Some states appreciated the rules, others did not.

Many environmental policies have changed under the administration of George W. Bush without any congressional action, thanks to broad legislation that permits the appointees of presidents—in this the EPA administrator—to make such alterations. Thus, during the Bush years, the EPA has eased federal rules on logging and relaxed power-plant pollution standards, leaving to the states the best management practices. With the change in responsibility, some critics have howled that the administrative changes will permit polluting industries "to completely undermine the Clean Air Act" without any moves by Congress to change the law.[22] But for the Bush administration, the paramount question is one of allowing the states to do best for themselves. Former EPA administrator Christie Todd Whitman argued that "those closest to the problem are often best-suited to finding solutions that get results."[23] Translation: States can solve these problems better than the federal government.

Judicial Activity

The courts rule on the use of power through their decisions and the expectation that the other branches and levels will carry out those decisions. Although the federal judicial system has three tiers, the U.S. Supreme Court has final say over lower court decisions. The Supreme Court is also the highest level of adjudication for state court decisions that bear upon the U.S. Constitution. Of the more than 300,000 court cases each year, perhaps one hundred or so will wind up before the U.S. Supreme Court during any annual term, taking many years to wend their way through the legal process. Of the decisions handed down by the Court during any term, only a few pertain to federalism, but those cases speak to the organizational structure of the union.

Scholars have followed the ebb and flow of the decisions of the U.S. Supreme Court since the Constitutional Convention. In broad terms, the Court's decisions have swayed over time, first favoring a strong national government in the first few decades of the Republic, then endorsing greater powers for the states from the 1830s through the 1930s.[24]

From the days of the New Deal until the 1980s, the Court again tended to favor the national government over the states. The deepening of the Great Depression to the point of great despair gave federal jurists reason to believe that the national government should assume responsibilities previously thought best managed by the states. *Helvering v. Davis* (1937), a case permitting the creation of Social Security, symbolized the Court's new behavior first on economic and later on social questions—behavior with an undertone that supported greater national authority. Not all cases were decided in the same direction. However, many were, including *Brown v. Board of Education* (1954), *Baker v. Carr* (1962), and *Roe v. Wade* (1973). In these and other key cases, state powers were minimized in the name of promoting national values through constitutional guarantees.

Since the mid-1980s, the Court has moved yet again on federalism. As with other eras, the direction has been neither uniform nor overly doctrinaire. At times, the Court has ruled against the states regarding the rights of juveniles, environmental protection issues, and medical marijuana. Nevertheless, the tendency has been to tilt in the favor of more state power, while curbing federal intervention. Some recent examples include:

- *Gregory v. Ashcroft* (1991), which stated that the Age Discrimination in Employment Act, designed to keep employers from denying employees work because of age, did not interfere with a state's mandatory retirement laws.
- *U.S. v. Lopez* (1995), which overturned the Gun-Free School Zones Act that prohibited firearms from within 1,000 feet of any public school.
- *Printz v. United States* (1997), which voided a provision of the Brady Act requiring state-conducted background checks of prospective gun owners.

- *Board of Trustees v. Garrett* (2001), which prevented state employees from suing for damages because of violations of the Americans With Disabilities Act, thereby enhancing the power of state governments.

These days, the Supreme Court now seems primed to take more definitive positions on federalism questions, resulting in "new constraints on congressional authority and a corresponding expansion of states' immunity from federal power."[25] The appointments of conservatives John Roberts, Jr., in 2005 and Samuel Alioto in 2006 suggest that "strict constructionists" now have a solid majority to interpret cases more in favor of the states than the federal government.[26]

State Resistance

As partners in the federal arrangement, states contribute considerably to the debate over orchestration and implementation of major public policies. This is especially true with respect to those that require state cooperation in their implementation. When states are called upon to participate in a federal policy, they may resist because of imposing financial burdens, new obligations that conflict with dominant state values, or because they believe their own circumstances call for approaches outside federal policies. On other occasions, states have been known to be proactive in policy areas that become templates for national action.

Financial Burdens

Sometimes, state leaders push for national relief from financial burdens that are imposed upon them as part of legislation, court orders, or regulations promulgated by the federal bureaucracy. The Unfunded Mandates Reform Act of 1995 was designed to limit such impositions, or at least give Congress in particular reason to pause. Nevertheless, despite the intentions of the national legislation, federal officials continue to pass laws with the implementation costs left to the states.

Consider the requirements associated with the No Child Left Behind Education Act. Although the legislation is intended to help states increase the competence of their school-age populations, some officials allege that the law is unnecessarily rigid and that federal government underfunded the states by $25 billion during the first three years of implementation.[27] In view of the absence of billions of dollars to carry out federally mandated programs at the state level, an observer recently noted that as a result of the numerous mandates coming from Congress, "the major battles this year [2005] may not be between Democrats and Republicans in Congress, but between the states and the federal government."[28] Shortly thereafter, Utah became the first state to reject parts of the No Child Left Behind legislation, jeopardizing the state's receipt of federal funds.[29] On a related front, the Connecticut attorney general sued the federal government for not providing enough funds to implement the act, while as many as twenty other states considered whether to refuse participation and forego federal funding.[30] The resistance took hold. In November 2005, the U.S. Department of Education shifted its criteria for measuring education success by agreeing to allow states to set objectives on a school-by-school basis, rather than a statewide basis as provided in the original program.[31]

Opposing State Values

Sometimes one or more institutions at the federal level will create a policy that simply does not sit well with the dominant political culture, or value system, of one or more states. Ira Sharkansky observes that "political cultures differ from one state and region to the next, and leave their imprint on public affairs."[32] When a federal prescription results in state discomfort, the state may well refuse to implement the new policy, risking a lawsuit or financial sanctions for doing so.

School prayer is an area where federal rules and state political culture often collide. In 2000, the U.S. Supreme Court ruled 6–3 that student-led prayers before public school football games violated the wall separating religion and state.[33] Yet, by the start of the next football season, several states permitted the very school prayers that had been declared unconstitutional.[34] Why does the federal government not step in to rectify such defiance? To do so in every case across the country would require tremendous political energy and exacerbate numerous conflicts. Thus, leaders at the national level must weigh the extent to which further attention is worth the effort and potential costs down the road—in other words, future elections.

Proposed Exemptions

Occasionally, there are instances where states have been known to lobby the federal government for exemption from national legislation because of matters unique to those states. When such objections are raised, they sometimes become the first steps to test-bed or beta site programs that later emerge as templates for national models. Such conditions arise, David Osborne writes, because states must deal with real, everyday problems, unlike the institutions of the federal government that focus on concepts.[35] But because states are small "laboratories" relative to the entire nation, their sizes allow easier experimentation of a new policy than if the entire nation pursued a new direction.

Environmental policy is an area where states often oppose federal standards because they simply do not fit in with state values. In California, state leaders have long argued for the right to adopt environmental regulations that are actually stronger than federal rules because of the state's history with smog. Such pleas have come from both Democrats and Republicans for more than thirty years, and have usually been granted by federal Environmental Protection Agency administrators.[36] Similar pleas have come from governors on the East Coast over the federal relaxation of power-plant pollution standards. After the George W. Bush administration made pollution requirements less onerous for businesses in 2003, the governors from several eastern states took the administration to court in an effort to block the new regulation.[37] Later that year, a federal court issued an order that kept the administration from carrying out the plan.

State Initiatives

On some occasions, states seize an issue that is too difficult for the federal government to deal with on a national basis. One such area has focused on the sexual relationships between consenting adults. Well before the U.S. Supreme Court determined that government does not have the right to interfere with such relationships, several states had taken the lead in eliminating sodomy laws affecting heterosexuals and homosexuals. As recently as 1960, all fifty states had anti-sodomy laws. David C. Nice writes that by the early 1990s, most states had removed laws governing sexual practices of adults because laws against such activities were difficult to enforce, they lacked public support, and they faced perennially strained police resources.[38] By 2003, sodomy laws remained on the books in thirteen states. Those were wiped out when the U.S. Supreme Court ruled by a vote of 6–3 that states could not criminalize private conduct between adults.[39] The collective action of so many states elevated the issue to a national debate, although to this day states have differing policies governing sexual relationships.

Immigration policy is another area where states have moved in the face of federal paralysis. In 2001, newly elected President George W. Bush asked the Congress to overhaul the nation's immigration law to deal with increasing numbers of illegal immigrants as well as the needs of businesses for immigrant labor. As Congress began to consider legislation, the nation was horrified by the terrorist attacks of September 11, 2001. Stunned by the events, Congress ceased all activity on immigration reform. But over the next twenty-four months, states acted, with at least thirty-seven states considering more than one hundred bills ranging from immigrants' rights to driver's licenses. The governors of two states, New Mexico and Arizona, actually declared emergencies, charging the U.S. Department of Homeland Security with abandoning its responsibilities, while freeing up special funds to deal with border problems.[40] Not all states passed tougher restrictions; in fact, some states eased the rules on university admissions, teaching credentials, and other activities. The final outcome, however, is that most states acted on their own.[41]

When it comes to revenue streams, the hard-pressed states have been active in pursuing income opportunities. The tobacco industry is a case in point. For decades, the tobacco companies and their products were regulated (some would say protected) by the federal government, particularly the Federal Trade Commission. Tobacco lobbyists worked hard to keep their industry under federal regulation because they appreciated lenient treatment under one federal roof, rather than the possibilities of suits in fifty states. During the 1980s and 1990s, evidence against tobacco as a direct cause of cancer became irrefutable, and the states saw an opportunity. After a few successful cases against tobacco companies in state courts during the mid-1990s, the attorneys general of forty-six states collaborated in an agreement with the major tobacco companies to collect more than $200 billion over a twenty-year period in exchange for protecting the companies against future lawsuits. While this agreement ended state disputes, it did nothing regarding federal claims against the industry. The federal government sued in 1999, and settled its issues in 2005 with the industry for a fraction of what the states had won,[42] leading some critics to praise the states for their political will and condemn the Bush administration for caving in to a major campaign contribution group.[43]

Aggressive state activity on pressing issues can sometimes be unsettling not only to the federal government but to private interests as well. For more than a century, the federal government has regulated major segments of food and food processing largely through two 1906 laws—the Food and Drug Act, which created the Food and Drug Administration, and the Meat Inspection Act. States, however, have been able to act in areas not covered by the federal legislation, such as labels that contain warnings of potentially harmful health risks associated with the packaged food. Thus, California requires disclosure of substances that may cause cancer or birth defects, while Connecticut and Michigan mandate warnings about allergy-causing preservatives. The various food policies may fit well with the needs of particular states, but they cause havoc for the food industry, whose representatives view the individual policies as confusing and unnecessarily costly. As a spokesperson has stated, "You could have two different labels, three different labels, 50 labels depending on inconsistent state requirements."[44] As a result of this tension, several bills have been introduced in Congress.

Clearly, the federal government wields great clout in creating policies that extend to the states and beyond. Nevertheless, states often are not idle in their reactions to federal policies, particularly if they conflict with state needs as perceived by their leaders or populations. Further, states are not shy about enacting laws in areas where the federal government has not acted. This dynamic underscores the uncertainty of federal/state government relations.

National/Local Federalism

It is an understatement to say that governments have expanded their roles and functions over the nation's history. From the national regulations on spent nuclear materials to state public education requirements to local speeding laws, governments have emerged as key participants in the lives of American citizens. Along with their expanded roles, governments have developed new relationships with each other. One such connection has emerged in the interaction between national and local governments. Federal policies on housing, urban crime, military base locations, and highway programs have intersected with local governments in ways unimaginable two hundred years ago. These are rather remarkable developments, given that the Framers did not even mention local governments in the Constitution.

Evolution of a Relationship

In the early years of the nation, cities were physically isolated and politically far removed from national and state politics. In 1800, urban areas contained about 300,000 of the nation's 5,300,000 inhabitants. With the industrial revolution, however, cities became centers of production and assembly plants. Urban living areas grew more dense and congested, leading to needs for water supplies, transportation networks, sewer systems, education facilities, police forces, fire departments, and other services.

By 1900, urban residents made up about 40 percent of the nation's population. Many city governments had fallen under the control of corrupt political machines that were more attentive to powerful, narrow interests than the needs of the cities. With the rise of the Progressive movement at the turn of the century, reformers demanded an end to patronage, the establishment of neutral civil service systems, and other means to restore government to popular rule. Still, local governments kept to themselves, relying upon property and user taxes as the means to finance their local needs. They were largely self-contained political units.

It was with the onset of the Great Depression that the national government began to focus upon cities and their populations. By the 1930s, cities had become centers of unemployment, displaced populations, and starvation. Bankrupt, neither city nor state governments were financially equipped to respond to the unprecedented economic devastation. The nation and its governments were in a collective state of near paralysis. Beginning in 1932, and continuing through 1936, candidate and then president Franklin D. Roosevelt focused upon the cities as open economic wounds in need of immediate treatment. Roosevelt asked for and Congress passed several programs emphasizing relief, including the Public Works Administration, Civilian Works Administration, and the Works Progress Administration. While these efforts were not tailored exclusively for urban populations, they had a disproportionate impact in the cities.

From those days on, the national and urban governments expanded political and economic ties. Presidential candidates pursued urban votes and local government leaders petitioned for federal assistance.[45] The national/local fiscal linkage has become a staple in American politics. Over time, the federal government has increasingly provided direct fiscal assistance to cities through myriad grant-in-aid programs. Over the past thirty years, the federal contribution to local coffers has varied between 5 and 15 percent of all city revenues. However, in the most recent period, the percentage has been toward the low end of the range.[46]

Along with more federal money for the cities has come the quest for more federal control over what transpires in the cities. In some cases, such as urban renewal programs, the federal government has provided criteria for local governments which, when implemented, destroyed some neighborhoods while rebuilding others. In other cases, federal programs for assisting small business development have operated at odds with urban housing efforts. Because of the dollars associated with these programs, the financially pressed cities have had to develop inconsistent policies in order to qualify for federal funds. That said, without the funds, the cities might be struggling even more.

The most current developments in the federal government/local government arrangement have centered on new types of federal commitments. While the dollar amounts have remained fairly constant, they have been directed toward different objectives. Thus, between 2003 and 2004, while federal funds for urban faith-based initiatives and organizations doubled, federal funds for traditional public programs such as public housing, energy subsidies, and other social services were slashed.[47] These nuances point to the ebb and flow of political values in the governmental process. They also show the extent to which federal objectives trickle all the way down to local arenas.

These changes have transformed the relationship between cities and the federal government. Because of the tremendous extent of reliance, Terry

Christensen notes, "local governments are no longer sovereign or autonomous. Rather, they are subnational and subordinate—dependent instead of independent."[48] Perhaps. More fundamentally, however, the transformation shows the extent to which federalism is an evolving enterprise.

Hurricane Katrina: Breakdown and Reassessment

On August 28, 2005, Hurricane Katrina assaulted the Gulf Coast, rewriting the meaning of "devastation" in the process. Designated a Category 4—next to the most serious category—hurricane, Katrina wiped out greater New Orleans as well as areas several hundred miles in each direction. In the wake of the September 11, 2001, terrorist attacks upon the East Coast, Katrina offered the first test of the United States' capability to respond to a disaster. Within days, Congress allocated more than $80 billion for repairs and restoration of everything from destroyed levees to destroyed and uninhabitable housing. Yet, the federal government moved at a snail's pace; government officials could not even match temporary housing with households even though thousands of unoccupied trailers awaited occupancy. Dollars notwithstanding, most critics believe that the government failed.[49]

One hundred days after Katrina, the Gulf Coast region remained in a daze. The unemployment rate hovered at 15 percent, triple the pre-Katrina rate. More significantly, electricity had been restored to only half of the homes, while only one of the New Orleans' public schools had reopened. Astoundingly, little changed very quickly. Six months after Katrina, more than 200,000 Gulf Coast families remained without any hope of returning home—whether to their old residences or replacement housing.[50]

With each day after Katrina, growing numbers of fingers pointed wildly in numerous directions of blame. So slow was the federal government's response through the Federal Emergency Management Agency (FEMA) that President George W. Bush apologized to the victims and promised an unprecedented federal relief effort that would restore the Gulf Coast to its previous condition. Yet, while the president accepted blame for a slow-responding federal government, the governors of Louisiana and Mississippi dueled with federal officials over control of the recovery process, while local mayors anguished in despair.[51] Meanwhile, the governors of "host" states wondered whether and when they would be compensated for the various costs—in some cases hundreds of millions of dollars—associated with sheltering Katrina refugees.[52] Who was to blame may never be fully known, but one inescapable conclusion is clear: The various levels of governments failed to assemble a coordinated, well-managed response to the nation's worst disaster since 9/11.

State/Local Relations

Bearing in mind that federalism focuses on the relationship between two or more governments, state/local linkages represent worthy areas of attention. Federal dollars to the state and local governments through grant-in-aid programs have leveled off at about $400 billion in recent years, underscoring the deep connection of state/local relationships. In addition, as devolution increases, state and local governments are gaining greater responsibilities and obligations for public policy issues that were once under greater control of or had more support from the federal government. Thus, on matters ranging from public education to the use of public lands, the state/local government relationship has reemerged as a critical cornerstone of federalism.

The Battle for Control

Historically, the state/local government power linkage has been rather one-sided. Bearing in mind that local governments are not acknowledged in the U.S. Constitution, local authorities have operated largely as appendages and with the permission of the states. The legal basis for this arrangement was crafted first in 1819, when the U.S. Supreme Court "upheld the power of states to define the powers and obligations of local governments."[53] In 1868, John F. Dillon, an Iowa judge, clarified the matter further by observing that given the absence of any constitutional foundation, municipal governments are "creatures of the state." As such, Dillon noted, cities may only carry out functions authorized by the state government.[54] States also set the conditions under which groups of people may organize populations into towns, cities, and other local jurisdictions. Most often, towns and cities fall under the responsibility of counties, which are the primary local governments that administer state laws.

So much for the constitutional explanation. The fact is that in most states, state and local leaders' struggle for power is similar to the battles witnessed between the federal government and the states. Often, the battles take place over public policy areas such as local taxation capabilities, welfare requirements, public education requirements, building codes, and infrastructure facilities such as power facilities and transportation. These battles carry considerable irony, given similar power struggles elsewhere. As Robert S. Lorch notes, "states seem to disregard the aspirations of local governments for local control with the same regularity that Washington habitually disregards 'state sovereignty.'"[55]

Although power issues regarding local control vary from state to state, in general:

- Increasingly, states have assumed larger roles in funding and shaping public education programs, generally the largest single financial commitment.
- Local governments have learned to circumvent statewide tax limits by creating special districts to fund dozens of programs ranging from fire protection to insect abatement.
- Newer states tend to cede more authority and self-governance to local governments than older states, chiefly because their constitutions are longer, more detailed, and more explicit in the assignments of authority.

Special Districts

The rise of **special districts** exemplifies the changing relationship between state and local governments. These narrowly constructed governmental units are designed to provide services and programs through targeted revenues. They collect taxes, have elected officials, and operate to serve narrow areas such as sewage removal, lighting, fire protection, insect control, cemetery maintenance, and other one-dimensional operations. Today there are more than thirty thousand of these units in operation.

Operating "outside the consciousness of the average citizen,"[56] special districts are often organized as creative ways to pay for local needs that traditional local governments or states choose not to fund, usually because of budget constraints or property tax limitations. The establishment of these governing bodies has added yet another facet to the concept of federalism, demonstrating once again its malleability.

Federal Grants-in-Aid as a Catalyst for Control

In Chapter 4, we introduced the concept of grants-in-aid as a form of fiscal federalism. Congress employs grants as a means to organize and promote national public policy. Dollars from these commitments flow to states and local governments that buy into the programs. Beyond establishing national priorities, grants-in-aid bind state and local governments to these programs by virtue of their acceptance of federal dollars (See Figure 6.1).

Categorical Grant-in-Aid Programs

The changes have been dramatic. As grants-in-aid proliferated during the 1960s and 1970s, Congress enacted hundreds of **categorical**, or specific, grant programs that provided aid, sometimes to states for distribution, but

Figure 6.1 **Summary Comparison of Total Outlays for Grants to State and Local Governments, 1940–2011**

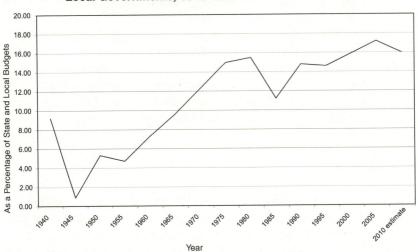

Source: Office of Management and Budget. Budget of the United States Government, Fiscal Year 2003. Section 12 Federal Grants to State and Local Governments. Table 12.1 Summary Comparision of Total Outlays for Grants to State Governments. www.whitehouse. gov/omb/budget/fy2007/pdf/hist.pdf

often directly from Washington to local governments. The programs are categorical because participation of state or local governments must fit into the various narrow categories of legislation. They usually include a matching federal component of anywhere between 5 percent and 50 percent, depending upon the program in question.

Most of the omnibus grant-in-aid programs have been reauthorized every few years. Beyond the availability of federal dollars for local projects, these fiscal relationships have created strong political ties between local members of Congress, federal bureaucrats, and local government officials. A recent example is the Safe, Accountable, Flexible, and Efficient Transportation Equity Act (SAFETEA), a six-year, $244 billion piece of legislation enacted by Congress in 2005. Under this legislation, cities, ports, and regional governments can apply to the Department of Transportation to participate directly in dozens of categorical programs ranging from school bus safety to road congestion relief.[57]

Block Grant-in-Aid Programs

Some opponents of categorical grants-in-aid have faulted the concept because of the specificity attached to most of the programs. They say that local governments can hardly squeeze into a "one size fits all template." Rather, these institutions and their populations have widely differing needs dependent upon factors such as densities, local economies, cultural imperatives, and geographical distinctions like rivers or mountains that define unique needs.

Let us return to the transportation issue. Suppose that a congressional grant-in-aid program similar to SAFETEA makes available funds for new bridges, but the local government needs high occupancy vehicle (HOV) lanes instead. With categorical grants-in-aid, there would be no assistance. Further, under the terms of these narrow approaches, local officials often have not been able to coordinate one grant with another, exacerbating inefficiencies rather than reducing them. There is a political cost as well. As a result of the enhanced national/local relationship, some state governments have lost a good deal of control over their own local governments.

The Growth of Federal Grants-in-Aid

Criticisms of the categorical approach have led Congress to enact **block** grant-in-aid programs, funding for general problem areas with local leaders deciding just how and where to spend the money. The impetus for this new direction began under the Reagan administration, when Congress converted about two dozen categorical grant-in-aid programs into block programs. Over the next decade or so, some areas such as criminal justice and welfare received block funding, with state and local governments given broad latitude over how to spend their allocations. But this approach raised another issue—the problem of accountability. With few requirements, state and local governments often spent funds on needs that Congress never intended. That independence has led Congress to recalibrate the block approach. Over time, David Walker observes, block grants "tend to acquire conditions, provided that Congress or the executive branch is really concerned over the goals of a particular block grant."[58]

The Problem of Formulas

Most grants-in-aid programs are formula based—that is the dollars are made available to state or local governments based on a preexisting set of conditions including population, cost-of-living indexes, percentages of poor people, average income levels, geographical considerations, and other factors. Sometimes these formulas are totally inappropriate because their assumptions are out of touch with reality. Nowhere has there been more controversy than over the formula for the funding of homeland security

Table 6.1

Federal Homeland Security Grants-in-Aid, Fiscal Years 2003 and 2004

State	Amount (in millions $)
California	317.1
New York	183.4
Texas	154.1
Florida	130.8
Illinois	113.8
Pennsylvania	111.0
Ohio	100.9
New Jersey	88.1
Michigan	75.8
Massachusetts	68.3
Georgia	67.6
Missouri	66.1
North Carolina	61.6
Washington	61.2
Minnesota	59.2
Maryland	58.9
Virginia	56.9
Indiana	54.5
Arizona	53.4
Tennessee	52.8
Wisconsin	51.3
Louisiana	51.2
Colorado	45.5
Kentucky	44.0
Connecticut	42.6
Oregon	40.6
Alabama	36.9
Nevada	36.8
South Carolina	35.2
Oklahoma	32.4
Iowa	29.9
Mississippi	29.6

sistance to the states. Table 6.1 lists the U.S. states and territories in order of homeland security dollars received in 2003 and 2004. Yet, there is little correlation in terms of homeland security risks. Note that Washington and Minnesota received nearly identical sums, even though Washington has a huge coastal seaport that receives ships from throughout the world, compared to a land-locked state on the border with Canada.

The issue is particularly revealing when examining homeland security funds as related to populations. During 2005, for example, Wyoming received the largest allocation on a per capita basis, while Virginia, located adjacent to politically sensitive Washington, D.C., received the least. Table 6.2 shows the five

Table 6.1 *(continued)*

State	Amount (in millions $)
Arkansas	28.9
Kansas	28.9
Utah	27.0
New Mexico	24.9
West Virginia	24.8
Nebraska	24.4
Idaho	22.7
Maine	22.4
New Hampshire	22.3
Hawaii	22.2
Rhode Island	21.3
Montana	20.7
Delaware	20.2
South Dakota	20.0
Alaska	19.5
North Dakota	19.4
Vermont	19.4
District of Columbia	19.1
Wyoming	18.8
National Capital Region*	32.1
Puerto Rico	34.0
US Virgin Islands	6.1
American Samoa	5.8
Guam	6.2
Northern Marianas	5.8

Note: Allocations include funds from the State Homeland Security Grant Program, the Law Enforcement Terrorism Prevention Program, the Citizen Corps Grant Program, and the Urban Area Security Initiative.

* Additional funds for Washington, D.C., and select counties in Maryland and Virginia.

Source: Shawn Reese, *FY2003 and FY2004 State Allocations for Selected Homeland Security Assistance Programs* (Congressional Research Service Report, July 2004).

states receiving the most homeland security funding and the five states receiving the least on a per capita basis. These funding processes have left critics up in arms over formula-based grant-in-aid allocations. Nevertheless many federal programs operate along lines similar to the homeland security funding system. Depending upon the urgency of the policy area, states often have to make up the difference—a situation that sometimes wreaks havoc on budgets.

Inequities notwithstanding, grant-in-aid programs now dominate the fiscal relationship between the national and state/local governments. And increasingly, conservatives and liberals differ not on whether there should be such programs, but rather the themes and forms of funding.

Table 6.2

Homeland Security Grants—State Allocations, Fiscal Year 2005

Highest		Lowest	
State	Per capita amount	State	Per capita amount
Wyoming	$27.80	Virginia	$5.23
Alaska	24.83	North Carolina	5.61
North Dakota	23.83	Tennessee	5.64
Vermont	23.83	Florida	6.07
Hawaii	19.35	Alabama	6.24

Note: The District of Columbia received $23.50.
Source: U.S. Department of Homeland Security, Office of Homeland Preparedness.

Grants-in-Aid and Local Power

Grants-in-aid have complicated the relationship between state and local governments. Politically, local governments still may be largely dependent upon the states for their existence and capabilities. Fiscally, however, the fact that local governments increasingly may acquire funds from another source—the federal government—has the potential for lessening local dependence upon state governments and weakening the control state governments have over local entities. This relatively new wrinkle in federalism may diminish the power of state governments over the long run, should grants-in-aid continue to grow in popularity.

National/Private Sector Relations

When the Framers designed the U.S. Constitution, it is hard to imagine they considered anything remotely close to a system where government provides direct assistance to the private sector. The early designers looked favorably upon property, but they were quick to avoid favoritism of one propertied class over another; to do so would undermine the cherished value of equality.[59] That is why the growing relationship between the national government and the private sector looms so large in a discussion of federalism. Surely, this connection would turn the heads of more than a few Framers; then, many other transformations of the Constitution would probably turn heads, too. Three examples are government commitments to employee pensions, corporate economic security, and subsidies.

Pension Benefits Guarantees

Pensions long have been part of the agreement between employers and their employees. Historically, these retirement payments have been the glue that kept the two primary components of capitalism on the same page. In return for working many years at the same company, the employee would receive annual payments in his or her retirement. These dollars would be put aside by the company during the length of the worker's employment, assuring funds after departure. The eligibility requirements and funding formulas varied dramatically, depending upon a variety of factors, but the pension concept simply was a way to promote loyalty, continuity, and productivity in the workplace. Differences notwithstanding, companies reduced their pension commitments by about 20 percent between 1980 and 1995 alone, leaving a collective shortfall of $262 billion.[60]

During the 1970s and 1980s, a few companies defaulted on their pension promises, causing financial problems for their retirees and worrying others in the workforce. In an effort to assure long-term stability, Congress created the Pension Benefit Guarantee Corporation (PBGC) in 1974. This governmental unit was intended as insurance that all pensions would be paid, regardless of any corporate problems. The program would be funded by corporations with more than twenty-five employees that provided pensions. By 2005, PBGC covered 44 million workers and retirees in 35,000 pension plans. About 20 percent of the active workforce was included among this group.

At first, the PBGC charged companies premiums of $1 per employee per month; by 2005, the premium had been readjusted several times to $19 per employee per year. This amount seemed to be rather an inexpensive insurance policy. According to the law governing the PBGC, the employees of any company no longer able to pay pensions would be awarded a maximum of $42,950 per year in the lieu of their pensions.

Still, the PBGC was not prepared for the economic avalanche about to occur. Beginning in 2002, several large companies declared bankruptcy. Thanks to accommodating bankruptcy laws, companies could forego debts to their creditors as well as retirement obligations to their employees, leaving the PBGC to fill in with respect to employee pensions. Several airlines led the way, but dozens of other major companies followed in their wake including Delphi Auto Parts, Bethlehem Steel, Kaiser Aluminum, Enron, and Cone Mills. Suddenly, millions of employees and retirees faced futures with no pensions and minimal federal compensation. So vast were the numbers of bankruptcies and corporate reorganizations that the PBGC was overwhelmed with obligations. Several economists pointed to dozens of other major companies that were underfunding their pension needs.[61] Nevertheless, bankruptcy had become a way of life, with the government left to pick up a sizable portion of the retirement tab. By 2004, the PBGC had assets of $39 billion and liabilities of $62.3 billion, leaving a deficit of $23.3 billion. But this was only the beginning. As of 2005, the Congressional Budget Office estimated that because of increasing numbers of corporate bankruptcies, by 2015 the deficit would grow to $86.7 billion, with an even larger deficit of $141.9 billion expected by 2025.[62]

Meanwhile, members of Congress began to craft a response. In 2005, bills were introduced to increase the annual premiums to $30 per worker and to give corporations extended periods of time to make up their deficiencies.[63] More important than the details of the policy response, however, was the built-in guarantee that the U.S. government would make up any deficits in order to provide the minimum guarantees associated with the PBGC. To this extent, the national government/private sector bond was unbreakable, giving an expanded meaning to federalism.

Corporate Bailouts

On a philosophical level, many observers of American politics believe that government and the private sector are separated by a tall fence. In their *Free to Choose,* Milton and Rose Friedman make the case that the best government is one that stays far away from individuals or organizations: "The system under which people make their own choices—and bear most of the consequences for their decisions—is the system that has prevailed for most of our history."[64] That may be the case in theory, but others are not so sure strong separations between government and private interests exist in fact. Thus, Grant McConnell writes, historically groups have lobbied for and received favored treatment by government, leading to the conclusion that some elements are conferred different benefits from others.[65] In fact, historical examples abound of governments benefiting private interests in the name of the "public good,"[66] all of which leads us to a discussion of modern linkages between the national government and corporate interests.

Over the past few decades, the federal government has had a closer relationship with corporations than in the past. In fact, a leading economist has written that the modern corporation "has won accommodation" by government on matters important to survival.[67] Consider some examples of where the federal government has thrown a financial life preserver to save corporations from going under:

- *Lockheed, 1971.* As the nation's largest defense contractor at the time, Lockheed had run out of money attempting to fund a new airplane. Proponents claimed that the company needed another $250 million to avoid bankruptcy and the loss of 60,000 jobs. In a close vote, Congress provided the loan guarantee and President Richard Nixon signed the bill into law. Lockheed repaid the loan.

- *Chrysler, 1980.* For more than a decade, Chrysler lost market share (its traditional portion of automobile sales) largely to Japanese automobile firms that made better cars at lower prices. Battered, in 1980, Chrysler asked for and received a government loan guarantee of $1.2 billion, courtesy of the U.S Congress and President Jimmy Carter. Chrysler eventually paid back the loan.

- *Banks and Savings and Loans, 1987.* Between 1980 and 1982, the federal government deregulated the conditions under which banks and savings and loans could operate.[68] Within the next four years, 140 banks went under, leaving depositors without any compensation. In 1987, Congress bailed out financial institutions by authorizing $10.8 billion in the Competitive Equality Banking Act. In this case, taxpayers were left to shoulder the burden.

- *Airline Industry, 2001.* Fierce competition in the airline industry emerged after Congress enacted the Airline Transportation Act of 1978. Regional carriers and start-ups cut into the long-established "legacy carriers," bringing about financial losses and, in some cases, mergers. Shortly after the 9/11 terrorist attacks, the airline industry asked for and received $5 billion in cash and $10 billion in loan guarantees.

The foregoing examples show the growing relationship between the federal government and the private sector. When major elements of the business community appear in jeopardy, the federal government provides relief with the intention of restoring stability.

Subsidies

In addition to industry-specific bailouts, the federal government provides an array of subsidies, or targeted payments, to the public and private sectors. Public subsidies are often seen in the forms of subsidized public housing and economic enterprise zones. Usually, distressed urban areas are awarded federal tax breaks as an inducement for attracting businesses. Note that federal political decisions are made to increase opportunities for economic success.

Federal subsidies for elements of the private sector are more pervasive and costly. In recent years, farmers of numerous crops, timber companies, and airplane manufacturers have been among the many private interests to benefit from government subsidies. Large farm interests and agribusiness corporations in particular have often been the most notable recipients of subsidies, with the public picking up the tab in the form of higher prices for farm products.[69] These forms of assistance are given either to shore up depressed sectors or help companies compete internationally. Here, too, we see direct relationships between government commitments and economic advancement. As with the public commitments, however, such decisions are targeted and made available to select recipients.

Vertical Federalism in Perspective

Clearly, vertical federalism is a mainstay in defining the power relationships between the national and state governments. However, contemporary political arrangements extend the concept beyond historic boundaries to other governments, and even the private sector. It is hard to know how many of these linkages were anticipated at the Constitutional Convention. It is also fair to say that some—notably national/local and national/private sector relationships—were in all likelihood well beyond the imaginations of the Framers.

Just because new applications of vertical federalism were not original creations does not denigrate their value or roles. Rather, these new wrinkles point to the extent that even the most recognized forms of federalism have the potential to evolve.

7

★ ★ ★ ★

Horizontal Federalism
Arrangements Among the States

Relationships among the American states are particularly complex, inconsistent, and unpredictable. The word "complex" comes to mind because of the multifaceted dealings between states on numerous public policy issues that occur simultaneously. Sometimes, the linkages are harmonious and complementary, with several states working to achieve the same general objective. At other times, however, intense rivalries smack of harsh competition for advantage, reflecting the dynamics of a zero-sum game. The latter is most often observed on economic matters, but may also be seen on questions ranging from competing social values to geographical boundary disputes.

On one level, states find it in their interests to cooperate with respect to both regional issues and in their petitions for assistance from the federal government. There is a strategic political reason for such mindfulness. So large and potentially dominating is the federal government that purposive coordination and collaboration among the states often become a fundamental necessity in thwarting what states often view as intrusive federal threats. Sometimes by banding together, state resistance becomes more difficult for the federal government to overcome.

On another level, states compete with each other nonstop in their efforts to improve their individual economies and fiscal well-being. Often one state will woo a major business or industry from another state with promises such as reduced taxes, infrastructure assistance, or free job training facilities for new employees. The outcomes of these battles can be compelling for the "winning" and "losing" states. When a manufacturing business with several thousand workers moves from one state to another, so go real estate prices, nearby supporting businesses, and state and local revenues from corporate profits, personal incomes, and consumer purchases.

Cooperation and competition among the states are contradictory by definition, yet these two themes go a long away toward explaining the bipolar dynamics of horizontal federalism. The same states that work hard together to thwart illegal immigration or organize a regional electricity power line grid may also simultaneously attempt to capture each other's water supply and battle for grants-in-aid and federal pilot programs. This rather unstable political environment makes it hard for states to plan long-term, resulting in a variety of economic and political issues.

This chapter focuses on the opportunities and challenges of horizontal federalism. We begin with a discussion of the cultural differences and similarities among the various states, the combination of which provides an unstable foundation for political linkages beyond state boundaries. Following that we will examine the impact of public opinion upon state issues. We will also discuss the various inducements for regional cooperation as well as the sources of political and economic competition.

State Political Cultures in the Federal Framework

Much has been said about "red" and "blue" states as participants in presidential elections. Red states tend to be toward the conservative end of the political spectrum, embodying traits such as fiscal restraint, states' rights, and religious evangelism. Most red states lie in the nation's interior and southern area. Blue states tend to be toward the liberal end of the political spectrum, reflecting characteristics such as government growth, national dominance, and secular values. Most blue states are found along the nation's coasts.[1] To be sure, the descriptions here and elsewhere in this chapter on cultural distinctions are generalizations—there are liberals in red states and conservatives in blue states, along with political moderates of various shades in between. Yet, as generalizations, these descriptions give us a handle on understanding some of the cultural differences among the states.

Defining Political Culture

Countries are held together by numerous bonds, one of which is **political culture**, or the loose set of basic attitudes and beliefs among the general population that underlies support of the political system and the processes under which it operates. Political culture is something akin to political glue for a society. People adhere to a set of general themes and propositions that more or less frame their approaches to the operation of their government. Cultural values, in turn, help to shape the terms of governments and their public policies. Lucian Pye points to political culture as "the product of both the collective history of a political system and the life histories of the members of that system. . . . In brief, political culture is to the political system what culture is to the social system."[2] All societies function to some extent in concert with their political cultures. This does not mean that everyone within the polity thinks and acts the same way; rather it suggests a general widespread agreement among most people about a broad-based pattern of political operation.

Some countries falter or fail altogether because no one set of values is strong enough to ensure consensus and deference among the population to a mutually agreed set of rules or principles. When that happens, they sometimes fall into civil war or a milder form of dysfunctional behavior. Samuel P. Huntington refers to these political arrangements as the conditions of "cleft countries," where deep cultural or religious divisions "can lead to massive violence or threaten a country's existence."[3] Political culture, then, is an important ingredient for promoting stability and order in society.

In addition to the national characteristics of political culture, states have their own dominant value systems, too. And yet, as we will see below, not all states adhere to the same sets of political values, helping to explain some of the fissures in American politics that often appear as policy disagreements.

Cultural Distinctions as Related to American Federalism

Historically, political culture has played an important role in framing the organization of the United States. Broad-based ingredients such as the collective desire for a republican form of government, support for the concept of political accountability, and endorsement of universal suffrage (eventually) are among the many beliefs that have been embraced by most Americans. Together, these and other elements weave together the nation's political tapestry. Of course, there have been regional, sectional, and even state-to-state differences that sometimes unravel the political tapestry at the edges. For the most part, however, the subsets of American political culture within the states have been sufficiently elastic and tolerant to accommodate competing views within the general overarching national governmental framework. Only in the instance of the Civil War were the value differences between Americans so great that the nation temporarily collapsed before repairing itself.

Earlier we discussed the conflicting themes of liberty and equality; historically, these have been "bookend" values of American federalism. Each has been both cultivated and balanced through the organization of and amendments to the United States Constitution. Ever since the earliest days at the Constitutional Convention in Philadelphia, public policy makers at the national and state levels have operated—sometimes with great difficulty—between these powerful magnets. Beyond equality and liberty, political scientists point to other values suggesting the existence of several political cultures under the umbrella of American government. Thus, Aaron Wildavsky writes, "though the United States is a single nation, Americans do not constitute a single culture."[4] In other words, although there are certain binding dominant values, differences exist on other issues.

In fact, some political scientists have described the coexistence of several political cultures in the United States, not unlike competing cultures in other nations.[5] Daniel Elazar explores the notion of competing values further in his work on federalism, where he contends that three political culture subsets coexist in the United States:

- The **individualistic** political culture, which emphasizes limited roles for government, voluntary relationships, and individualism over any collective benefits provided by political parties.
- The **moralistic** political culture, which views government commitments to the public as more important than private relationships, with a strong reliance upon public participation in the political process.
- The **traditionalistic** political culture, which focuses on government activities as limited to protecting the existing social order and carried out by elites, those who have the most at stake and who understand the process.[6]

These cultures tend to occupy different geographical areas of the United States. In general terms, most southern states exhibit the traditionalistic model, northern states from the Great Lakes to the Pacific operate largely under the moralistic model, and states from Appalachia to the plains characterize the individualistic model.

Elazar notes that the patterns of political cultures are dynamic rather than static. Whatever their origins, value systems change over time particularly in response to immigration, economic development, demography, social change, and the development of cultural norms. Thus, whereas California was once dominated by the moralistic model, in recent years it exhibits a good deal of the individualistic approach largely because of changing immigration patterns. And whereas Florida was once dominated by the individualistic approach, in recent years it has been influenced increasingly by the moralistic model with an influx of retirees.

All of this supports something akin to a cultural kaleidoscope of unpredictable dimensions. Elazar concludes that "changes occur internally within particular cultural groups, movement occurs from group to group, cultures borrow from one another, and cultural syntheses take place over time."[7] Fundamentally, however, the United States is the home to several political cultures that distinguish themselves differently from state to state, but are not so different that their values tear the nation apart. At the same time, these differences underscore the point that states often respond to similar economic, social, and political issues with different public policies.

Public Opinion and Policy Differences

Because states contain populations with different dominant value sets, their leaders sometimes chart different courses. As a result, an issue handled one way in some states may be administered quite differently in others. The controversial issues of capital punishment, abortion, immigration, and public education help to make the point.

Capital Punishment

In 1972, the U.S. Supreme Court suspended capital punishment on the grounds that it was applied with radically different standards from state to state.[8] Four years later, the Court allowed resumption of capital punishment if states separated the trial phase from the punishment phase.[9] Since then, thirty-eight states have reinstated capital punishment as part of their sentencing alternatives.

An examination of data gathered between 1976 and 2005 shows that a handful of states have administered most of the nation's executions. At the same time, twelve states have refused to execute anyone over the same period. Table 7.1 shows the ten leading capital punishment states during the thirty-year period.

Of interest is that eight of the top ten states are in the South, with the remaining two being "border states," suggesting a strong regional pattern.

Equally interesting is the collection of twelve states that choose not to use capital punishment (Table 7.2). A glance at this shows a different regional connection. All of the states except one, West Virginia, are in the North, with several clustered in the Midwest. Conclusion: States behave very differently on this compelling "life and death" question.

Abortion

Abortion is an issue that leaves the nation very divided. Although most people agree on the right to an abortion, opinions vary dramatically from state to state. In addition, public opinion is fractured over the conditions and timing of such events. A CNN/USA/Gallup Poll taken of a randomly selected sample in 2005 typifies the recent responses to the abortion question (see Table 7.3).

The same question on abortion was asked of a national sample in 1975, with answers almost identical to the results generated thirty years later. Clearly, national public opinion has moved little on this issue.

Closer examination of the abortion question on a state-to-state basis (see Table 7.4) shows wide differences, revealing the impact of political culture on a public policy issue. Although the nation as a whole is "pro-choice," substantial "pro-life" majorities can be seen in Alabama, Arkansas, Idaho, Mississippi, Utah, and West Virginia—all states with substantial rural-based populations.

Table 7.1

Capital Punishment—Leading States, 1976–2005

State	Number of Executions
1. Texas	355
2. Virginia	94
3. Oklahoma	79
4. Missouri	66
5. Florida	60
6. Georgia	39
7. North Carolina	39
8. South Carolina	35
9. Alabama	34
10. Arkansas	27
Total	838
All others	164
Grand total	1,002

Source: U.S. Department of Justice

Table 7.2

Non-Capital Punishment States

1. Alaska	7. Minnesota
2. Hawaii	8. North Dakota
3. Iowa	9. Rhode Island
4. Maine	10. Vermont
5. Massachusetts	11. West Virginia
6. Michigan	12. Wisconsin

Source: U.S. Department of Justice

Table 7.3

A Question of Abortion

"Do you think abortions should be legal under any circumstances, legal only under certain circumstances, or illegal in all circumstances?"

Sometimes legal	53%
Always legal	30%
Always illegal	15%
Uncertain	2%
Total	100%

Source: Gallup Poll as cited in *Newsweek*, May 8–11, 2006.

Table 7.4

Public Opinion on Abortion in the Fifty States

"Do you consider yourself pro-choice or pro-life?"

State	Pro-life	Pro-choice
1. Alabama	54%	36%
2. Alaska	37%	58%
3. Arizona	39%	56%
4. Arkansas	55%	40%
5. California	28%	65%
6. Colorado	34%	61%
7. Connecticut	26%	68%
8. Delaware	31%	63%
9. Florida	36%	58%
10. Georgia	43%	52%
11. Hawaii	35%	57%
12. Idaho	55%	41%
13. Illinois	33%	58%
14. Indiana	50%	47%
15. Iowa	41%	56%
16. Kansas	45%	50%
17. Kentucky	51%	42%
18. Louisiana	57%	36%
19. Maine	33%	63%
20. Maryland	29%	65%
21. Massachusetts	28%	68%
22. Michigan	42%	55%
23. Minnesota	39%	56%
24. Mississippi	53%	39%
25. Missouri	48%	45%
26. Montana	42%	53%
27. Nebraska	47%	49%
28. Nevada	32%	64%
29. New Hampshire	29%	67%
30. New Jersey	31%	63%
31. New Mexico	39%	56%
32. New York	27%	66%
33. North Carolina	44%	47%
34. North Dakota	47%	47%
35. Ohio	42%	52%
36. Oklahoma	48%	47%
37. Oregon	33%	62%
38. Pennsylvania	44%	51%
39. Rhode Island	32%	63%
40. South Carolina	43%	47%

continued

Table 7.4 *(continued)*

State	Pro-life	Pro-choice
41. South Dakota	49%	47%
42. Tennessee	51%	42%
43. Texas	43%	52%
44. Utah	61%	33%
45. Vermont	25%	70%
46. Virginia	39%	54%
47. Washington	32%	63%
48. West Virginia	53%	39%
49. Wisconsin	39%	57%
50. Wyoming	39%	57%
Weighted Average	38%	56%
Unweighted Average	41%	54%

Note: "Weighted Average" means each state is weighted proportionally to its share of U.S. population. For example, California, the most populated state, is given 71 times the weight of Wyoming, the least populated state, in a weighted average.

"Unweighted Average" means each state is given equal weight; population density is not taken into account.

Finally, we can examine the abortion question in terms of state laws. Even though abortion is legal according to *Roe v. Wade*, states deal with implementation of the policy in many different respects. Nowhere is the issue more disputed than with regard to minors. Some states require parental consent, others require parental notification, and others still have no requirements. Regarding the time between the decision and surgery, twenty-two states require a waiting period of anywhere between 1 hour and 72 hours. Table 7.5 shows the extent to which states differ over application of the abortion right for minors.

That abortion may be a constitutional right has not kept states from all but attempting to eliminate that right. The most direct confrontation came in 2006 when legislators in South Dakota passed a law that declared abortions illegal except when a mother's life is in jeopardy. Missouri and Mississippi were considering similar legislation. Clearly aware of precedent, South Dakota governor Mike Rounds stated that he signed the legislation with the hope that the U.S. Supreme Court would overturn *Roe v. Wade* just as the Court had declared segregation illegal with *Brown v. Board* reversing *Plessy v. Ferguson.* Opponents of the new South Dakota law promised to meet the governor in the hearing room of the U.S. Supreme Court for final resolution.[10] Yet these new legislative forays showed the extent that some states were willing to challenge established national law.

Table 7.5

Abortion Parental Consent/Notification and Mandatory Waiting Period Laws

State	Mandatory Waiting Period	Delay
Alabama	Currently enforced	24-hour delay
Alaska	Currently enforced	No delay
Arizona	No	
Arkansas	Currently enforced	24-hour delay. Requires woman to receive state-directed counseling and the option to view state-prepared materials, "prior to and in no event on the same day as the abortion."
California	No	
Colorado	No	
Connecticut	No	
Delaware	Enforcement stayed by federal court	24-hour delay
District of Columbia	No	
Florida	Enforcement stayed by state court	No delay. Requires woman to receive information in person from a health-care provider. (In litigation.)
Georgia	Currently enforced	24-hour delay
Hawaii	No	
Idaho	Currently enforced	24-hour delay
Illinois	No	
Indiana	Currently enforced	18-hour delay. Requires woman to receive information in person from a health-care provider. (In litigation.)
Iowa	No	
Kansas	Currently enforced	24-hour delay
Kentucky	Currently enforced	24-hour delay
Louisiana	Currently enforced	24-hour delay. Requires woman to receive information in person from a health-care provider.
Maine	No	
Maryland	No	
Massachusetts	Enforcement stayed by federal court	24-hour delay
Michigan	Currently enforced	24-hour delay
Minnesota	Currently enforced	24-hour delay
Mississippi	Currently enforced	24-hour delay. Requires woman to receive information in person from a health-care provider.

continued

Table 7.5 *(continued)*

State	Mandatory Waiting Period	Delay
Missouri	Currently enforced	24-hour delay
Montana	Enforcement stayed by state court	24-hour delay
Nebraska	Currently enforced	24-hour delay
Nevada	No	
New Hampshire	No	
New Jersey	No	
New Mexico	No	
New York	No	
North Carolina	No	
North Dakota	Currently enforced	24-hour delay
Ohio	Currently enforced	24-hour delay. Requires woman to receive information in person from a health-care provider.
Oklahoma	Currently enforced	24-hour delay
Oregon	No	
Pennsylvania	Currently enforced	24-hour delay
Rhode Island	No	
South Carolina	Currently enforced	1-hour delay
South Dakota	Currently enforced	24-hour delay
Tennessee	Enforcement stayed by state court	2-day delay (excluding the day on which information is given and day of procedure).
Texas	Currently enforced	24-hour delay
Utah	Currently enforced	24-hour delay. Requires woman to receive information in person from a health-care provider.
Vermont	No	
Virginia	Currently enforced	24-hour delay
Washington	No	
West Virginia	Currently enforced	24-hour delay
Wisconsin	Currently enforced	24-hour delay. Requires woman to receive information in person from a health-care provider.
Wyoming	No	

Source: Mandatory Delays and Biased Information Requirements, December 9, 2005, from the Center for Reproductive Rights, www.crlp.org/pub_fac_manddelay1.html.

Public Education

From the standpoint of budget expenditures, no issue is more important to states than public education. States and their local governments routinely pay more than

Table 7.6

Education Expenditures Per Pupil, 2001–2002

State	Expenditures per pupil	Rank
New York	$11,029	1
District of Columbia	$11,009	2
Connecticut	$10,528	3
Rhode Island	$10,193	4
Massachusetts	$9,949	5
New Jersey	$9,875	6
Vermont	$9,675	7
Delaware	$9,612	8
Alaska	$9,406	9
West Virginia	$8,716	10
Michigan	$8,678	11
Wisconsin	$8,649	12
Pennsylvania	$8,619	13
Maine	$8,393	14
Ohio	$8,323	15
Oregon	$8,290	16
Wyoming	$8,191	17
New Hampshire	$8,102	18
Indiana	$8,022	19
Maryland	$7,849	20
Minnesota	$7,780	21
Georgia	$7,633	22
Illinois	$7,603	23

continued

90 percent of the public education bill, with less than 10 percent contributed by the federal government. In recent years, as local governments have encountered more difficulties in paying for public education, states have become the single largest source of funding. Today, numerous challenges confront public education, ranging from the requirements of the No Child Left Behind federal legislation to proposals for voucher programs and charter schools. The latter proposals have emerged in part because of concerns about the public education "product" that more times than not fails to live up to the public's expectations.[11]

Although the concern for quality public education is almost universal, the attention paid to this policy area by the respective states is not. Data provided by the American Legislative Exchange Council suggest vast differences both in state commitments to public education and student performance.[12] According to information for the 2001–2 academic year, the national average for per pupil expenditures was $7,557. State-by-state differences varied wildly, however, from $11,029 in New York to $4,769 in Utah, as seen in Table 7.6.

Table 7.6 *(continued)*

State	Expenditures per pupil	Rank
Nebraska	$7,579	24
Virginia	$7,450	25
Washington	$7,231	26
Iowa	$7,203	27
Montana	$7,081	28
New Mexico	$7,006	29
California	$6,997	30
South Carolina	$6,946	31
Kansas	$6,875	32
Texas	$6,803	33
Hawaii	$6,775	34
Missouri	$6,591	35
South Dakota	$6,490	36
North Carolina	$6,490	37
Kentucky	$6,443	38
Louisiana	$6,280	39
Colorado	$6,244	40
Florida	$6,243	41
North Dakota	$6,221	42
Oklahoma	$6,167	43
Nevada	$6,121	44
Alabama	$5,937	45
Idaho	$5,779	46
Arkansas	$5,764	47
Tennessee	$5,653	48
Arizona	$5,373	49
Mississippi	$5,229	50
Utah	$4,769	51

Source: Report Card on American Education: A State-by-State Report Card, 2004, p. 74. http://www.alec.org/meSWFiles/pdf/2004_Report_Card_on_Education.pdf

While funding is often considered the best measure of state support, it is not necessarily the best measure of student performance. The findings of the American Legislative Exchange Council show that the states with the highest national academic test scores were in many cases different than the best-funded states. These data are presented in Table 7.7.

Note that of the top ten funded states, only two—Massachusetts and Vermont—were among the ten highest achievement states. Of the bottom ten funded states, only three—Alabama, Arkansas, and Mississippi—were also among the ten lowest achievement states. What, then accounts for discrepancies in performance? Several possible answers exist, including resident income levels, percentages of immigrants and/or second language students, and other social and cultural factors that are not always easy to see.[13] What

Table 7.7

Rankings of States Based on Academic Achievement, 2001–2002

State	Rank	State	Rank
Minnesota	1	Idaho	27
Wisconsin	2	Nevada	28
Massachusetts	3	Colorado	29
New Hampshire	4	Michigan	30
Iowa	5	North Carolina	31
Montana	6	Pennsylvania	32
Vermont	7	Rhode Island	33
Washington	8	Delaware	34
Kansas	9	Oklahoma	35
South Dakota	10	California	36
Oregon	11	Illinois	37
Nebraska	12	West Virginia	38
Wyoming	13	Kentucky	39
North Dakota	14	Tennessee	40
Connecticut	15	Texas	41
Ohio	16	South Carolina	42
Virginia	17	Arkansas	43
Alaska	18	Hawaii	44
Missouri	19	Florida	45
Utah	20	Georgia	46
New Jersey	21	Alabama	47
Arizona	22	Louisiana	48
Maine	23	New Mexico	49
Maryland	24	Mississippi	50
Indiana	25	District of Columbia	51
New York	26		

Source: Report Card on American Education: A State-by-State Report Card, 2004, p. 14.
http://www.alec.org/meSWFiles/pdf/2004_Report_Card_on_Education.pdf

we do see, however, is an education network that is anything but consistent either in state funding or student performance.

The Consequences of State-to-State Policy Differences

Capital punishment, abortion, and public education are only three of dozens of public policy areas that strike different chords among the various states. Similar discussions could just as easily take place on sizzling questions such as gun ownership regulations, campaign finance laws, welfare rules, toxic waste laws, and affirmative action policies, to name a few. On a wide range of issues, collective values within the states often yield dissimilar policies.

Local political cultures may be well served with different applications of the same general question, reminding us of the value of liberty in the federalism debate. At the same time, specially tailored public policy responses to the same question suggest that not all options are available to all people in the fifty states, reminding us of the trade-off with equality. To the extent that some states treat a controversial issue differently than others, surely the residents of other political jurisdictions are likely to perceive greater or fewer benefits from different treatments. Simply put, if one state allows the purchase of discounted pharmaceutical drugs from Canada while a neighboring state does not, what does this say about "equal protection of the law," a venerable guarantee of the Fourteenth Amendment? Likewise, if one state permits abortion for a teenager without any questions while another requires physician consultations and parental permission, what do such interpretations say about the "right to privacy"? The tension between liberty and equality is never too far away from a discussion on federalism.

Cutting-Edge Issues in the Twenty-first Century

The issues chronicled above have been centers of debate for many years. But with the growth of technology and the evolution of society, new issues of contentiousness join others already on the public agenda. A recent addition has been the "death with dignity" concept that has been adopted in Oregon. Enacted first in 1994 and again in 1998, this legislation allows a terminally ill individual to acquire a lethal prescription from a physician under very strict conditions. After the law was upheld by the U.S. Supreme Court in 2006, some states moved in a similar direction; others specifically outlawed what some people term "death with dignity."[14]

Another instance of cutting-edge activity has occurred in California on the issue of passive or "secondhand" smoke. In 2006, the state's Air Resources Board accepted a scientific finding that links secondhand smoke with premature births, asthma, heart disease, and several forms of cancer. As a consequence, the policymaking authority declared secondhand smoke a toxic air pollutant and vowed to take steps to protect people from exposure.[15] The findings led some advocates to push for an end to smoking in private automobiles.[16]

Neither assisted suicide nor banning secondhand smoke is likely to be adopted as public policy by a majority of states in the near future. Nevertheless, their emergence as cutting-edge issues reveals the extent to which some states continuously mine new ideas and sometimes adopt new policies. As these states move in new directions, they strike very different chords from others nearby.

State-to-State Competition

Although the fifty states all share political space under the same federal tent, they are extraordinarily competitive in protecting their turf from one another. Their struggles for preeminence extend well beyond the pages of inviting travel magazines, often taking on the appearance of corporate warfare. So daring are these efforts that states often advertise in other states about their economic climates, prepared workforce, cost of living, education systems, and a variety of other virtues. Sometimes governors even take trade missions to other states, where they attempt to induce businesses to relocate in their states.

Battling for Businesses

The outreach programs by states often occur in the form of joint efforts between major business associations and state economic development agencies. Committees of well-known leaders from the private and public sectors constantly peruse the national economic landscape in hopes of finding major companies looking to improve their bottom line—profits. One way of enhancing corporate profitability is through lowering the cost of doing business.

With this in mind, states attempt to attract businesses from other states by offering economic packages with better conditions than those under which the companies currently operate. In 2004, when California governor Arnold Schwarzenegger spent several days campaigning up and down the famous Las Vegas Strip of huge casinos touting that "California is open for business,"[17] his effort symbolized the activities of numerous governors engaged in hand-to-hand economic combat in states across the nation.

As states battle for companies and their attendant jobs, they also compete to keep workers. Laws regarding mandatory health insurance, workers' compensation, and disability are among the many components that differentiate some states from others in an effort to keep strong labor pools. In recent years, seventeen states have enacted minimum wage legislation above the federal minimum, which is far below the official poverty level. Their purpose has been to make sure that workers have a livable income floor. The outcome of these changes is that the federal minimum wage is the minimum for some, but not others. As of 2006, nearly half of the labor force throughout the nation benefited from higher minimum wages, pitting the states against each other as competitors for labor.[18]

Tax Breaks and Employee Incentives

The costs for attracting new industry can be substantial, although defenders of the process point to long-term state revenue gains that can accrue. One such example occurred in 2004, when several states competed for a new Dell Computer assembly plant expected to employ 1,500. North Carolina, already suffering from massive job losses in the textile and furniture industries, prevailed over other states by offering $225 million in income tax credits to Dell over a fifteen-year period. As part of the state package, the city of Winston-Salem and Forsyth County added another $37 million in various benefits, including 200 acres of free land. These costs notwithstanding, state economists considered the deal a bargain, estimating that North Carolina would receive four dollars in economic development revenue for every dollar in tax breaks.[19]

Rewriting the Laws

Some states are so anxious to bring in new industries that they often rewrite existing laws to accommodate new business. Consider the efforts of Tennessee to bolster its economy. In order to encourage the relocation of the North American headquarters of Nissan Motor Co. from Los Angeles, Tennessee officials changed the state's tax laws in 2004. Less than a year later, the state offered Nissan $197.6 million in tax credits and other incentives, gaining 1,300 new jobs and $20 million in annual tax revenues. The sting did not escape the attention of Los Angeles officials. The senior economist of the local development corporation complained that "the loss of a [Nissan] corporate headquarters is something that other states will be able to use against us" as they attempt to recruit other companies.[20]

Uneven Economic Outcomes

While individual states may benefit to some degree from garnering additions to their economy, the overall benefits from the competition may have a downside over the long term. The more that states undercut each other with economic incentives, the fewer tax dollars accrue collectively to the various state treasuries. Thus, what benefits the private sector may actually hurt the states and their ability to provide services and programs. Then there is the question of the costs of these inducements. If states give special benefits to some, how fair is this to those companies already operating under a different set of rules? As a state legislator complained, state incentives "are out of control.... The perfect scenario would be if incentives were outlawed nationally."[21] Given the fierce nature of state-to-state competition, however, such cooperation does not appear likely in the near future.

Battling for Tax Dollars

At the same time that states provide economic incentives to attract new businesses, they are also looking for ways to collect more tax dollars. Often they do so through the development of new revenue streams, thereby alleviating pressure on traditional revenue sources such as income, sales, and property taxes.

Indian gaming has become a revenue staple for many states in the twenty-first century. Until the late 1980s, fifteen states permitted the operation of casinos, mostly with video poker or slot machines. State tax rates on casinos varied between 6.25 percent and 35 percent, yielding much more money in some states than others.[22] Some states have done well. In South Dakota, for example, enough revenue accrued from casinos to permit the legislature to reduce property taxes by 20 percent. At the same time, competition from the recent installations of slot machines in Pennsylvania and Maryland has threatened future collection of state tax revenues in Delaware, which amounted to $120 million, or 8 percent of total tax collections, in 2004.[23]

Passage of the Indian Gaming Regulatory Act by the U.S. Congress in 1988 cleared the way for federally recognized tribes to negotiate with the states for the types of gaming once found only in Nevada and Atlantic City, New Jersey. Revenue-starved states and long-impoverished Indian tribes joined to forge casino development compacts. The leaders of state governments hoped that the compacts would add to their coffers along the lines of gaming revenues in other states, although the sovereignty of Indian tribes has provided a different environment for obtaining tax dollars.

The results from Indian gaming have been astounding, although one-sided. In 1995, total revenues from 215 Indian casinos across the states amounted to $5.4 billion. By 2004, casino revenues from 352 establishments rose to $19.4 billion.[24] However, a closer look at the data shows an uneven distribution of casinos, with little of the money going to the states in the form of new revenues. Of the 352 Indian casinos operating in 2004, more than one hundred were in just three states—California (53), Washington (27), and Arizona (22).

Meanwhile, the benefits for Indian residents from gaming have varied wildly. For example, a recent study shows casinos in five states with half of the nation's native American population—Montana, Nevada, North Dakota, Oklahoma, and South Dakota—generating annual revenues of about $400 per Indian. Yet, casinos in California, Connecticut, and Florida—states with 3 percent of the Indian population—produced revenues of about $100,000 per Indian.[25] At the same time, Indian casino revenues have been a big revenue bust for the states. Despite gaming proceeds of $19.4 billion in 2004, states collected a paltry $101 million the same year,[26] leaving state leaders disappointed. Much of the disappointment revolved around unrealistic expectations, given complicated state and federal tax laws. For example, in 2004, California governor Arnold Schwarzenegger signed gaming agreements with several Indian tribes that, according to Schwarzenegger, would bring in annual revenues of $150 million to $200 million.[27] Yet, one year later, state officials acknowledged that only $18.7 million had been received,[28] a small fraction of the original estimate.

Battling for Better Environments

In recent years, people have become interested in preserving their quality of life, with states often taking the lead in this public policy area. Much of the discussion has boiled down to improving general environmental conditions particularly in terms of air pollution, acid rain, and toxic waste in the land and water. Whereas these issues once were clearly dominated by federal legislation and regulations, some states have begun to move independently on environmental policy matters. Others, notably "rust belt" or older states with less efficient manufacturing facilities, have not followed suit in fear of chasing away valued industries because of costs associated with retrofitting old emissions-control systems. Of interest here is the way that the environmental policies of some state impact others.

The Question of Auto Emissions

When it comes to environmental degradation, automobile emissions are most responsible for creating air pollution.[29] On this subject, the federal government and several states have been heading in different directions. In 2002, for example, the Justice Department under President George W. Bush sided with carmakers in a court suit designed to prevent the state of California from adopting new fuel efficiency standards. One year later, the Environmental Protection Agency adopted new rules that allowed power plants, oil refineries, and other industrial units to avoid installing expensive antipollution equipment. The decisions represented a major departure from the environmentally sensitive Clinton administration.[30] As a result, many states anticipated more air pollution.

Meanwhile, some states have moved in their own independent direction. In 2004, state regulators in California adopted an ambitious plan far beyond the guidelines set out by the EPA. Unlike other states, California has certain flexibility in writing regulations that exceed federal requirements because its air quality rules predated federal laws.[31] In 2004, the state enacted a new regulation that requires the automobile industry to reduce carbon dioxide and other emissions by 30 percent between the 2009 and 2016 model years.

Although the Bush administration and automobile makers have challenged the new state regulations, the size of California's purchasing power has forced the industry to consider new production methods.[32] Pressure has mounted as other states have followed California's lead. Shortly after California's new rules, New York adopted similar regulations, with nine additional states also poised to join with their own tough new rules.[33] Together the population of the ten states amount to nearly one-third of national purchasing power for automobiles. That market share has served as the impetus for forcing automobile manufacturers to alter their production process.

Water Pollution

Despite the activity of the federal Environmental Protection Agency in numerous aspects of environmental policy, some jurisdictions remain outside the agency's responsibility. One such area is gold mining. Unlike coal or oil extraction, there are no federal guidelines for gold mining practices or post-mining clean-up costs. Gold mining is an active, lucrative enterprise in Nevada, where the process includes pumping out water from gold-laden areas to capture the metal. As a result, however, mining companies have drained an underlying aquifer for the water necessary to soak the ore and separate the gold, placing the "used" water into an artificial lake.

With the extraction of gold, large amounts of mercury have surfaced on the land, in the air, and in the water, often moving beyond Nevada's border to nearby states, particularly Idaho. Mercury is a cause of concern because high levels of the chemical have been associated with several neurological maladies affecting fetuses, infants, and children. "There are things crossing state lines here [in Nevada] that don't know anything about political boundaries,"[34] an Idaho State Department of Environmental Quality research scientist has said, noting that mercury levels at the Nevada/Idaho border are ten times higher than anywhere else in the state. Meanwhile, Idaho scientists expect that the new artificial lake will contain large deposits of arsenic and selenium, leaving the driest state in the union with an unusable supply of water,[35] thanks largely to the economic activity in Nevada.

Battling for Leadership

Many states labor to assume leadership positions in various policy areas. They do so in hopes of attracting talented researchers, entrepreneurs, leading-edge businesses, major manufacturing, energy-efficient facilities, and other enterprises whose presence will add to the reputations of the states. Realizing that they cannot be all things to all people or even their own populations, states often specialize in specific areas such as technology, sports, tourism, or even international trade.[36] By becoming leaders in one or more of these areas, states hope to draw in related industries to bolster their economies, thereby increasing their desirability as places to live.

Stem Cell Research

In some respects, President George W. Bush did the states a favor when he announced in 2001 that the federal government would expend very few resources on stem cell research. Stem cells have been praised by most scientists in the field as promising opportunities for the regeneration of malfunctioning body organs. They have been viewed as possible cures for more than 700 diseases. Yet the use of the most common sources of stem cells, aborted human embryos, is controversial. After much soul-searching on the subject, the president shied away from federal involvement in the cutting-edge industry because stem cells are taken from what he described as "by-products of a process that creates life,"[37] and human life "is a sacred gift from our creator."[38] His decision basically removed the U.S. government from the stem cell research business,[39] although other nations quickly began to fill the research gap.[40]

In addition to competing global efforts, several states quickly seized upon stem cell research as a way to assert hegemony in the relatively new scientific subfield. In 2004, voters in California approved an initiative providing $3 billion for stem cell research. This followed a modest commitment in Ohio of $19.5 million in 2003. Shortly after the California commitment, the states of Illinois ($10 million), New Jersey ($20 million), and Connecticut ($100 million) added government support for stem cell research programs, with seven other states also moving forward to endorse stem cell research projects. Not all states have jumped onto the stem cell research bandwagon, however. A few—notably Arizona, Nebraska, and South Dakota—have passed legislation specifically limiting the possibilities for stem cell research, revealing the extent to which states are divided on this issue.

California's massive investment in stem cell research is yet to bear results either in economic or health benefits. Long research lead times and two court suits challenging the legality of the initiative have slowed progress.[41] Nevertheless, California "really led the nation [on the stem cell issue] and drove awareness," according to the spokesperson of a national stem cell advocacy group.[42] As a leader in the field, it may well profit more than other states in the future by attracting the next wave of bio-tech companies.

Regional Cooperation

Thus far, we have chronicled various conditions of state-to-state competition in several areas of public policy. But there is another side to the interaction of states. Although states often struggle in an economic environment of hand-to-hand combat, there are occasions where they cooperate to obtain mutual benefits. Regional cooperation through interstate compacts offers these governments opportunities to collaborate on important issues that transcend their respective borders. Through these efforts, states deal with and often overcome problems jointly in ways they cannot do individually.

Regional agreements are tough to operate for three reasons: First, as prescribed in Article I, Section 10, of the Constitution, states may not enter into these arrangements without the consent of Congress. Second, states often find it difficult to surrender sovereignty en route to solving mutual problems. Third, states sometimes have difficulty staying the course when they are adversely impacted by the decisions of other states in the organization. Thus, David Nice and Patricia Fredericksen observe, "most regional organizations have a relatively limited record of accomplishment, in part because neither national officials nor state officials have had sufficient confidence in the regional organizations to trust them with substantial power, whether legal or financial."[43]

Multi-State Policymaking Organizations

Political hurdles notwithstanding, regional organizations offer an alternative approach to problem-solving, particularly in an environment characterized by scarce economic resources. More than two hundred interstate compacts exist today.

Port Authority of New York and New Jersey

Ever since their admissions to statehood, New York and New Jersey have had a contentious relationship over the waters that both join and divide the two states. In 1921, the two eastern powerhouses agreed to establish the Port Authority of New York and New Jersey, with each side appointing six members to the twelve-person governing board. The bi-state agency has control over transportation infrastructure including bridges, tunnels, airports, and seaports within the boundaries of the district. Millions of people are transported daily through the system. In addition, the Port Authority is a major conduit of commerce and moves over $100 billion in goods annually.

Most of the time, issues are addressed by the twelve-person Port Authority governing board with little incident. By the end of the twentieth century, however, the two states had numerous grievances against each other, threatening to prevent work on billions of dollars of improvement and expansion projects important to each state. The two governors, New York's George Pataki and New Jersey's Christine Todd Whitman, were beside themselves with disgust over differing opinions on transportation, funding, and construction priorities.

As the governors and their advisors struggled for solutions, planning work of the Port Authority came to a standstill. Nevertheless, the authority remained in place as an institution through which the governors and their staffs could negotiate. Billions of dollars of improvements and new construction remained on standby. They included leasing rights to a marine terminal, air rights over the Port Authority bus terminal, dredging operations to improve ship navigation through local rivers, and funding responsibilities for future projects.

Finally, after eighteen months of intense negotiations, the two state chief executives agreed to an eighteen-point plan that offered projects for both states, while establishing new collective sources of funding and shared expenses. Governor Pataki released a statement praising the agreement for "creating more jobs and opportunities for New Yorkers," while Governor Whitman added that the agreement would "provide a foundation for the long-term stability of the port region."[44] Peace was restored, yet without the framework of the two-state regional organization, it is hard to know whether any common ground would have been found, and if so, at what additional cost.

The Colorado River Compact

In the West, where intermittent scarcity of water threatens everything from high tech to agriculture, seven states participate in an agreement that is now more than eighty years old. The Colorado River Compact includes the states of Arizona, California, Colorado, Nevada, New Mexico, Utah, and Wyoming. The compact has the unique challenge of overseeing the distribution of the region's major water source—the Colorado River and its massive underground aquifer—to the fastest growing region of the nation. According to a long-standing agreement, every state has an assigned amount of water it can draw from the Colorado River basin. California's share amounts to about one-fourth of the water, or 4.4 million acre-feet, a significant number given that hardly any of the state touches the 1,400-mile-long Colorado River Basin.

Over the existence of the compact, skirmishes between the states have broken out particularly during drought years. Because the compact awards surplus water to farm-rich California, the drought years have tested the resolve of all partners. But as the other six states gained population and their own water-dependent industries, they seized upon the surplus river water routinely claimed by California. Representatives from the other six states claimed persistent allotment violations by California of as much as one million acre-feet annually regardless of the water conditions.[45] California resisted.

Matters came to a boil in 2000 toward the end of the Clinton administration, when Secretary of the Interior Bruce Babbitt convened a summit of the compact partners to arbitrate the water war. Discussions carried over to the Bush administration where, after two years of negotiations, new Secretary of the Interior Gail Norton ordered California to draw down to its 4.4 million acre-feet limit, effective January 1, 2003, or face stiff financial penalties.[46] Although the order was not met with glee in the Golden State, the framework of the Colorado River Basin Compact allowed the decision and its implementation to take place. Without the compact, hostility among the participating states could have gone without resolution, leading to ugly political and economic outcomes for all concerned.

Informal Networks

In addition to specific policymaking bodies, state representatives from the executive, legislative, judicial, and bureaucratic sectors meet periodically to forge new links on key questions of the day. These groups meet both regionally and nationally on regular bases. Some, such as the National Governors Conference or the National Conference of State Legislators, have staff and research offices and attract a good deal of attention at their annual gatherings, where attendees discuss everything from agricultural pests to domestic terrorism. The presence of major leaders assures a strong media presence at these meetings.

Other, small organizations, such as the Western Region of Lieutenant Governors or the Southern State Treasurers Conference, tend to operate well beneath the radar of the public or media. Whether well known or hardly known, these voluntary groups of government leaders meet to exchange ideas, share the results of new programs, pursue collaborative projects, and mine areas of common interests.

Horizontal Federalism in the Twenty-first Century

After more than two centuries, horizontal federalism continues to zigzag through the complex federal arrangement of American politics. Like virtually every other aspect of American government, this arrangement has exhibited its own evolutionary qualities. In the 1780s, operating under the Articles of Confederation, Jack Rakove recounts, "neither state legislatures nor their constituents could be relied upon to support the general interests of the union."[47] The value of state sovereignty over any other form of governmental association contributed to an environment of political distrust and severe economic competition among the states, ultimately rendering them weak, dysfunctional, and desperately in need of repair. The concern of some state representatives over too much national control set the tone for corrective measures that emerged at the end the Constitutional Convention, particularly in the form of the Bill of Rights. But while the national/state power debate was addressed at least in part, state-to-state relations continued to touch raw nerves.

Today relations among the states are far more harmonious than they were during the first years of the Republic. States are united by a set of federal rules that both confer opportunities and impose limits. Operating as viable governments within their prescribed spheres of authority, they have learned the benefits of cooperation in areas where various combinations of states may work toward agreed-upon objectives. In honoring Article IV of the Constitution, particularly the "full faith and credit" clause of Section 1, states respect each other's laws and procedures.

Nonetheless, states continue to operate with their own sets of political and social values, often leading them to take different approaches to similar issues. Their economies depend upon different mixes of industries, population subsets, and environmental frameworks, underscoring different challenges and contributions. For these reasons, states often produce conflicting policies, some of which are tolerated and others of which are tested at higher levels along the vertical chain of governmental authority.

Clearly, horizontal federalism remains a key part of the federal structure, but to what degree? Daniel Elazar once defined states as the glue of American federalism. He wrote, "The 50 American states, located between the powerful federal government and the burgeoning local governments in a metropolitanized nation, are the keystones of the American governmental arch. This was the case when the Constitution was adopted in 1789 and remains true despite the great changes that have taken place during the intervening years."[48] Few observers of American politics share Elazar's credentials, yet, given so many changes in the American political system, one wonders whether his assessment is true today, or whether even he might offer a revision.

8

★ ★ ★ ★

The International
Dimension of Federalism

At first blush, the political exchanges among nations seem far removed from any discussion of federalism. After all, federalism centers largely on the political interaction between the elements of a large government and several smaller government units within established, self-contained boundaries in which struggles over and assignments for governance take place. Nevertheless, once-compartmentalized relationships within national boundaries are no longer easy to categorize because of the multiple levels of growing interdependence and unprecedented connectivity among nations, their subgovernments, and private enterprise. Numerous elements from commerce to pollution to human rights spill over from one nation to the next and beyond, showing little regard for official lines of political demarcation.

International economic activity, now most commonly described as **globalization**, transcends political boundaries. The products of innovation, labor, and distribution in one part of the world often wind up elsewhere; companies that are owned by investors in capital-intensive nations often operate with their employees located in emerging nations thousands of miles away. And consumers who purchase the products of international companies and workforces often live in parts of the world far from where the labor occurs. It is a new paradigm of dizzying proportions and uncertainties. As Jack Behrman and Dennis Rondinelli explain, "The increasing integration of the world economy means a virtual elimination of debates over autarchy, national self-sufficiency, and economic independence. The only question remaining is how far and in what ways nations will be interdependent."[1] These economic balancing acts impact the well-being of nations in ways that include government surpluses or deficits, the movement of jobs, and the transfer of wealth.

But far more than international economics is at stake. Pollution and toxic waste, while perhaps originating in certain parts of the world, can affect populations far away. Acid rain that develops in China often falls on Japan similar to the way acid rain produced in America's rust belt descends upon Canadian soil. Likewise, the holes in the ozone layer over Australia and northern Canada are generated, in all likelihood, not by those countries but by other of the world's industrialized and industrializing nations. Back on earth, as pollutant-caused global warming melts ice caps near the North and South Poles, all nations with coasts brace for rising shorelines, while people everywhere struggle to understand and deal with new weather patterns.

Then there is the issue of disease. Acquired Immune Deficiency Syndrome (AIDS) may have originated in Africa, yet the potentially lethal infection has ravaged tens of millions of lives around the world. An outbreak of Avian flu may have been discovered most recently in East Asia, but the disease has threatened both the food supply and lives of people the world over. With more people and goods able to travel greater distances today than ever before, our interconnectivity and interdependence grow proportionally. Along the way, governments jockey for a variety of political, economic, and social advantages.

Determining which levels of American government should negotiate matters relating to international economy links us to the subject of federalism. As with other aspects relating to this method of political organization, most lines of distinction are rather blurred except for the most obvious examples. True, when it comes to international relations, the national government has sole responsibility for negotiating treaties with other nations as well as declaring war and providing for the national defense. Beyond these clearly stated constitutional imperatives, however, states may become involved collaboratively and competitively. Commonly, states send trade delegations in hopes of attracting foreign investment and jobs, both of which will contribute to their tax bases. States also assume responsibility for environmental safety, international shipping ports, and new business tax incentives. Some states even look to nearby countries for medical care and supplies.

In this chapter we will look at international issues as they apply to national/state relationships. Globalization, immigration, and domestic security will be examined in the context of federalism, allowing us to understand how the cooperative, competitive, and ever-changing conditions are approached and managed by the federal and state governments.

The Many Faces of Globalization

To the extent that countries break down or minimize barriers to ideas and commerce, they become enveloped in globalization. Globalization has long been appreciated as an economic concept, referring to the expansion of international trade and foreign investment among nations, particularly from developed nations to emerging nations. But globalization today is a conceptual umbrella for myriad activities that transcend national boundaries, including human rights, environmental protection, and the movement of labor as well as goods.[2]

Trade

Like subsidies, welfare, and tax incentives, international trade attracts governments and the private sector. Most nations develop trade policies to advance opportunities for their producers and consumers.[3] Within the framework of those government policies, companies and workers attempt to benefit from the conditions that have been established. Trade does not occur in a perfectly balanced environment; in fact, most nations have an imbalance relative to others. Moreover, the advantages and disadvantages change over time, sometimes swiftly and dramatically. As Graham Wilson explains, "the impact of globalization on each country is not necessarily the same, just as a storm passing over a forest has a different impact on different trees."[4] This is the uncertain world of today's global economy. Depending upon whether exports exceed imports or vice versa, nations will have trade surpluses or deficits.

For years, the United States has operated with a trade deficit.[5] In 2005, for example, the U.S. trade imbalance exceeded a record $700 billion, of which more than $200 billion alone was accumulated with China.[6] The ever-growing transferability of technology and manufacturing capabilities between nations combined with fewer trade barriers has made American trade deficits a permanent international fixture.[7] Meanwhile, with Americans buying more from abroad than sending abroad, we are producing less at home, which relates to the jobs issue discussed below.

In many respects, battles between nations in the twenty-first century are different from any point in recent history. More times than not, warfare is not cast in a military light; instead, it is defined in terms of the economic battles. As Marcus Ethridge and Howard Handelman note, "Supercomputers and efficient auto assembly lines now appear to count for more than missiles or aircraft carriers in calculating national strength."[8] International organizations such as the World Trade Organization (WTO), which is supported by 149 nations, promote agreements that work toward a "level playing field" that attempts to keep some nations from undercutting others through secret government price dumping, farm subsidies, and selling products at artificially low prices.

Sometimes, national and state objectives clash on matters of international trade. For example, in 2004, when California legislators sought to pass an environmentally friendly law providing incentives to incorporate a 32 million annual supply of used tires into the asphalt mix, federal officials warned that the program would violate the rules of the North American Free Trade Association (NAFTA) by placing Mexican and Canadian recyclers at a competitive disadvantage.[9] Bowing to the terms of the multinational agreement, state leaders had to find other, more costly ways of disposing of the tires.

Jobs

For some time, American companies have shifted their manufacturing and service facilities from state to state to take advantage of tax breaks and other economic incentives. As noted in Chapter 7, states compete for these businesses. This internal hodgepodge pattern has been replaced by offshoring, an offshoot that ships jobs to other countries while leaving employees behind. Offshoring has become a bane for American workers. With increasingly skilled people abroad willing to work for a fraction of American salaries, several U.S. professions have been depleted of their workforces. A large portion of the garment industry has been relocated from New York to Mexico, Central America, and China. Textiles, once the cornerstone of the North Carolina economy, now come from China. Data entry and engineering jobs have left California for India. Even part of the legal profession has shifted from American shores to India,[10] underscoring the transfer of services as well as products.

In some cases, American-owned companies have exported the jobs, while in others, new companies or subsidiaries of existing companies have been formed in developing countries. The changes are dramatic. A recent study estimates that more than 3 million American jobs will be sent offshore by 2015;[11] other calculations project that as many as 14 million U.S. jobs could be lost to other countries within the next decade.[12] Some areas of the country have the potential for a complete "economic makeover," such as in Silicon Valley in California, where a recent study estimated that one in six jobs were at risk of being sent offshore.[13]

In his book *The World Is Flat*, *New York Times* columnist and author Thomas Friedman attributes changing global dynamics to the inevitable evening out of technology and capabilities. But it is more than the relocation of jobs or economic clout. Offshoring has the potential of rearranging not only economic leverage but also international political power. Friedman argues:

> You cannot maintain rising standards of living in a flattening world when you are up against competitors who are getting not only their fundamentals right but also their intangibles. China does not only want to get rich. It wants to get powerful. China doesn't just want to learn how to make GM cars. It wants to be GM and put GM out of business.[14]

Add to China places such as India, Malaysia, Mexico, parts of a resurgent Eastern Europe, and countless others. Suddenly, the United States finds itself in an economic environment of cutthroat competition.

The changes described above have affected states in different ways and to different degrees. In some instances, the economic transformations have been cataclysmic. Nowhere is this more evident than in Michigan, a state whose automobile industry has been ravaged by high costs, old plants, and various inefficiencies. Between 2001 and 2005, Michigan lost a quarter of its automobile manufacturing jobs to foreign companies, driving the state's unemployment rate well above the national average.[15] Another example can be seen with North Carolina, where between 2000 and 2005 alone the once venerable furniture industry lost 20,000 jobs to manufacturing facilities in Asia, shrinking industry employment by 27 percent.[16] Clearly, the impact of international dynamics on the domestic workforce is almost beyond imagination.

Meanwhile, state governors have become aggressive about attracting new business from abroad. Seizing upon her state's core competence, in 2005 Michigan governor Jennifer Granholm induced the state legislature to pass a $50 million tax incentive package, as part of an effort to convince Toyota, a Japanese automobile manufacturer, to locate a $150 million design center in the state.[17] This facility would be in addition to the 2,000 research employees and $500 million worth of investment already working in Michigan under the banners of Honda, Nissan, Toyota, and Hyundai—all foreign automakers.[18] California also has had a bit of success in this area. In 2006, after losing Nissan's headquarters to the state of Tennessee, the state attracted the new design center of Acura Automobiles, a division of the Honda Motor Company.[19]

Still, the globalization issue may not be one-sided. For example, a study by the Department of Commerce found that foreign employers added 3.4 million workers to American payrolls between 1996 and 2001. A more recent Department of Commerce study estimated $82 billion worth of investment by foreign companies in 2003 alone, generating 400,000 jobs in the United States.[20] Many are paid well. According to the Organization for International Investment, compensation for U.S. employees of foreign-owned companies is 34 percent higher than for employees of American-owned companies.

Jobs are moving between and among nations and states like never before. And given that some industries are rapidly vanishing in several states, their leaders are working feverishly to replace their losses. During the first three months of 2005 alone, 112 bills were proposed by state legislators to discourage the exodus of American jobs.[21]

Another way of expanding a state's economy is through trying to attract more foreign interest in the state's products. By convincing foreign governments and their companies to purchase local goods, state leaders assure more employment at home. In 2005, California governor Arnold Schwarzenegger exemplified this outreach effort by leading a trade delegation of state government and business leaders to China. Private sector participants included seventy-five CEOs and other high-ranking executives from the pharmaceutical, high tech, energy, agriculture, and transportation sectors. Their objective was to persuade Chinese leaders to buy California goods and services. Governor Schwarzenegger viewed the trip as an opportunity for California to expand business: "It [the trip] means more jobs and more opportunities for my state."[22]

Environmental Issues

With respect to international environmental policy, the United States often has maintained policies independent of other nations. A recent example is the American response to the Kyoto Protocol of 1997, a United Nations–orchestrated agreement that negotiated significant decreases in carbon dioxide and other so-called greenhouse gas emissions from the industrialized nations, while temporarily exempting the developing nations. With 4 percent of the world's population, the heavily industrialized United States generates about a fifth of the world's pollutants and nearly one-fourth of the world's carbon dioxide, whose heat-keeping effect is believed by scientists to be a major cause of global warming.[23] Thus, the Kyoto Protocol would affect the United States and its manufacturing sector more than any nation.

Because of the dependence upon industrial production and fears that such emissions reductions would hamstring the U.S. economy, the George W. Bush administration refrained from signing the Kyoto Protocol. In the words of Energy Secretary Spencer Abraham, "No nation will mortgage its growth and prosperity to cut greenhouse gas emissions."[24] The Bush administration also is uncertain about the cause-and-effect relationship between greenhouse gasses and global warning. Stephen Johnson, head of the U.S. Environmental Protection Agency, notes that "there's a lot of debate over the science [and whether] global warming is natural or manmade."[25] Rather than require changes, the Bush administration has asked for voluntary emissions reductions from polluting industries.

Meanwhile, states have moved in their own directions independent of the national government, both in terms of challenging polluting industries and rewriting their own standards. Seizing upon the unwillingness of the Bush administration to accept the Kyoto accord, in 2004 the attorneys general from eight states in the Northeast sued their largest utilities to force conformance with international reduced emission standards. The movement has spread elsewhere as well. As of 2005, states employed a variety of techniques to encourage their companies and customers to "turn green." Among the environmental initiatives: renewable energy equipment tax incentives for corporations (16 states), personal income tax credits (14 states), property tax incentives (25 states), and sales tax incentives (15 states).[26] At the local level, officials in 180 American cities pledged to reduced carbon monoxide and other harmful emissions. Such movement comes in the absence of a federal commitment to protecting a flagging environment. "In the absence of any congressional leadership and action by the Bush administration, we have decided to set climate change on our own," New Mexico governor Bill Richardson has said.[27]

The most aggressive response has been in California, where Governor Arnold Schwarzenegger in 2004 pledged to reduce state greenhouse emissions by 80 percent by 2050.[28] Two years earlier, the California state legislature passed a law requiring automobile manufacturers to reduce carbon dioxide emissions by 30 percent between 2009 and 2015. As Alan Lloyd, the state's environmental protection secretary explained, "We [Californians] can't control what the national government is doing. [But], we are big enough to effect change, and we are still looked upon as a leader on these issues due to our decades of work on air pollution."[29] Automakers contested California's claim that reduced emissions would curtail greenhouse gasses and argued that the new requirements would drive up the costs of new cars. Nevertheless, the state's Air Resources Board, the agency responsible for environmental protection, accepted the findings of a scientific report that rising temperatures would impede the state's ongoing battle with smog, intensify forest fires, and lead to early melting of the state's snowpack, which in turn would simultaneously increase the likelihood of flooding while harming the state's multibillion-dollar agriculture industry.[30] With that major step, California public policy makers aligned the state with a key Kyoto Protocol objective.

Immigration

Immigration issues traditionally have fallen within the policymaking bailiwick of the federal government. Since 1891, the federal government has assumed responsibility for national policies relating to the flow of people into the United States.[31] Periodically, the federal government has revisited the immigration issue, scaling back or liberalizing entries to the United States depending on the nation's needs and values at the time.

Federal Management of Immigration

By most accounts, that effort has failed. Nobody knows how many illegal or undocumented immigrants live in the United States today, although most are comfortable with the number of about 11 million, which is about as many as the legal immigrant residents who reside here.[32] A study conducted by the Pew Hispanic Center in 2006 reports that 6.2 million, or more than half of all unauthorized or illegal immigrants, come from Mexico, with another 2.5 million coming from the rest of Latin America.[33] Virtually all of these immigrants have entered the United States through the states bordering Mexico, placing a huge strain on the U.S. Border Patrol. In 2005 alone, U.S. Border Patrol agents along the Mexican border caught and returned more than 155,000 people attempting to enter illegally, twice as many as in 2004.[34] Still, this number did not come close to equaling the approximately 500,000 illegal immigrants who enter the United States every year.

Huge debates have ensued over whether illegal immigrants are a plus to American society or a minus. Some experts have argued that undocumented immigrants provide voluminous amounts of labor in low-paid jobs that are difficult for employers to fill, including construction jobs and service occupations such as farming and cleaning.[35] For this reason, many leaders of the corporate sector have discouraged any serious effort to curb illegal immigration.[36] Others contend that illegal residents drain social system elements such as hospitals, schools, and even penal facilities of scarce resources.[37] The truth may be somewhere in between; a 2006 study by the nonpartisan Congressional Budget Office found that legalization of illegal immigrants would cost $54 billion in government benefits while raising $56 billion in new government revenues and taxes.[38]

Plagued by competing assessments and objectives, leaders at the federal level have been paralyzed between the alternatives of accepting illegal immigrants for their economic value and rejecting illegal immigrants because of social concerns and potential terrorist threats.

In 1996, Congress enacted the Illegal Immigration Reform and Responsibility Act, yet another effort by the federal government to control illegal immigration into the United States. The legislation doubled the size of the Border Patrol to 2,000 agents, added stiff penalties for illegal entries, and created sanctions against employers who knowingly hire illegal immigrants. While the law seemed to curb illegal immigration, it failed to do so, largely because of voluntary provisions that reduced any enforcement capabilities. An example is a voluntary employee identification system that verifies employee documents such as Social Security cards. In operation since 1997, the program works to the extent that it is utilized, yet a study in 2006 found that only 5,479 of the nation's 8.5 million employers participated.[39] As a result, illegal immigrants now account for about 5 percent of the U.S. workforce, with more than 400,000 working in low-wage assembly and manufacturing jobs.

Immigration has become particularly problematic in the context of homeland security issues. Citing the poor tracking of illegal immigrants in the United States, in 2005, President Bush proposed a program that would allow illegal residents in the United States to remain, while increasing the difficulty of additional immigration except for a "guest worker" program, but the issue remained unresolved.[40] In 2006, several members of Congress proposed competing bills that would allow foreigners to work in the United States, while requiring them to return to their native countries after a specified period of time. The bill languished, largely over the issue of illegal immigrants who are already in the United States. Whereas the Senate version of the immigration bill allowed for guest workers and the eventual possibility of citizenship, the House version insisted on the deportation of all illegal immigrants in the United States. Meanwhile, the lack of federal response has left the states with day-to-day responsibilities for coping with illegal immigration.

State Management of Immigration

Given inconsistent federal direction and little consensus, the states have moved in variety of directions on the immigration issue and produced a "hodgepodge of results."[41] Some have embraced undocumented immigrants as important elements of a labor pool in short supply. Eleven states, for example, have enacted legislation that permits illegal residents to obtain driver's licenses.[42] At least nine states have enacted legislation allowing undocumented immigrants to attend public colleges and universities on the grounds that they will become productive, taxpaying members of society upon graduation. In the words of a state legislator, "These children didn't bring themselves. . . . It's only a good investment on our part to make certain they are productive citizens."[43] Other states, notably Illinois and Wisconsin, have created housing programs to help illegal immigrants obtain home mortgages.[44]

At the same time, several border states, notably New Mexico, Arizona, and California, have not only refused to grant driver's licenses but have beefed up patrols at the border with Mexico in hopes of preventing illegal immigration. In 2004, voters in Arizona went so far as to pass a proposition that blocks public services for illegal residents.[45] In 2005, California governor Arnold Schwarzenegger demanded that the federal government increase enforcement of laws regarding illegal immigration,[46] and yet at the same time California farmers complained that tighter borders had resulted in a dearth of workers to pick time-sensitive crops.[47]

As more immigrants move into the nation's heartland, other states are reacting to the immigration issue. As a way of eliminating immigrants, in some cases, state officials have looked to punish those who harbor immigrants. In Idaho, for example, officials have filed civil suits under the Racketeer Influenced and Corrupt Organizations (RICO) Act to target companies that have employed illegal immigrant labor as a means to cut prices. A similar lawsuit was successful in Washington State.[48] Both of these suits are likely to be tied up in the courts for some time, but they nevertheless reflect novel approaches by states to dealing with the controversial issue of illegal immigration.

The struggle over illegal immigration has extended to local government, where authorities are often on the front lines in dealing with the issue. In New Hampshire, a local police chief has arrested illegal immigrants on criminal trespassing charges for entering the United States.[49] But perhaps the most novel response has occurred in Oregon, where a local sheriff, after arresting several illegal immigrants, sent a letter to then Mexican president Vicente Fox requesting $318,843 for the incarceration of 360 Mexican illegal immigrants at a cost of $63 per day each![50]

In Search of Direction

Illegal immigration has become a lightening rod for some people, particularly many American citizens along the 2,000-mile-long porous U.S.-Mexican border who are concerned that both the U.S. and state governments have done too little in this area. In 2005, several hundred activists in Arizona formed the Minutemen, a self-appointed citizen's border patrol to assist U.S. agents in spotting illegal entrants and informing agents through two-way radio communication. Before long, organizations loosely affiliated with the Minutemen were organized in Texas and California. The success of the organization's efforts is debatable. At the end of a month-long intercept effort in March 2005, a Minuteman leader claimed that the group assisted in apprehending 146 illegal immigrants. Nevertheless, President Bush referred to the group as a bunch of vigilantes and Mexican Vicente Fox worried about the loss of innocent lives; additionally, Border Patrol officials and others feared that the group would harm the civil liberties of U.S. citizens by tramping private property and misidentifying illegal immigrants.[51] The Minutemen controversy notwithstanding, the existence of this organization shows not only frayed nerves but the willingness of some people to engage the political process head on.

Meanwhile, the immigration issue remains murky for several groups. With state governments enacting policies that often conflict with each other, many immigrants—particularly undocumented or illegal immigrants—remain uncertain of their treatment and acceptance as they move from state to state. In addition, employers have often scratched their heads over conflicting laws, while banks, phone companies, and even health insurance plans move forward with services for the growing purchasing power of 11 million undocumented immigrants.[52] The result has been confusion and uncertainty, with illegal immigrants being the Ping-Pong ball between two wildly swinging rackets.

Security

It is an understatement to assert that people need to feel safe both in their individual lives and as citizens of a nation. Physical security is the extension of the psychological notion of comfort. Long ago, sociologist Talcott Parsons wrote that people feel secure when they believe that their routine activities occur in an environment of predictability, safety, and stability.[53] With the evolution of modern society, we have come to depend upon governments as guarantors of security. This protection comes in many forms, whether in terms of personal threats such as robbery or murder; threats to the environment such as a tainted water supply or toxic land; or the military threat to a nation through war or unexpected organized physical assaults. Because governments at all levels strive to provide security, their roles, both separately and collaboratively, are important to understanding federalism. In this section, we examine threats to security on a variety of levels with various possibilities of potential harm.

International Terrorism

In recent years, nothing has shaken American society more than the threat of terrorism. Political scientist Walter Laqueur defines terrorism as the illegitimate use of force against innocent people to accomplish a political objective.[54] To that, Brian M. Jenkins adds, the purpose of terrorism "is to instill fear and alter a political situation."[55] Terrorism focuses on the potential of unknown harm. More than anything else, the uncertainty of terrorism is what gives those who promise it tremendous leverage over those who fear it.

The events of 9/11 brought terrorism to the United States in a dramatic, punishing fashion unequaled by any other act on American soil. As Jonathan White recalls, "routines were shattered as people in households, offices, and stores with television displays focused on the horror unfolding in New York City, Washington, D.C., and the Pennsylvania countryside."[56] To be sure, Americans had been attacked by internationally based terrorists before, but always in places far from our shores,[57] except for the 1993 World Trade Center attack that killed six people. But this time, 3,000 people perished from a well-coordinated series of attacks, with a financial price tag of $150 billion. Most significantly, the 9/11 attacks exacted a severe psychological cost to this nation's once-confident sense of invulnerability. So massive was the devastation from the 9/11 events that governments at all levels were compelled to respond in unprecedented ways.

National Government Responses

Predictably, the bulk of the government action in response to 9/11 came from the federal government. About a year after the attacks, Congress created the Department of Homeland Security, a cabinet-level agency with 170,000 employees and an initial budget in excess of $35 billion. Most of the new department's employees were integrated from twenty-two federal agencies ranging from the Federal Emergency Management Agency to the Coast Guard and Secret Service.[58] As part of its effort to provide improved security, the new department established tight rules for foreigners seeking to enter the United States. Shortly after 9/11, Congress also passed the USA Patriot Act, legislation that provides federal officials with sweeping new powers to conduct wiretapping with fewer restraints, detain immigrants without any official charges, and investigate bank records for international money-laundering schemes.

Even so, huge security gaps remain in the federal government's efforts to protect the nation from international terrorism. Consider the nation's 361 seaports that receive about 25,000 shipping containers each day, amounting to 95 percent of all goods that enter the United States. Five years after 9/11, records showed that the U.S. Customs Bureau, the chief monitoring agency, examined the contents of less than 6 percent of the arriving containers, leaving port security as little more than a "house of cards," according to a former Coast Guard official.[59]

Policy architects hoped that security changes undertaken through post-9/11 legislation would restore a sense of public safety. Carrying out such changes, however, has been another matter altogether. As a result, experts and the public alike remain skittish on homeland security. In fact, nearly three years after 9/11, the bipartisan 9/11 Commission warned that federal agencies were not responding to the continued threats of international terror.[60] Further, in a CBS News Poll conducted in 2005, 40 percent of those interviewed expressed little or no confidence in the government's ability to protect citizens from terrorism, compared to 19 percent who expressed a great deal of confidence.[61]

State and Local Government Responses

In addition to the federal government's efforts to put new security policies into place, states have assumed much of the day-to-day grunt work. Much of their efforts have taken place through federal grant-in-aid allocations from the Department of Homeland Security. Many states have complained about the basis of the formula and the amounts provided. During fiscal year 2005, for example, the allocations varied between $27.80 per capita in Wyoming and $5.23 in Virginia, a state bordering Washington, D.C., the nation's political nerve center (see Chapter 6). Further, according to at least one study of the allocations, the vast majority of the funds have been distributed "with no regard for the threats, vulnerabilities and potential consequences" confronting various areas of the country.[62]

Meanwhile, governors and mayors have struggled to protect public safety with costs that well exceed the amount of federal funding. More than two years after 9/11, a study of more than two hundred mayors found that an astounding 76 percent had not received any of the $1.5 billion in federal homeland security funds set aside for police and fire departments.[63] Because of the lack of federal support and stretched local funds, in many cases states have not treated national security alerts with the required "heightened readiness"; in other cases, they have done so at a price beyond security.[64] The result has been an uncomfortable shifting of priorities away from traditional public programs and services to services focusing on police and fire protection because of security alerts and antiwar protests.[65]

Domestic Terrorism

In the post-9/11 world, we often think of terrorism as devastation brought by people from other countries. However, terrorism can be caused by individuals within the United States just as easily as by those from abroad. Some of it has come from white supremacists who have carried out murders and seized land. Other terrorist activities have been conducted by vengeful people opposed to physicians who perform abortions.[66] The destruction of the Murrah Federal Building in Oklahoma City and loss of 168 lives in 1995 was caused by a disgruntled American citizen, not a foreigner with fanatical religious values. Likewise, when the federal government indicted eleven Americans in 2006 for planning acts of "environmental terrorism," once again the focus was on Americans bringing terror to other Americans. In fact, the ability of people to threaten the well-being of others knows no boundaries. Nevertheless, the federal government spends disproportionate resources focusing on threats to the United States from foreign shores; states and cities operate with less discrimination, worrying instead about threats from anywhere.

States and local governments have also increased their preparedness levels against terrorism and any other forms of potential harm to their populations. In the wake of 9/11, these governments have developed emergency plans for a variety of potential dangers including conventional weapons, hazardous materials, chemical attacks, and biological attacks. Their preparedness is an extension of ongoing activities that focus on floods, earthquakes, mining accidents, mosquito infestations, and other potential events. As a result, these governments now dedicate major resources to patrolling airport perimeters, power transmission lines, water resources, bridges and tunnels, and numerous other facilities that, if damaged, could bring about havoc beyond imagination. Most of these efforts, while more critical than ever in the post-9/11 environment, have been funded largely by the states and local governments, with little financial support from the federal government. As a local disaster management expert concludes, "The local government emergency manager is confronted with a series of competing demands and a very limited source of local funding and federal support to meet those demands."[67] As a result, these governments have been forced to alter their priorities, with less money available for traditional expenditure areas such as public education, roads, and health care.

Pandemic Threats

Diseases have always found their way around the world. Shortly after explorer Christopher Columbus and his party set foot in Hispaniola in 1492, local natives died from diseases for which they had no resistance. Likewise, when the European influenza pandemic reached American shores in 1918, 675,000 people lost their lives to the imported disease—ten times the number of Americans who died in combat during World War I. In the twenty-first century, disease travels easier than ever. The combination of increased global commerce and relatively inexpensive transcontinental transportation has eased global movement to the point that seas and huge land masses no longer keep people apart. Thus, AIDS, first discovered by American researchers in 1978 in a handful of countries, quickly spread within a matter of months. Within fifteen years, the disease had infected more than 22 million people around the world.[68]

Pandemic threats are always on the horizon. Because they are often widespread in their attack, they require attention from all levels of government, particularly those at the state and local levels. Avian flu is the most recent example of a disease with the capability of wiping out large populations. During 2005 alone, a resurgence of this virus led to the preventive destruction of 200 million birds, while causing the deaths of more than eighty people in countries spanning from China to Turkey. Congress authorized $3.3 billion for research in 2005, but made available only $350 million for local health departments for purchases of vaccines and other preparations. Local health officials were dismayed over the congressional allocation: "That $350 million sounds like a lot, but divided among 5,000 health departments, it's only $70,000 each," lamented the chief of communicable diseases in Seattle's King County Health Department. [69] In fact, as of 2006, few states or cities were prepared to handle a possible epidemic.

The unpreparedness of states extends to virtually all forms of disaster, regardless of the cause or source. A survey of state disaster officials in 2006 found that twenty-six states were unprepared for situations with mass casualties; moreover, only fourteen states expressed confidence in their ability to manage such events.[70] Operating with far too few financial resources, states and local governments remain vulnerable to unexpected assaults on their populations, regardless of the sources.

International Dimensions in a Domestic Context

International developments today impact American governments on a variety of levels. While the federal government may be consumed with global issues ranging from trade to tourism, states and local governments have plenty to contend with as well. Surely, the federal government has its hands full with the threat of international terrorism and other intrusions into the United States. Yet, those and other issues affect the states as well. More than ever, states confront a variety of problems including potentially lost jobs to other countries, programs and services for illegal immigrants, and uncompensated homeland security costs. On these and other policy areas, states must often fend for themselves.

Although all governments in the United States share the concern of security, they do not necessarily operate with the same objectives in other areas, such as trade. Thus, discouragement of individuals by the federal government from purchasing inexpensive drugs from foreign sources may satisfy protectionist demands of U.S.-based pharmaceuticals but harm people on fixed incomes. Likewise, those who welcome low-priced foreign labor for their businesses may undermine federal immigration policy. The result can be a conflicting cacophony of policies that do not necessarily complement one another, while giving mixed messages to all affected.

The examples above suggest a public policy network that is not particularly well linked on matters of international concern. They also show the endless number of new issues relating to federalism. Some, if not resolved, could bring substantial harm to all concerned in the years to come. Fundamentally, however, this discussion highlights the extent to which international issues have become the twenty-first-century concerns of all levels of government in the United States.

Part IV

Continuity and Change

9

✩ ✩ ✩ ✩

Explaining American Federalism in the Twenty-first Century

Here is a trivia question. How many nations are governed by the same set of written rules today that were used more than two hundred years ago? You probably have already figured out the answer: One, the United States. In fairness, that answer should come with an asterisk, for although the United States can boast the world's oldest constitution, it has been amended, or altered, on twenty-seven occasions.

The Constitution organized this nation in several respects, ranging from the creation of political institutions, to opportunities for and restraints upon the use of power, to defining the relationship between citizen and government. Much of the new framework focused upon the assignment of authority to and among various levels of governments; the resulting series of relationships has come to be known as federalism.

Remarkably, the basic architecture crafted at the Constitutional Convention remains in place. Two strong levels of government—the nation as a whole and its many parts—operate today as they did two centuries ago. The divisions of powers among the three major branches at the national level also endure. Those elements of continuity notwithstanding, any suggestion that the federal arrangement functions now exactly as it did in 1787 would be overly simplistic and downright inaccurate, for amidst governing continuity has coexisted the concept of political change.

The idea of change to accommodate several blossoming interests and evolving values should not be a surprise, for pressures to do so first emerged with the very adoption of the Constitution. Stanley Elkins and Eric McKitrick chronicle that even before the Constitutional Convention of 1787 disbanded, delegate George Mason and others demanded guarantees beyond the scope of the document, many of which appeared shortly thereafter in the form of the Bill of Rights.[1] Thus, the twin messages of continuity and change became early complementary themes of the Constitution and federalism—an odd combination, given that these two phenomena reside at opposite ends of the activity spectrum. All of which takes us back to the design of this book.

American federalism, it turns out, resides as a curious combination of contradictions. Along with a strong strain of conservatism designed to protect the status quo, our political system at times has moved boldly in new directions, often recalibrating the status quo in the process. Juxtaposed against efforts to promote individual liberty has been a current to protect the collective interests of all irrespective of where they reside. A political environment built on a delicate compromise has housed conflict within that framework, often instilling a new consensus through evolution. What does this all mean? That as much as most people agree upon the basics of federalism, it is the details and applications that often refine governing relationships as we struggle to cope with social, economic, political, and international events. If that is true, our understanding of federalism today may be quite different from how the concept will operate fifty or a hundred years from now.

In this chapter we rethink federalism in terms of its malleability and capacity for change. We do so carefully, bearing in mind that the original framework still very much dominates our governmental environment and collective political values. Clearly, the world is a different place today in so many respects, yet the general themes upon which this nation was constructed—while sometimes stretched, twisted, and amended—remain largely in place. Adjusting our governmental system to present-day experiences with a mindful eye to the past is both a tribute and challenge to American federalism.

Problem-Solving in a Defined Political Structure

Whatever the varying shades of philosophical values that accompanied the delegates to Philadelphia in 1787, almost all agreed on the need to leave the meeting with a new workable plan for governance to replace the old system. Clearly, they jousted for positions on numerous topics to the very end, but overwhelmingly the delegates agreed to a different arrangement, flaws included. Benjamin Franklin, at eight-one years of age by far the most senior of the delegates in attendance, put the framework in perspective when he wrote at the Convention's end, "I agree to this Constitution with all its faults—if they are such—because I think a general government is necessary for us."[2] He noted that no other group of individuals assembled at such a meeting in the future was likely to improve upon the outcome, given the profound differences likely to exist among the participants. It was, Franklin concluded, the best compromise that could possibly emerge under such trying circumstances.[3] This observation was important, because it acknowledged that from the outset the Constitution would be anything but a perfect document. Yet the political agreement represented a new start for Americans and their governments.

Within the document, the Constitution contained a prescription for federalism, the design for simultaneously organizing, distributing, and managing political power. Some elements were clearly arranged and remain without change to this day. Other elements have shifted over time. Much of the political debate since 1787 has focused on finding the balance between boundaries of governance and accommodation to reflect changing ideas and needs.

Established Boundaries

Some concepts became firmly ingrained in the new governmental structure with precious little dissent. Learning from the weaknesses that stemmed from the Articles of Confederation, the Framers established dominance of the national government on questions relating to national defense and military security; no longer would states be allowed to operate their own foreign policies independently at the peril of nation. The assignment of military authority and other foreign affairs responsibilities to the national level was articulated in Article I, Section 8, of the Constitution, along with other rights placed firmly within the province of the Congress and president. On this there would be firm agreement.

States, too, were given unambiguous reign in several areas of governance. As described in Article IV, their boundaries were established as sovereign along with activities within. At the same time, they were given the security of respect by other states on matters relating to laws and rules of conduct. Lest anyone wonder whether Congress might legislate away state authority in the future, the Tenth Amendment of the Bill of Rights clarified that all powers not assigned to the national level by the Constitution would reside with the states and their populations.

And what about the people? How would their rights be protected? The answer to this question evolved with the rights as well as the growing numbers of people entitled to them. The earliest attention focused on protection from a potentially overreaching national government, but this notion expanded to protection from the states, too, over time. Through constitutional amendments and court decisions, the guarantees against unwarranted government intrusions grew in scope and depth.

Some matters were so difficult to resolve that the Framers basically ignored them. Chief among these was the issue of slavery. Pitting the urban north against the rural south, this sectional dispute threatened to undue the series of fragile alliances necessary to gain agreement on the Constitution. Taking the issue head-on contained another risk, namely reopening the representation question that had been a particularly thorny issue. With so much on the line, the delegates largely ignored the slavery issue to the point that the word "slavery" was not even included in the Constitution.[4]

Whatever the omissions, the boundaries distinguishing the powers of the national and state governments were carved much differently with the Constitution in 1787 from the Articles of Confederation a scant six years earlier. The new division created much more of a balance, to the delight of most but to the concern of some who feared excessive power at the national level. Even the Bill of Rights failed to convert those who worried that the new system of government could overwhelm the inherent interests of the individual.[5] That tension remains to this day.

Elasticity of the System

Although many questions related to governance were answered with the provisions of the Constitution, others languished without immediate resolution. Some have been sorted out over time in concert with development of the nation; others have persisted because of unbridgeable conflicting values.

One level of expansion has centered on the growth of government in general. The modernization of society has produced with it demands for programs and services unimaginable even a hundred years ago. But the Great Depression brought the national government into our lives in a string of areas ranging from home mortgage guarantees to old age security. Many of these changes were justified under the terms of the "necessary and proper clause" found in Article I, Section 8, of the Constitution, although not all agreed with such a generous interpretation. The events surrounding and following World War II moved government further into our lives in terms of protection from outside forces. Finally, the post-9/11 environment has contributed to an expectation that government play a larger, not smaller, role in our lives. Today, Theodore Lowi and his colleagues write, "the national government is an enormous institution with programs and policies reaching into every corner of American life."[6] Further, it is hard to imagine doing without these programs and services.

Another element of change has been the growing relationship between the national government and local governments. Completely ignored at the meeting in Philadelphia, local governments have emerged as vital institutions. At first, they operated as subservient partners to state governments. However, over the past half century local governments have become important independent centers of political power, often collaborating directly with the national government on key issues. Today, the issues expressed by mayors of large cities such as New York, Los Angeles, and Chicago often are the harbingers of discussions that take place at the national level. Additionally, the leaders of suburban communities have gained prominence for raising issues that previously escaped the national spotlight. No longer are public education, health, local transportation, and the environment simply matters for local governments to "work out" on their own.[7] Particularly to the extent that the federal government has shied away from funding these areas, they have emerged as important national matters of public policy.

A third factor, the liberty/equality dichotomy cited at various junctures throughout this volume, has inched toward resolution, although hardly in linear fashion without its own controversy. Constitutional amendments, the cleanest of the directives, have cemented basic political participation rights of minorities, women, and young adults. Less clear have been the answers to questions focusing on the definitions of life and the conditions related to an individual's decision to end it, specific remedies for discrimination, and the conditions under which governments might deprive an individual of his or her existence through capital punishment. In these and other instances, resolution of various issues through laws, executive orders, court decisions, and regulations has sometimes moved erratically in concert with changing values and the times. On a related track, at times recent state laws on abortion, religion in the schools, eminent domain, and natural resources have traveled along distinctly unique paths, challenging the right of the national government to interfere with their objectives.

If all of this seems a bit sloppy, it is because it *is* sloppy. Federalism operates best as a basic design or a general blueprint for the political system. But anyone who has worked with blueprints appreciates the host of issues that ensue as builders attempt to convert the plans into an actual structure. So it is with federalism. Application of the values to specific policies can be inconsistent and confusing because of so many elements that test the boundaries of the political system.

In Search of Balance

Specific areas of policy notwithstanding, operation of the federal system in the United States is largely about determining limits of authority in both vertical and horizontal dimensions of government power. On the question of vertical relationships, there exists a vigorous, ongoing debate. Some scholars contend that modern federalism operates with all levels having more authority today than in the past, referring to the natural accumulation of authority for all governments with the increasing complexity of a modern society. Nowhere is this more profound than with the expansion of the national government, according to James Anderson, who notes that "the reach and power of the national government has undergone continual expansion since the Constitution's adoption. . . . National policies now apply to many areas once regarded as the domain of the states; examples include public education, social welfare, and highway construction and maintenance."[8]

Others contend that federalism operates within a zero-sum environment, meaning that to the extent the national government gains power, the states automatically lose it and vice versa. As William Morrow explains, "Even in cases in which states and localities are not asked to provide resources and change policies to accommodate federal initiatives, federalism encourages resistance to programs that are incompatible with local interests. Or that threaten the ability of a state to protect the welfare of its residents."[9] These approaches to power help to explain the debate over the very definition of federalism and the difficulties associated with determining application limits by various authorities.

The horizontal dimension presents its own set of challenges. In matters of executive-versus-legislative clout, an examination of recent policy initiatives suggests the executive branch gaining power over the legislative branch both at the national and state levels. This is particularly evident with the executive branch which, some argue, has been transformed from a muted institution with a relatively weak leader to one "in which the president, not the Congress, is viewed by the American people as the nation's chief agenda setter and the nation's leader."[10] That said, the judiciary cannot be discounted with its emergence as the ultimate referee in horizontal and vertical clashes. Here we are reminded of the power stemming from judicial review, originally defined more than two hundred years ago in *Marbury v. Madison*. With this tool, G. Alan Tarr notes, "judges are more involved in policymaking today than in the past" at both the national and state levels.[11] By clarifying thorny questions through their decisions, courts may have emerged as the most important of all the federalism components in the twenty-first century.

Whether viewing the horizontal or vertical dimensions, checks and balances among these political actors remain as critical today as at any moment in American history. The disputes are easily observed in the horizontal dimension through the assorted and diverse battles between the various branches of authority. They also occur vertically, although in more indirect ways, commonly defined by the political outcomes of elections. Combined, this information shows us the fluidity associated with efforts to determine the limits of federalism.

Emerging Themes, New Directions, Unanswered Questions

Along with the ongoing debates about roles of government and levels of distribution, new issues have further complicated the meaning and direction of federalism. Three particularly controversial questions in the early moments of the twenty-first century focus on the control of resources, the changing impact of science and technology, and globalization—all of which have raised new questions about the workings of federalism.

Few authorities could predict the emergence of these issues two-hundred years ago, yet they have become critical to the modern operation of federalism as a means of governance.

Controlling Natural Resources

Air, water, land, and other natural resources have become bargaining chips in the struggle over defining and operating federalism. Decades ago, this nation was less populated, less developed, and less aware of the ecological damage we can bring upon ourselves; there was little concern about the environment or which level of government would be best suited to manage precious environmental resources. All that has changed. The once generally cooperative relationship between the national government and states has deteriorated into contentiousness and competition. At the same time, the roles of governments have changed as many observers recognize the devastating effects of global warming.[12]

From the days of Teddy Roosevelt and the first environmentalists to about the end of the twentieth century, those concerned with preserving natural resources relied upon the federal government for protection. Through federal preemption of state regulatory activities, Congress routinely enacted legislation that set aside land, pursued cleaner air, and cleansed the soil of toxics.[13] While these efforts were not always to the standards of some environmentalists, they reflected a value of the national government protecting the public good. Some states that would set lower standards for land use or permitted pollution as a necessary by-product of private enterprise found themselves limited by federal policies. Such conditions no longer exist.

Beginning with the return of conservatives to power in Congress during the mid-1990s, coupled with the election of a conservative president in 2000, roles have reversed. Since then, congressional legislation and federal regulatory activity have moved to lessen national control, favoring instead self-management of environmental issues by the private sector. A few states have welcomed this change, believing that the benefits from exploiting the land more than offset the potential harm to the environment.[14] Others, however, have felt abandoned, if not betrayed, by the federal government. Acting in response to the void, some states have assumed aggressive postures toward environmental protection. In fact, by 2006, more than half of the states adopted "climate action" plans designed to lessen reliance upon fossil fuels, while the mayors of 218 cities containing 44 million Americans pledged to adopt programs designed to meet the Kyoto Protocol targets for the United States.[15] Rather than endorse these efforts, the federal government has taken states to court to block such efforts as harmful to national standards.[16]

This struggle involves more than determining power relationships. Many states, once viewed as protectors of the private sector in the name of economic benefits for their populations, now view protecting the environment as a greater good, with the federal government moving in the opposite direction. Such a reversal of values shows the fluidity of the national/state relationship.

Science, Technology, and Health

In the twenty-first century, scientific breakthroughs are challenging the roles of governments and their relationships with citizens. The changes are startling not only because of their potential magnitude, but because of the speed with which they are unfolding. New inventions now allow women to terminate potential pregnancies within hours of possible conception, courtesy of RU-486 (the "morning after" pill). Modern medical technology can now keep body fluids flowing and organs functioning on life support for years as scientists attempt to revive the mental capacities of incapacitated people. At the same time, stem cell research is opening up the possibility of replacing degenerated nerves and organs. These and other rapidly developing breakthroughs are raising fundamental questions relating to the ways we define life and death, as well as which governments will define and protect the guarantees of the individuals involved.

On these topics, the struggles for governmental dominance remain. One only has to recall the agonizing situation of Terri Schiavo in 2005, a woman who suffered extensive brain damage in 1990 and who never regained consciousness. Beginning in 2000, a Florida state court agreed with the request of her husband to remove a feeding tube that, he argued, had been keeping her artificially alive. In the end, the U.S. Supreme Court decided not to intervene in the case, allowing the decision of a Florida State Supreme Court to stand. Fundamentally, however, the debate was over which level of authority would prevail in defining and guaranteeing various rights.[17]

Then there is the matter of health-care costs in general. With the costs for medical services and hospitalization rising at rates well beyond the cost of living, new questions are emerging about paying for medical care. As many as 45 million Americans were without health insurance in 2003, an increase of more than 5,200,000 since 2000.[18] At first blush, any health-care problem would seem to be the concern of only the individual affected. But what if the person in need of hospitalization has no health insurance or money to pay for medical care? And what about the huge number of "baby boomers," people born between 1946 and 1964, who are not only becoming senior citizens, but living longer than any previous generation? In 1965, public programs paid for 25 percent of all medical costs in the United States. A respected estimate forecasts that by 2014, governments will be required to pay 49 percent of all health-care costs.[19] Should this prediction come true, which governments will pick up the tab, the national or states and their local governments? Will Social Security and other economic "safety nets" undergo fundamental change? The answers to these questions will tell us much about the direction of federalism in the next century.

Globalization

More than ever, significant issues relating to federalism extend well beyond our shores. Nowhere is this more evident than with globalization. Not so many years ago, states competed with each other for the right to make products for American companies. Many of those companies still are "American," however they have moved their assembly lines and service centers offshore.[20] Intel, IBM, and even Boeing may have U.S. names, but substantial percentages of their work are carried out offshore by people whose wages are considerably less than the wages in the United States. Nowadays, states compete to be the local production sources for foreign companies instead of representing American companies. The altered landscape is monumental both psychologically and economically. Sony and Toyota have replaced RCA and GM. As they have moved production to the United States, these and other companies have established facilities in states with lower labor costs and special tax benefits. States still compete with each other, but under radically different circumstances than in the past. In the process, many state governments are giving away more and getting less.

Beyond corporate changes, globalization has affected federalism in other ways. Dealing with illegal immigration has created a great chasm within the national government and between the national government and the states, leading to unprecedented finger-pointing over responsibilities. Not only are there border-patrol-related matters, but there are several spillover issues that include additional education costs, public health and other social services, low-cost housing, and added incarceration costs for undocumented residents. In all of these cases, many states are assuming huge financial burdens with little or no compensation from the federal government.

Responding to terrorism stands out as a third major area of concern relating to federalism. Since 9/11 the federal government has taken many steps to protect U.S. soil, ranging from legislation such as the USA Patriot Act to creation of the Department of Homeland Security. Considerable federal effort has been directed to protection of most airports. Still, the states have been left with enormous responsibilities with respect to protecting electricity transmission lines, rivers and water quality, ports of entry, and food production. On these and other areas the federal response has been tepid in some cases and absent in others.

The Bottom Line

The issues discussed above present new challenges to the federal government and the states. Beyond funding, they raise questions about the most efficient levels of service, distributions of public authority, and responsibilities for protecting individual rights. Most have been addressed partially or in piecemeal fashion, with others too controversial to settle. Greater attention will be required by public policy makers in the future, although their outcomes remain uncertain.

The Future of American Federalism

Sometimes the best hint at predicting the future comes from understanding the past. However, the conditions of the past may not necessarily be the same at other times. Such are the bookends of American federalism. Assuming the past to be a valuable indicator of upcoming political challenges and opportunities, it is reasonable to expect that the basic foundations of American federalism will remain in place. More than two hundred years of vertical and horizontal interaction shows that the "checks and balances" of our system work remarkably well, although hardly consistently or in a particular direction.

But there is another side of this political paradox. It is also reasonable to assume that changes in the relationship between the governments will also occur as events and circumstances require. Sometimes, these rearrangements may come about because of technological breakthroughs, global changes, or scientific developments; other times they may take place as a result of changing social values such as women participating in the workplace or the emergence of domestic partnerships. Regardless, the world is hardly static. As events alter the conditions in which we live, governments must respond accordingly.

Looking ahead, experimentation with various policy themes will continue to take place, notably at the state and local levels of authority because of their relatively nimble organizations and entrepreneurialism.[21] On this topic, David Nice points out, accommodating political environments have produced "widespread and in some cases dramatic" changes in state public policies and procedures.[22] Some, like welfare reform in Wisconsin during the early 1990s, will become national models. Others, such as public education vouchers first employed in Milwaukee and Cleveland, will gain grudging national recognition and operate tentatively in a cloud of debate. Others still, such as Oregon's "death with dignity," will remain on the cutting edges of social controversy and roaring political debates, with reaction and judgments uncertain.

And so many more remain on the horizon of American federalism. It remains to be seen what will become of state initiatives in the areas of medical marijuana decriminalization, stem cell research, and illegal immigration, three particularly hot topics in the first decade of the twenty-first century. These and others no doubt will add to the items on the federalism agenda in the coming years.

Finally, a word about perfection. Their efforts notwithstanding, the Framers did not create a perfect political system for Americans, nor do we have one today. Two major reasons help to explain this outcome. First, political perfection, like beauty, lies in the eye of the beholder. One whose values are disposed toward less national control and more state powers might be quite pleased with the diminution of national welfare and increased state authority on matters such as environmental protection and affirmative action; one whose values tilt toward more national standards and less state government authority on these issues would feel just as disappointed. In this sense, federalism does not overcome differences. Rather, federalism provides an organizational vehicle for accommodating differences.

Second, the exercise of power by a particular level of government that seems appropriate at one moment in time may well take on a different look at another time because of changing political values or circumstances. It would have been difficult to imagine the national government adopting the Social Security system prior to the Great Depression; now, most people consider this program an essential part of their "social contract" with government. Likewise, the thought of states negotiating with representatives of other countries for location of their companies or production facilities might have been viewed as heretical in the late 1780s, given the tumult surrounding such activities prior to the Constitutional Convention; today these activities are commonplace. Times and public values change, and so do the behaviors of governments.

Buried in all this cacophony lies the central theme of this book—that federalism is the guiding, if often misunderstood, force for government in the United States. It is a force that sometimes moves in curious directions and sometimes no direction at all. The struggles to define, organize, and carry out political power by governments in the name of the people are just as pronounced today as at any other moment in American history. The stakes for the nation and its people can be substantial, depending upon which level of government prevails upon a given issue. The conflicts can take disputing sides to the brink of political stalemate, if not dysfunctionalism. Yet, in spite of all of these and other concerns, the system stays intact as we debate the best ways to manage the issues and values of the day.

Notes

Notes to Chapter 1

1. Among the many comparative treatments on the subject, see Pradeep Chhibber and Ken Kollman, *The Formation of National Party Systems: Federalism and Party Competition in Canada, Great Britain, India, and the United States* (Princeton, NJ: Princeton University Press, 2004).

2. "Sunnis See Iran's Hand in Call for Federalism," *Los Angeles Times,* August 21, 2005, p. A9.

3. "Debate on Kenya's Future: Serious Talk and Fruit Tossing," *New York Times,* October 16, 2005, p. 3.

4. Leslie Lipson, *The Democratic Civilization* (New York: Oxford University Press, 1964), p. 143.

5. Seymour Martin Lipset offers this term as an explanation for the novel practices and institutions embraced by the founders of the United States at the time of the American Revolution. See his *The First New Nation* (New York: Anchor, 1967).

6. For a rich discussion of the development of representation as a concept, see Hannah Fenichel Pitkin, *The Concept of Representation* (Berkeley: University of California Press, 1978).

7. Steven J. Rosenstone and John Mark Hansen, *Mobilization, Participation, and Democracy in America* (New York: Macmillan, 1993), pp. 234–48.

8. James J. Harrigan and David C. Nice, *Politics and Policy in States and Communities,* 8th ed. (New York: Pearson Longman, 2004), pp. 74–88.

9. Theodore J. Lowi, *The End of Liberalism,* 2nd ed. (New York: W.W. Norton, 1979), pp. 61–63. Lowi is actually critical of expanded representation, particularly to the extent the pursuit of interest group objectives takes place in a closed bureaucratic environment rather than the elected political process.

10. E.E. Schattschneider, *The Semisovereign People* (New York: Holt, Rinehart, and Winston, 1966), p. 7.

11. G. Ross Stephens and Nelson Wikstrom, *American Intergovernmental Relations: A Fragmented Federal Polity* (New York: Oxford University Press, 2007), p. 271.

12. See Thomas R. Dye, *American Federalism: Competition among Governments* (Lexington, MA: Lexington Books, 1990), p. 21.

13. Burdett A. Loomis, *The Contemporary Congress,* 3rd ed. (Boston: Bedford/St. Martin's, 2000), pp. 1–14.

14. This argument is persuasively made by Ira Sharkansky in his *The Maligned States,* 2nd ed. (New York: McGraw-Hill, 1978).

15. For a discussion of various models of power distribution, see David C. Nice and Patricia Fredericksen, *The Politics of Intergovernmental Relations,* 2nd ed. (Chicago: Nelson-Hall, 1995), pp. 3–6.

16. "Web Merchants Gear Up for Busy 'Black Monday,'" *Wall Street Journal,* November 21, 2005, p. A1.

17. "States Covet Web Tax Revenues," *San Francisco Chronicle,* February 8, 2003, pp. A1, A10.

18. Harold D. Lasswell, *Politics: Who Gets What, When, How* (New York: McGraw-Hill, 1936).

19. In 2005, Congress passed and President George W. Bush signed emergency legislation taking jurisdiction of the case of Terri Schiavo, a woman in a deep coma and showing no visible signs of life, away from the Florida courts to the federal courts, in hopes that the federal courts would order the reinsertion of a feeding tube that had been removed under state court guidance. Ironically, the federal courts upheld the state court decisions. See "U.S. Court Begins Consideration of Schiavo Case," *New York Times,* March 22, 2005, pp. A1, A14; and "Judge Declines to Order Feeding in Schiavo Case," *New York Times,* March 23, 2005, pp. A1, A14.

20. Jonathon Walters and Donald Kettle, "The Katrina Breakdown," *Governing,* December 2005, pp. 20–25.

21. "Bush Visit Sees More Cleanup Progress," *Wall Street Journal,* April 28, 2006, p. A6.

22. There are numerous works that emphasize one school of federalism over another. For an approach that sides largely with the states, see Robert F. Nagel, *The Implosion of American Federalism* (New York: Oxford University Press, 2001). A considerably different approach emphasizing national government involvement is found in Lester C. Thurow, *The Zero-Sum Society* (New York: Penguin, 1980).

23. Monte Palmer makes this point in his *Dilemmas of Political Development,* 4th ed. (Itasca, IL: F.E. Peacock, 1989), chap. 4.

24. Joseph F. Zimmerman, *Contemporary American Federalism* (Westport, CT: Praeger, 1992), p. 204.

25. "30 Years after Abortion Ruling, New Trends but the Old Debate," *New York Times,* January 20, 2003, pp. A1, A16.

26. "Washington Washes Its Hands," *Newsweek,* August 12, 1996, p. 42.

27. See Virginia Gray and Peter Eisinger, *Politics in the American States and Cities,* 2nd ed. (New York: Longman, 1997), pp. 18–22.

28. See "Limits on Stem-Cell Research Re-emerge as a Political Issue," *New York Times,* May 6, 2004, pp. A1, A23.

29. For a comparison of the attitudes toward stem cell research in the 2004 presidential campaign, see "Hopes Now Outpace Stem Cell Science," *New York Times,* July 29, 2004, p. 4. Meanwhile, in November 2004, California voters passed a $3 billion measure that provides ten times more money than the national government for stem cell research.

30. See "A Halt to Execution Gaining in States," *Los Angeles Times,* November 8, 2002, p. A28.

31. "A Battle over the Morning-After Pill," *Time,* June 2, 2003, p. 8.

Notes to Chapter 2

1. Walter Isaacson makes this point in his *Benjamin Franklin: An American Life* (New York: Simon & Schuster, 2003), p. 161.

2. The four acts passed in 1774 were the Boston Port Act, the Massachusetts Government Act, the Administration of Justice Act, and the Quartering Act, the last of which removed the governor of Massachusetts and placed the colony under command of the British army.

3. The concept of virtual representation and colonial opposition is discussed in Pauline

Maier, Merritt Roe Smith, Alexander Keyssar, and Daniel Kevees, *Inventing America: A History of the United States*, vol. 1 (New York: W.W. Norton, 2003), pp. 160–63.

4. For an excellent overview of the conditions leading up to the American Revolution, see James West Davidson, William E. Gienapp, Christine Leigh Heyrman, Mark H. Lytle, and Michael B. Stoff, *Nation of Nations: A Narrative History of the American Republic*, vol. 1 (New York: McGraw-Hill, 1994), pp. 104–140.

5. In his *The Strength of a People* (Chapel Hill: University of North Carolina Press, 1996), Richard D. Brown describes the connection between Locke and those European political philosophers who preceded him. See pp. 1–25.

6. Some men of his day actually accused Jefferson of plagiarizing Locke, a charge Jefferson denied. Regardless, the tie was clear. See Noble E. Cunningham, Jr., *The Life of Thomas Jefferson* (New York: Ballentine, 1987), p. 48.

7. For an analysis of Montesquieu's impact on democracy and federalism, see Melvin Richter, *The Political Theory of Montesquieu* (Cambridge: Cambridge University Press, 1977).

8. *Spirit of the Laws, XI*, edited by Franz Neumann, translated by Thomas Nugent (New York: Hafner, 1949), pp. 151–52.

9. Cunningham, *The Life of Thomas Jefferson*, p. 30.

10. Daniel J. Boorstin, *The Lost World of Thomas Jefferson* (New York: Henry Holt, 1948), p. 190.

11. Seymour Martin Lipset, *The First New Nation* (New York: Basic Books, 1963), p. 30.

12. For a discussion of the extent to which states abused one another, see Maier et al., *Inventing America*, vol. 1., pp. 232–36.

13. See Jack N. Rakove, *Original Meanings: Politics and Ideas in the Making of the Constitution* (New York: Vintage, 1997), p. 101.

14. David B. Walker, *The Rebirth of Federalism*, 2nd ed. (New York: Chatham House, 2000), p. 45.

15. Rakove, *Making of the Constitution*, pp. 26–30.

16. Ibid., p. 48.

17. For a comprehensive treatment of Madison's role before, during, and after the Constitutional Convention, see Robert A. Goldwin, *From Parchment to Power* (Washington, D.C.: AEI Press, 1997).

18. Rakove, *Making of the Constitution*, pp. 73–75.

19. See Joseph Tussman, *Obligation and the Body Politic* (New York: Oxford University Press, 1960), who writes: "To be an agent [representative], is thus to accept authority or assume responsibility. . . . It involves for the agent the subordination of private interest to public interest" (p. 60). Of course, defining the "public interest" was as difficult in 1787 as it is today. Like beauty, it is often in the eye of the beholder.

20. Beyond the general description above, numerous nuances accompany the concept of representation. For a rich overview, see Carl J. Friedrich, *Constitutional Government and Democracy*, revised ed. (New York: Blaisdell, 1950), pp. 259–76.

21. Cunningham, *The Life of Thomas Jefferson*, p. 53.

22. Ibid.

23. These issues are summarized in Saul Cornell, *The Other Founders* (Chapel Hill: University of North Carolina Press, 1999), pp. 26–33.

24. See "The Plan Presented by Alexander Hamilton, June 18, 1787," in Michael Kammen, ed., *The Origins of the American Constitution: A Documentary History* (New York: Penguin, 1988), pp. 36–38.

25. James David Barber, *The Book of Democracy* (Englewood Cliffs, NJ: Prentice Hall, 1995), p. 388.

26. Rakove, *Making of the Constitution*, p. 109.

27. Robert A. Dahl, *Pluralist Democracy in the United States: Conflict and Consent* (Chicago: Rand McNally, 1967), p. 24.

28. See Samuel H. Beer, *To Make a Nation: The Rediscovery of American Federalism* (Cambridge, MA: Belknap, 1993), p. 5.

29. Walker, *The Rebirth of Federalism*, p. 58.

30. Rakove, *Making of the Constitution*, p. 170.

31. Beer, *Rediscovery of American Federalism*, p. 389.

32. For a complete collection of all eighty-five essays in the Federalist Papers and thoughtful interpretation, see Clinton L. Rossiter, *The Federalist Papers: Alexander Hamilton, James Madison, John Jay* (New York: Mentor, 1992).

33. Rakove, *Making of the Constitution*, pp. 139–40.

Notes to Chapter 3

1. Karl W. Deutsch, *Nationalism and Social Communication* (Cambridge, MA: MIT Press, 1953), p. 99.

2. Amitai Etzioni writes of people clinging to traditional patterns because of their fear of "potentially slippery slopes," or falling to a less desirable place. See his *The Spirit of Community* (New York: Crown, 1993), pp. 176–77.

3. Richard Hofstadter, *The American Political Tradition* (New York: Vintage, 1948), pp. 8–9.

4. Hofstadter discusses this dilemma and the response to it in his *American Political Tradition*, pp. 10–11.

5. Robert F. Nagel, *The Implosion of American Federalism* (New York: Oxford University Press, 2001), p. 16.

6. Michael D. Reagan and John G. Sanzone, *The New Federalism*, 2nd ed. (New York: Oxford University Press, 1981), p. 14.

7. Op cit., p. 7.

8. Samuel H. Beer, *To Make a Nation: The Rediscovery of American Federalism* (Cambridge, MA: Belknap, 1993), p. 285.

9. James Madison, "The Federalist #10," in Alexander Hamilton, John Jay, and James Madison, *The Federalist* (New York: Modern Library 1951), p. 61.

10. Richard D. Brown, *The Strength of a People* (Chapel Hill: University of North Carolina Press, 1996), p. 103.

11. Saul Cornell, *The Other Founders* (Chapel Hill: University of North Carolina Press, 1999), p. 70.

12. A.E. Dick Howard, "Garcia: Federalism's Principles Forgotten," in Lawrence J. O'Toole, Jr., ed., *American Intergovernmental Relations*, 2nd ed. (Washington, D.C.: CQ Press, 1993), p. 175.

13. In recent years, Maine (1972) and Nebraska (1996) have broken away from the winner-take-all Electoral College selection. In each state, whoever gets the most votes within a congressional district is awarded a delegate, and whoever wins the overall vote statewide earns the remaining two delegates allowed for the U.S. composition.

14. James P. Pfiffner, *The Modern Presidency*, 4th ed. (Belmont, CA: Thomson Wadsworth, 2005), p. 10.

15. James A. Henretta, W. Elliot Brownlee, David Brody, and Susan Ware, *America's History*, vol. 1, 2nd ed. (New York: Worth, 1993), p. 203.

16. David B. Walker, *The Rebirth of Federalism*, 2nd ed. (New York: Chatham House, 2000), p. 53. In *McCulloch v. Maryland* (1819), a case about whether the United States could establish a national bank, the Supreme Court held that Congress has "implied" powers

beyond those listed in the Constitution. This issue is discussed further in Chapter 4.

17. Jack N. Rakove, *Original Meanings: Politics and Ideas in the Making of the Constitution* (New York: Vintage, 1996), pp. 244–87.

18. See Joseph A. Pika and John Anthony Maltese, *The Politics of the Presidency*, 6th ed. (Washington, D.C.: CQ Press, 2004), p. 13.

19. For a description of these narrow judicial bodies, see Christopher E. Smith, *Courts, Politics, and the Judicial Process*, 2nd ed. (Chicago: Nelson-Hall, 1997), pp. 39–41.

20. David W. Neubauer and Stephen S. Meinhold, *Judicial Process*, 3rd ed. (Belmont, CA: Thomson Wadsworth, 2004), p. 64.

21. Walker, *The Rebirth of Federalism*, p. 50.

22. The five occasions were Vermont from New York (1791), Kentucky from Virginia (1792), Tennessee from North Carolina (1796), Maine from Massachusetts (1820), and West Virginia from Virginia (1863).

23. Beer, *Rediscovery of American Federalism*, pp. 305–6.

24. Cornell, *Other Founders*, p. 11.

25. Quoted in ibid., p. 59.

26. The case, *Gitlow v. New York*, 268 U.S. 652, was the first of many over the course of several decades to gradually extend the guarantees associated with the entire Bill of Rights to the states.

27. Michael Kammen, ed., *The Origins of the American Constitution: A Documentary History* (New York: Penguin, 1986), pp. xix–xx.

28. Quoted in Cornell, *Other Founders*, p. 29.

29. Nobel E. Cunningham, Jr., *The Life of Thomas Jefferson* (New York: Ballantine, 1987), p. 44.

30. Daniel Elazar, *American Federalism: A View From the States*, 3rd ed. (New York: Harper and Row, 1984), p. 11.

31. Michael S. Greve, *Real Federalism* (Washington, D.C.: AEI Press, 1999), p. 5.

32. "School Vouchers to Start by Fall," *Washington Times*, January 29, 2004, p. B-1.

33. *New State Ice Company v. Liebmann*, 285 U.S. 262, 1932.

34. For a discussion of equality on the context of civil rights, see Vernon Van Dyke, *Equality and Public Policy* (Chicago: Nelson-Hall, 1990).

35. Quoted in Hamilton, Jay, and Madison, *The Federalist*, p. 143.

36. Rakove, *Making of the Constitution*, p. 29.

37. Reagan and Sanzone, *The New Federalism*, p. 175.

38. William E. Hudson, *American Democracy in Peril*, 3rd ed. (New York: Chatham House, 2001), p. 221.

39. See Thomas G. Walker and Lee Epstein, *The Supreme Court of the United States* (New York: St. Martin's, 1993), pp. 143–46.

Notes to Chapter 4

1. For a description of the "traditional" political system with primitive, unresponsive political institutions, see Samuel P. Huntington, *Political Order in Changing Societies* (New Haven, CT: Yale University Press, 1968), pp. 140–46.

2. Robert A. Dahl, *Pluralist Democracy in the United States: Conflict and Consent* (Chicago: Rand McNally, 1967), p. 373.

3. Like many American traditions, the concept of judicial review has English roots, notably in a 1610 decision known as *Dr. Bonham's Case*, where chief justice of the Court of Common Pleas, Sir Edward Coke, ruled that the proceedings in the case were void because they violated the dictates of an earlier case. For a discussion of this moment, see Michael Les Benedict, *The Blessings of Liberty*, 2nd ed. (Boston: Houghton Mifflin, 2006), p. 4.

4. An endless stream of scholarship has flowed over the meaning and constitutional intent of judicial review. Two of the best sources are Benjamin N. Cardozo, *The Nature of the Judicial Process* (New Haven, CT: Yale University Press, 1921), who argued affirmatively, and Edward S. Corwin, *The Doctrine of Judicial Review: Its Legal and Historical Basis and Other Essays* (Princeton, NJ: Princeton University Press, 1914), who argued to the contrary.

5. Henry J. Abraham, *The Judicial Process*, 6th ed. (New York: Oxford University Press, 1993), p. 315.

6. R. Kent Newmyer, *The Supreme Court under Marshall and Taney* (New York: Thomas Y. Crowell, 1968), p. 19.

7. Jeffrey A. Segal and Harold J. Spaeth, *The Supreme Court and the Attitudinal Model Revisited* (Cambridge: Cambridge University Press, 2002), p. 43.

8. Robert F. Nagel, *The Implosion of American Federalism* (New York: Oxford University Press, 2001), pp. 43, 46.

9. Much of the discussion in this and the following sections draws from the demarcations suggested by David B. Walker in his *The Rebirth of American Federalism*, 2nd ed. (New York: Chatham House, 2000); and Michael D. Reagan and John G. Sanzone, *The New Federalism*, 2nd ed. (New York: Oxford University Press, 1981).

10. Saul Cornell, *The Other Founders* (Chapel Hill: University of North Carolina Press, 1999), p. 283.

11. Newmyer, *The Supreme Court under Marshall and Taney*, p. 92.

12. Ibid., p. 114.

13. David B. Walker makes this point. He writes that by handcuffing both levels of government, "the power vacuum enhanced the position and power of corporate America." *The Rebirth of American Federalism*, p. 76.

14. For thorough analyses of this critical period, see Robert H. Jackson, *The Struggle for Judicial Supremacy* (New York: Knopf, 1949); and Leonard Baker, *Back to Back: The Duel between FDR and the Supreme Court* (New York: Macmillan, 1967).

15. Reagan and Sanzone, *The New Federalism*, p. 23.

16. The Warren Court also ordered redistricting of state upper houses in *Reynolds v. Sims* (1964) and redistricting of congressional districts in *Wesbury v. Sanders* (1964).

17. Among the many decisions handed down during this period were *Mapp v. Ohio*, 1964 (search and seizure); *Gideon v. Wainwright*, 1963 (right to counsel); *Miranda v. Arizona*, 1966 (self-incrimination); and *Griswald v. Connecticut*, 1965 (privacy).

18. Abraham, *The Judicial Process*, p. 70.

19. Jeffrey Segal and Harold J. Spaeth, "Decisional Trends on the Warren and Burger Courts: Results from the Supreme Court Data Base Project," *Judicature*, vol. 73, 1992, pp. 103–7.

20. Walker, *The Rebirth of American Federalism*, pp. 180–81.

21. David W. Neubauer and Stephen S. Meinhold, *Judicial Process: Law, Courts, and Politics in the United States*, 3rd ed. (Belmont, CA: Thomson Wadsworth, 2004), p. 321.

22. The Eleventh Amendment prevents state questions from being decided in federal courts.

23. Quoted in "High Court Curbs Federal Lawsuits against the States," *Los Angeles Times*, March 28, 1996, pp. A1, A12.

24. See *Atkins v. Virginia* (2002) and *Roper v. Simmons* (2005), both of which were decided on Eighth Amendment grounds.

25. See Neubauer and Meinhold, *Law, Courts, and Politics*, p. 21.

26. "New Conservative Activism Sweeps the Federal Courts," *Los Angeles Times*, June 22, 1999, pp. A1, A13.

27. "High Court Upholds Oregon Law Backing Doctor-Assisted Suicide," *Wall Street Journal*, January 18, 2006, pp. A3, A4. The case was *Gonzales v. Oregon*, 04–623.

28. Stanley M. Milkis and Michael Nelson, *The American Presidency: Origins and Development, 1776–2002* (Washington, D.C.: CQ Press, 2003), p. 205.

29. The case was *Youngstown Sheet & Tube Company v. Sawyer.*

30. Kenneth R. Mayer, *With the Stroke of a Pen: Executive Orders and Presidential Power* (Princeton, NJ: Princeton University Press, 2001), p. 4.

31. Richard A. Harris and Sidney M. Milkis, *The Politics of Regulatory Change*, 2nd ed. (New York: Oxford University Press, 1996), p. 261.

32. Cornelius M. Kerwin, *Rulemaking: How Government Agencies Write Law and Make Policy*, 3rd ed. (Washington, D.C.: CQ Press, 2003), p. 61

33. Mark K. Landy, Marc J. Roberts, and Stephen R. Thomas, *The Environmental Protection Agency*, expanded ed. (New York: Oxford University Press, 1994), p. 250.

34. Aaron Wildavsky, *The New Politics of the Budgetary Process* (Clearview, IL: Scott, Foresman, 1988), p. 173.

35. Bert A. Rockman, "Conclusions: An Imprint but Not a Revolution," in B.B. Kymlicka and Jean V. Matthews, eds., *The Reagan Revolution?* (Chicago: Dorsey, 1988), p. 197.

36. Kerwin, *Rulemaking*, pp. 218–33. Also see Joseph A. Pika and John Anthony Maltese, *The Politics of the Presidency*, 6th ed. (Washington, D.C.: CQ Press, 2004), p. 328.

37. This is discussed at length in Harris and Milkis, *The Politics of Regulatory Change*, pp. 128–33.

38. See Marshall R. Goodman and Margaret T. Wrightson, *Managing Regulatory Reform: The Reagan Strategy and Its Impact* (New York: Praeger, 1987), pp. 106–8.

39. Kerwin, *Rulemaking*, pp. 228–29.

40. George C. Edwards III and Stephen J. Wayne, *Presidential Leadership*, 6th ed. (Belmont, CA: Thomson Wadsworth, 2003), p. 417.

41. Kymlicka and Matthews, eds., *The Reagan Revolution?* p. 193.

42. Columnist Andrew Sullivan expresses this concern in his "We Don't Need a New King George," *Time*, January 23, 2006, p. 74.

43. Roger H. Davidson and Walter J. Oleszek, *Congress and Its Members*, 3rd ed. (Washington, D.C.: CQ Press, 1990), p. 18.

44. Jack N. Rakove, *Original Meanings: Politics and Ideas in the Making of the Constitution* (New York: Vintage, 1997), p. 53.

45. The most dramatic of all of the civil rights legislation enacted during the presidency of Lyndon Johnson was the Civil Rights Act of 1965, which empowered the U.S. attorney general to replace state officials with federal authorities for the purpose of registering African Americans to vote.

46. See Oliver H. Woshinsky, *Culture and Politics* (Englewood Cliffs, NJ: Prentice-Hall, 1995), pp. 151–55.

47. "Jupiter Research Reports U.S. Online Retail Will Reach $65 Billion in 2004, Increase over 2003, With Continued Heavy Growth in Home and Personal Care Categories," Jupiter Research, Inc., Press Release, January 20, 2004.

48. Reagan and Sanzone, *The New Federalism*, p. 38.

49. For a thorough analysis, see David C. Nice and Patricia Fredericksen, *The Politics of Intergovernmental Relations*, 2nd ed. (Chicago: Nelson-Hall, 1995), pp. 54–70.

50. David Walker offers an excellent summary of grant history. *The Rebirth of American Federalism*, pp. 78–80.

51. See Peter Gottschalk, "Retrenchment in Antipoverty Programs in the United States: Lessons for the Future," in Kymlicka and Matthews, eds., *The Reagan Revolution?* pp. 131–45.

52. Timothy Conlon, *From Federalism to Devolution* (Washington, D.C.: Brookings Institution, 1998), p. 260.

53. Ibid.

54. The law exempted civil rights, disaster relief, and social security programs.

55. "Study: Unfunded Federal Mandates Growing," United Press International, March 8, 2005.

56. John Boehner, "No Child Left Behind: Spending More Than Ever—And Expecting More Than Ever," Fact Sheet prepared by the House Education and the Workforce Committee, July 23, 2003, p. 2.

57. "Bush Administration 2005 Budget Fails Education," *Education News*, February 5, 2004.

58. Walker, *The Rebirth of American Federalism*, p. 27.

Notes to Chapter 5

1. Talcott Parsons, *The Social System* (New York: Free Press, 1951), p. 121.

2. See Monte Palmer, *Dilemmas of Political Development*, 4th ed. (Itasca, IL: F.E. Peacock, 1989), pp. 67–78.

3. See Samuel P. Huntington, *Political Order in Changing Societies* (New Haven, CT: Yale University Press), pp. 143–46.

4. Jack N. Rakove, *Original Meanings: Politics and Ideas in the Making of the Constitution* (New York: Vintage, 1997), p. 168.

5. For a discussion of the various dimensions of political parties, see Samuel J. Eldersveld and Hanes Walton, Jr., *Political Parties in American Society*, 2nd ed. (Boston: Bedford/St. Martin's, 2000), pp. 2–4.

6. For an explanation of different party arrangements and the consequences for governance, see Gregory S. Mahler, *Comparative Politics: An Institutional and Cross-National Approach*, 4th ed. (Upper Saddle River, NJ: Prentice Hall, 2003), pp. 80–88.

7. Frank Sorauf and Paul Allen Beck describe the American political party as having three major components: the party as an organization, the party as an electorate, and the party in government. The emphasis here is mostly on the latter. For a comprehensive explanation, see their *Party Politics in America*, 6th ed. (Glenview, IL: Scott, Foresman, 1988).

8. See William J. Keefe and Marc J. Hetherington, *Parties, Politics, and Public Policy in America* (Washington, D.C.: CQ Press, 2003), pp. 148–53.

9. Malcolm Jewel and Sarah Morehouse, *Political Parties and Elections in American States*, 4th ed. (Washington, D.C.: CQ Press, 2001), p. 283.

10. L. Sandy Maisel, *Parties and Elections in America: The Electoral Process*, 3rd ed. (Lanham, MD: Rowman & Littlefield, 1999), p. 17.

11. Alan Rosenthal, *The Decline of Representative Democracy* (Washington, D.C.: CQ Press, 1998), p. 187.

12. See John R. Wright, *Interest Groups and Congress* (Needham Heights, MA: Allyn and Bacon, 1996), p. 27.

13. Some states, particularly in the South, have laws that do not protect or recognize unions. In these "open shop" states, unions often lobby for laws that facilitate automatic membership. Similarly, in some "closed shop" states, business-oriented groups have been known to try to change policies to non-union "open shop" settings. One such effort occurred in California in 2005 when voters were asked to make it more difficult for unions to use members' contributions for political campaigns. The voters rejected the proposal, keeping the "closed shop" conditions unchanged.

14. Brian Anderson and Burdett A. Loomis, "Taking Organization Seriously: The Structure of Interest Group Influence," in Allan J. Cigler and Burdett A. Loomis, eds., *Interest Group Politics*, 5th ed. (Washington, D.C.: CQ Press, 1998), p. 93.

15. Four departing unions included the International Brotherhood of Teamsters, Service

Employees International Union, United Food and Commercial Workers, and UNITE-HERE, which represents hotel, casino, restaurant, and garment workers. Their new organization is called the Change to Win Federation. See "Breakaway Unions Start New Federation," *New York Times*, September 28, 2005, p. A16.

16. For a discussion of the interface of foreign policy and domestic policy issues, see James M. McCormick, *American Foreign Policy and Process*, 4th ed. (Belmont, CA: Thomson Wadsworth, 2005), pp. 193–98.

17. "Trade Groups Join Bush on Social Security," *Los Angeles Times*, April 11, 2005, pp. A1, A8.

18. See Clive S. Thomas and Ronald J. Hrebenar, "Interest Groups in the States," in Virginia Gray and Russell L. Hanson, eds., *Politics in the American States*, 8th ed. (Washington, D.C.: CQ Press, 2004, pp. 104–5.

19. "The Tobacco Sham," *Newsweek*, August 19, 2002, p. 33.

20. "Few Tobacco Settlement Dollars Used for Tobacco Control," *Los Angeles Times*, December 15, 2000, pp. A1, A20.

21. "States' Tobacco Settlement Has Failed to Clear the Air," *Los Angeles Times*, November 9, 2003, pp. C1, C4.

22. Thomas and Hrebenar, *op. cit.*, pp. 118–19.

23. For a history of this issue and the Court's responses, see Robert J. Spitzer, *The Politics of Gun Control* (Chatham, NJ: Chatham House, 1995), pp. 25–61.

24. "Gun Violence Renews Legislative Debate," *Los Angeles Times*, March 21, 2005, p. A11.

25. Judy Zelio, "Tribes Bet on Gaming," *State Legislatures*, March 2005, pp. 26–28.

26. "For a Tribe in Texas, an Era of Prosperity Undone by Politics," *New York Times*, June 13, 2005, p. A11.

27. See "Class Action Crackdown," *U.S. News and World Report*, February 25, 2005, pp. 46–47.

28. For a history of this interesting period, see Larry N. Gerston, Cynthia Fraleigh, and Robert Schwab, *The Deregulated Society* (Belmont, CA: Wadsworth, 1988), p. 115–41.

29. U.S. General Accounting Office, *Financial Audit: Resolution Trust Corporation's 1995 and 1994 Financial Statements* (Washington, D.C., 1996), p. 13.

30. See "Statement of Senator Dianne Feinstein on Finalizing an Agreement to Preserve the Headwaters Forest," Washington, D.C., March 2, 1999.

31. "Lumber Dispute Coming to a Head," *San Francisco Chronicle*, June 12, 2005, pp. E1, E4.

32. Anthony Downs, *Inside Bureaucracy* (Santa Monica, CA: Rand, 1966), p. 26.

33. David C. Nice and Patricia Fredericksen, *The Politics of Intergovernmental Relations*, 2nd ed. (Chicago: Nelson-Hall, 1995), pp. 5–6.

34. Walter A. Rosenbaum, *Environmental Politics and Policy*, 6th ed. (Washington, D.C.: CQ Press, 2005), p. 87.

35. *Zelman v. Simmons-Harris*, 122 S. Ct. 2460.

36. "Florida Supreme Court Blocks School Vouchers," *New York Times*, January 6, 2006, p. A14.

37. Gerston, Fraleigh, and Schwab, *The Deregulated Society*, pp. 51–53.

38. "Redrawing the Lines: Bush's Rules Czar Brings Long Knife to New Regulations," *Wall Street Journal*, June 11, 2002, pp. A1, A6.

39. For a discussion of the picket fence approach and other cooperative models, see Nice and Fredericksen, *The Politics of Intergovernmental Relations*, pp. 11–15.

40. "The New Face of Medicaid," *Business Week*, February 21, 2005, pp. 58–59.

41. "Long Resistant, Police Now Start Embracing Immigration Enforcement," *New York Times*, March 15, 2002, p. A11.

42. See "Overcoming Homeland Insecurity," *Newsweek*, December 13, 2004, pp. 26–30.

43. Randall B. Ripley and Grace A. Franklin, *Congress, the Bureaucracy and Public Policy*, 5th ed. (Pacific Grove, CA: Brooks/Cole, 1991), pp. 68–69.

44. "Bush Gives His Backing for Limited Research on Existing Stem Cells," *New York Times*, August 10, 2001, pp. A1, A16.

45. "Why Bush's Ban Could Be Reversed," *Time*, May 23, 2005, p. 30.

46. John W. Kingdon, *Agendas, Alternatives, and Public Policies*, 2nd ed. (New York: Addison-Wesley, 1995), p. 65.

47. For an examination of state capacity and willingness to undertake new policy directions, see David Osborne, *Laboratories of Democracy* (Boston: Harvard Business School Press, 1988).

48. "Debate's Tone Worries Legal Immigrants, Poll Finds," *San Francisco Chronicle*, March 29, 2006, p. A4.

49. "Immigration Debate Reaches Heartland," *Wall Street Journal*, April 13, 2006, p. A4.

Notes to Chapter 6

1. Jeffrey Henig, *Public Policy and Federalism: Issues in State & Local Politics* (New York: St. Martin's, 1985), p. 10.

2. Joseph F. Zimmerman, *Contemporary American Federalism* (Westport, CT: Praeger, 1992), pp. 4–5.

3. William H. Riker, "A Note on Ideology," in Laurence J. O'Toole, ed., *American Intergovernmental Relations*, 3rd ed. (Washington, D.C.: CQ Press, 2000), p. 97.

4. Zimmerman, *Contemporary American Federalism*, p. 5.

5. Aaron Wildavsky, *Federalism and Political Culture*, David Schleicher and Brendon Swedlow, eds. (New Brunswick, NJ: Transaction, 1998), p. 17.

6. This argument is made by Timothy Conlan in *From New Federalism to Devolution* (Washington, D.C.: Brookings Institution, 1998).

7. Cornelius M. Kerwin, *Rulemaking: How Government Agencies Write Law and Make Policy*, 3rd ed. (Washington, D.C.: CQ Press, 2003), p. 29.

8. For some examples of congressional emphasis on national control during this period, see Vernon Van Dyke, *Equality and Public Policy* (Chicago: Nelson-Hall, 1990); C. Lawrence Evans and Walter J. Oleszek, *Congress Under Fire* (Boston: Houghton Mifflin, 1997); and Gary C. Bryner, *Blue Skies, Green Politics*, 2nd ed. (Washington, D.C.: CQ Press, 1995).

9. Adam Clymer, "Role Reversal: Switching Sides on States' Rights," *New York Times*, June 1, 1997, p. 4.

10. For a discussion on the variations associated with implementation of this welfare reform legislation, see B. Guy Peters, *American Public Policy: Promise and Performance*, 6th ed. (Washington, D.C.: CQ Press, 2004), pp. 305–13.

11. "Dizzying Dive to Red Ink Poses Stark Choices for Washington," *New York Times*, September 14, 2003, pp. 1, 18.

12. "State Deficits Could Sink Bush's Plan," *San Francisco Chronicle*, January 8, 2003, pp. A1, A8.

13. "Class Action Crackdown," *U.S. News & World Report*, February 21, 2005, p. 46.

14. Alan Greenblatt, "The Washington Offensive," *Governing*, January 2005, p. 27.

15. See "Abortion Restrictions Were Efforts Long on the Rise," *Los Angeles Times*, November 21, 2004, p. A21.

16. "Model in Utah May Be Future for Medicaid," *New York Times,* February 24, 2005, p. A1.

17. Marc Landy, Marc J. Roberts, and Stephen R. Thomas, *The Environmental Protection Agency,* expanded ed. (New York: Oxford University Press, 1994), pp. 30–31.

18. Richard E. Neustadt, *Presidential Power: The Politics of Leadership from FDR to Carter* (New York: John Wiley & Sons, 1980).

19. Quoted in "Bush Decries Racial Preferences," *Wall Street Journal,* January 16, 2003, p. A4.

20. *Grutter v. Bollinger,* No. 02–241, 288 F 3d. 732.

21. This is the central point of Kerwin's book, *Rulemaking.*

22. "States to Fight Relaxation of Power-Plant Pollution Standards," *New York Times,* August 30, 2003, p. A17.

23. "States, White House, at Odds on Environment," *Los Angeles Times,* December 29, 2002, p. A23.

24. For a comprehensive review of these periods, see Michael Reagan and John Sanzone, *The New Federalism,* 2nd ed. (New York: Oxford University Press, 1981), pp. 20–23.

25. "In Year of Florida Vote, Supreme Court Also Did Much Other Work," *New York Times,* July 2, 2001, p. A12.

26. See "Bush Taps Roberts for Supreme Court," *Wall Street Journal,* July 20, 2005, pp. A1, A8; and "Alito Stirs Up Abortion Divisions," *Wall Street Journal,* November 5–6, 2005, p. A7.

27. Alan Greenblatt, "The Washington Offensive," p. 27.

28. James Dao, "Rebellion of the States: Red, Blue and Angry All Over," *New York Times,* January 16, 2005, section 4, p. 1.

29. "Utah Vote Rejects Parts of Education Law," *New York Times,* April 20, 2005, p. A14.

30. "A Revolt at the School Door," *BusinessWeek,* September 5, 2005, p. 47.

31. "A Chance for Flexible 'No Child' Program," *San Francisco Chronicle,* October 20, 2005, p. A1.

32. Ira Sharkansky, *The Maligned States,* 2nd ed. (New York: McGraw Hill, 1978), p. 38.

33. The case was *Santa Fe Independent School District v. Jane Doe,* 530 U.S. 290.

34. "Revival of School Prayer Has Limited Success," *New York Times,* October 23, 2001, p. A16.

35. David Osborne, *Laboratories of Democracy* (Boston: Harvard Business School Press, 1988), p. 9.

36. "States, White House at Odds on Environment," *Los Angeles Times,* December 29, 2002, p. A23.

37. "States to Fight Relaxation of Power-Plant Pollution Standards," *New York Times,* August 29, 2003, p. A17.

38. David C. Nice, *Policy Innovation in State Government* (Ames: Iowa State University Press, 1994), p. 115.

39. The 2003 case was *Lawrence and Garner v. Texas,* 539 U.S. 558.

40. "Border Troubles Divide U.S., States," *Los Angeles Times,* August 18, 2005, pp. A1, A15.

41. See "States Take the Lead on Policies for Immigrants," *Los Angeles Times,* June 9, 2003, pp. A1, A13.

42. For an excellent review of the tobacco saga, see Martha A. Derthick, *Up in Smoke,* 2nd ed. (Washington, D.C.: CQ Press, 2005).

43. See "U.S. to Consider Settling Suit Against Tobacco Companies," *New York Times,* June 20, 2001, pp. A1, A17; and "In Reversal, U.S. to Seek Tobacco Suit Settlement," *Los Angeles Times,* June 20, 2001, pp. A1, A11.

44. Quoted in "Caveat Eater: A Fight over Food Warnings," *Wall Street Journal,* January 9, 2006, p. A4.

45. See Dennis R. Judd and Todd Swanstrom, *City Politics: The Political Economy of Urban America,* 5th ed. (New York: Pearson Longman, 2006), p. 128.

46. Dennis L. Dressang and James J. Gosling, *Politics and Policy in American States and Communities* (New York: Pearson Longman, 2004), p. 80.

47. Bernard H. Ross and Myron A. Levine, *Urban Politics: Power in Metropolitan America,* 7th ed. (Belmont, CA: Thomson Wadsworth, 2005), p. 465.

48. Terry Christensen, *Local Politics: Governing at the Grass Roots* (Belmont, CA: Wadsworth, 1995), p. 6.

49. "Katrina Damage Estimate Hits $125B," *USA Today,* September 9, 2005, p. A1.

50. "Turf Wars," *U.S. News & World Report,* February 27, 2006, p. 70.

51. Jonathan Walters and Donald Kettl, "The Katrina Breakdown," *Governing,* vol. 19, no. 3, December 2005, pp. 20–25.

52. "Host States Look to Tighten Belts," *Arkansas Democrat Gazette,* January 2, 2006, pp. 1A, 3A.

53. Judd and Swanstrom, *City Politics,* p. 38. The case was *Dartmouth College v. Woodward,* 4 Wheaton 518.

54. For a discussion of Dillon's Rule, see John J. Harrigan and David C. Nice, *Politics and Policies in States and Communities,* 6th ed. (New York: Pearson Longman, 2004), pp. 130–32; and Ross and Levine, *Urban Politics,* pp. 133–35.

55. Robert S. Lorch, *State and Local Politics,* 6th ed. (Upper Saddle River, NJ: Prentice Hall, 2001), p. 229.

56. Kevin B. Smith, Alan Greenblat, and John Buntin, *Governing States and Localities* (Washington, D.C.: CQ Press, 2005), p. 350.

57. For a description of this legislation, see Federal Highway Administration, "A Summary of Highway Provisions in SAFETEA-LU" (Department of Transportation: Washington, D.C.), August 25, 2005.

58. David P. Walker, *The Rebirth of Federalism,* 2nd ed. (New York: Chatham House, 2000), p. 242.

59. See Richard Hotstadter, *The American Political Tradition* (New York: Alfred A. Knopf, 1948), p. 12.

60. "Rising Tensions over Pensions," *BusinessWeek,* May 16, 2005, p. 70.

61. "25 Most Underfunded Pensions," *USA Today,* July 18, 2005, p. B6.

62. "Whoops! There Goes Another Pension Plan," *New York Times,* September 18, 2005, section 3, pp. 1, 9.

63. "Pension Agency Deficit Could Swell Threefold," *Los Angeles Times,* June 10, 2005, p. C3.

64. Milton Friedman and Rose Friedman, *Free to Choose* (New York: Avon, 1980), p. 129.

65. Grant McConnell, *Private Power and American Democracy* (New York: Alfred P. Knopf, 1967), p. 29.

66. See Seymour Martin Lipset, *The First New Nation* (New York: Basic Books, 1973), pp. 58–61.

67. John Kenneth Galbraith, *The New Industrial State* (New York: Houghton Mifflin, 1967), p. 313.

68. For a history of the decline of the financial institutions industry leading up to the federal response, see Larry N. Gerston, Cynthia Fraleigh, and Robert Schwab, *The Deregulated Society* (Pacific Grove, CA: Brooks/Cole, 1988), pp. 115–41.

69. See Charles F. Bonser, Eugene B. McGregor, Jr., and Clinton V. Oster, Jr., *American Public Policy Problems,* 2nd ed. (Upper Saddle River, NJ: Prentice Hall, 2000), p. 304.

Notes to Chapter 7

1. For a recent analysis of the alignment patterns of American politics, see James W. Ceaser and Andrew E. Busch, *Red Over Blue* (Lanham, MD: Rowman & Litchfield, 2005), pp. 24–26, 135–40.

2. Lucian W. Pye, *Aspects of Political Development* (Boston: Little, Brown, 1966), p. 105.

3. Samuel P. Huntington, *The Clash of Civilizations and the Remaking of World Order* (New York: Simon & Schuster, 1996), p. 137.

4. Aaron Wildavsky, *Federalism and Political Culture* (New Brunswick, NJ: Transaction, 1998), p. 49.

5. For a comparative overview, see Marcus E. Ethridge and Howard Handelman, *Politics in a Changing World* (New York: St. Martin's, 1994), pp. 72–87.

6. Daniel J. Elazar, *American Federalism: A View From the States*, 3rd ed. (New York: Harper & Row, 1984), pp. 110–41.

7. Ibid., p. 134.

8. The case was *Furman v. Georgia*, 408 U.S. 238.

9. The case was *Gregg v. Georgia*, 428 U.S. 153.

10. "South Dakota Bans Abortion, Setting up Battle," *New York Times*, March 7, 2006, pp. A1, A14.

11. See Ann O'M. Bowman and Richard C. Kearney, *State and Local Government*, 6th ed. (Boston: Houghton Mifflin, 2005), pp. 418–19.

12. The data in the rest of this section come from Andrew T. LeFevre, *Report Card on American Education: A State-by-State Analysis, 1981–2003* (Washington, D.C.: American Legislative Exchange Council, 2004).

13. For a discussion of some of the factors behind inconsistent education performance, see Steven L. Nock and Paul W. Kingston, *The Sociology of Public Issues* (Belmont, CA: Wadsworth, 1990), pp. 144–60.

14. "Is California Next in Line?" *Los Angeles Times*, January 18, 2006, pp. A1, A14.

15. "California Puts Passive Smoke on Toxic List," *New York Times*, January 27, 2006, p. A12.

16. "Boost for Bids to Curb Smoking," *Sacramento Bee*, January 27, 2006, p. A1.

17. "Schwarzenegger Tries to Bring Nevada Jobs Back to California," *Reno Gazette-Journal*, August 3, 2004, p. 1.

18. "States Take Lead in Push to Raise Minimum Wages," *New York Times*, January 2, 2006, pp. A1, A9.

19. "States Pay Steep Price to Attract Industry," *Wall Street Journal*, June 20, 2005, p. A4.

20. "Nissan to Leave Southland," *Los Angeles Times*, November 10, 2005, pp. C1, C10.

21. "States Pay Steep Price to Attract Industry."

22. For an excellent overview of legalized gambling in the states, see Melissa Schettini Kearney, *The Economic Winners and Losers of Legalized Gambling* (Washington, D.C.: Brookings Institution, February 2005).

23. "As Gambling Grows, States Depend on Their Cut," *New York Times*, March 31, 2005, pp. A1, A24.

24. Data in this paragraph are from the National Indian Gaming Commission, www.nigc.gov.

25. "Wheel of Misfortune," *Time*, December 16, 2002, p. 47.

26. "Tribes Bet on Gaming," *State Legislatures*, March 2005, p. 28.

27. "5 Tribes, Gov. Sign Gaming Compacts," *Los Angeles Times*, June 22, 2004, pp. B1, B10.

28. "Governor Reaches Casino Deals with 2 Tribes," *San Francisco Chronicle*, June 17, 2005, B1, B6.

29. Walter A. Rosenbaum, *Environmental Politics and Public Policy*, 6th ed. (Washington, D.C.: CQ Press, 2005), p. 186.

30. "Draft of Air Rule Is Said to Exempt Many Old Plants," *New York Times*, August 22, 2003, pp. A1, A17.

31. See Gary C. Bryner, *Blue Skies, Green Politics*, 2nd ed. (Washington, D.C.: CQ Press, 1995), p. 101.

32. "California Backs Plan for Big Cut in Car Emissions," *New York Times*, September 25, 2004, pp. A1, B3.

33. "Battle Lines Set as New York Acts to Cut Emissions," *New York Times*, November 26, 2005, pp. A1, A14. The nine additional states are Maine, New Jersey, Vermont, Massachusetts, Oregon, Washington, Rhode Island, Connecticut, and Pennsylvania.

34. Quoted in "A Drier and Tainted Nevada May Be Legacy of a Gold Rush," *New York Times*, December 30, 2005, pp. A1, A20.

35. Ibid.

36. For a categorization of major state economic initiatives, see Bowman and Kearney, *State and Local Government*, pp. 396–408.

37. "Research Offers . . . Great Promise and Great Peril," *Los Angeles Times*, August 10, 2001, p. A18.

38. "Bush OKs Limited Stem Cell Funding," *Los Angeles Times*, August 10, 2001, pp. A1, A18.

39. "Limits on Stem-Cell Research Re-emerge as a Political Issue," *New York Times*, May 6, 2004, pp. A1, A23.

40. Robert G. Thobaben, Donna M. Schagheck, and Charles Fenderburk, *Issues in American Political Life*, 6th ed. (Upper Saddle River, NJ: Pearson Prentice Hall, 2006), pp. 180–81.

41. "California Stem-Cell Agency Gets Off to Inauspicious Start," *Wall Street Journal*, July 5, 2005, p. A11.

42. "Stem-Cell Vision Far from Reality," *San Jose Mercury News*, November 27, 2005, pp. E1, E2.

43. David C. Nice and Patricia Fredericksen, *The Politics of Intergovernmental Relations*, 2nd ed. (Chicago: Nelson Hall, 1995), p. 134.

44. "Governors Resolve Port Authority Dispute," *New York Times*, June 2, 2000, p. A23.

45. "Western States Blast California over Water Use," *Las Vegas Review Journal*, May 22, 1999, p. 5B.

46. "In a First, U.S. Officials Put Limits on California's Thirst," *New York Times*, January 5, 2003, pp. 1, 14.

47. Jack N. Rakove, *Original Meanings: Politics and Ideas in the Making of the Constitution* (New York: Vintage, 1997), p. 47.

48. Elazar, *American Federalism*, p. 1.

Notes to Chapter 8

1. Jack N. Behrman and Dennis A. Rondinelli, "Urban Development Policies in a Globalizing Economy: Creating Competitive Advantage in a Post–Cold War Era," in William Crotty, ed., *Post–Cold War Policy: The Social and Domestic Context* (Chicago: Nelson-Hall, 1995), p. 214.

2. Gregory S. Mahler, *Comparative Politics: An Institutional and Cross-National Approach*, 4th ed. (Upper Saddle River, NJ: Prentice Hall, 2003), pp. 64–65.

3. For an interesting discussion of the conditions that elicit government involvement, see Marc L. Busch, *Trade Warriors* (Cambridge: Cambridge University Press, 1999).

4. Graham K. Wilson, *Business and Politics*, 3rd ed. (New York: Chatham House, 2003), p. 158.

5. Alfred E. Eckes, Jr., chronicles the history of U.S. foreign trade policy in his *Opening America's Market: U.S. Foreign Trade Policy since 1776* (Chapel Hill: University of North Carolina Press, 1995).

6. "U.S. Trade Deficit Ballooned to a Record in 2005," *Wall Street Journal*, February 11–12, 2006, pp. A1, A10.

7. Sylvia Ostry and Richard R. Nelson, *Techno-Nationalism and Techno-Globalism: Conflict and Cooperation* (Washington, D.C.: Brookings Institution, 1995), pp. 100–102.

8. Marcus E. Ethridge and Howard Handleman, *Politics in a Changing World* (New York: St. Martin's, 1994), p. 536.

9. "States' Rights vs. Free Trade," *BusinessWeek*, March 7, 2005.

10. "More U.S. Legal Work Moves to India's Low-Cost Lawyers," *Wall Street Journal*, September 28, 2005, pp. B1, B2.

11. "Job Security a Worry in Changing Economy," *Boston Globe*, July 26, 2004, p. C16.

12. "Help Not Wanted," *Newsweek*, March 1, 2004, p. 33.

13. "Offshoring's Giant Target: The Bay Area," *San Francisco Chronicle*, March 7, 2004, pp. A1, A14.

14. Thomas L. Friedman, *The World Is Flat* (New York: Ferrar, Straus and Giroux, 2005), pp. 335–36.

15. "The Oracle Has Spoken," *The Economist*, January 11, 2006, pp. 30–31.

16. "More Furniture Production Moves Overseas," *San Francisco Chronicle*, February 12, 2006, p. J5.

17. "Michigan's Job #1: Recovery," *New York Times*, December 27, 2005, pp. C1, C6.

18. "Big Three May Be Shrinking but U.S. Auto Business Isn't," *Los Angeles Times*, December 18, 2005, pp. C1, C4.

19. "State to Get Acura Site for Design," *Los Angeles Times*, January 6, 2006, p. C2.

20. Carl Guardino, "Offshoring Also Brings Jobs Here," *San Jose Mercury News*, April 7, 2004, p. 7B.

21. "Outsourcing Outrage," *San Francisco Chronicle*, November 17, 2005, pp. C1, C6.

22. "Governor Takes Execs on Selling Spree to China," *San Francisco Chronicle*, November 16, 2005, p. A3.

23. "Kyoto Pact Takes Effect without U.S.," *Los Angeles Times*, February 16, 2005, p. A3.

24. "Global Warming," *BusinessWeek*, August 16, 2004, pp. 60–69.

25. "Signs of Hope on Warming, Poverty," *San Francisco Chronicle*, July 16, 2005, pp. A13, A14.

26. "The Allure of Initiatives," *State Legislatures*, April 2005, pp. 16–19.

27. "State Looks to Lead Pollution Fight," *Los Angeles Times*, December 6, 2005, pp. B1, B9.

28. Ibid.

29. Ibid.

30. "California Backs Plan for Big Cuts in Car Emissions," *New York Times*, September 25, 2004, pp. A1, B3.

31. Vernon M. Briggs, Jr., *Mass Immigration at the National Level* (Armonk, NY: M.E. Sharpe, 1992), p. 1.

32. "Embracing Illegals," *BusinessWeek*, July 18, 2005, pp. 56–64.

33. Jaffrey S. Passel, *The Size and Characteristics of the Unauthorized Migrant Population* (Washington, D.C.: Pew Hispanic Center, 2006), p. i.

34. "Tight Immigration Policy Hits Roadblock of Reality," *New York Times*, January 20, 2006, p. A12.

35. Passel, *Unauthorized Migrant Population*, p. 11.

36. "Who Left the Door Open?" *Time*, September 20, 2004, pp. 51–66.

37. For two different approaches to the immigration issue, see Roy Beck, *The Case against Immigration* (New York: W.W. Norton, 1996); and John Isbister, *The Immigration Debate: Remaking America* (West Hartford, CT: Kumarian, 1996).

38. "Immigration Costs Move to Fore," *Wall Street Journal*, May 24, 2006, p. A4.

39. "Business Groups Fault U.S. Plan to Identify Illegal Workers," *Wall Street Journal*, March 16, 2006, pp. B1, B13.

40. "Guest-Worker Proposals Prove Divisive," *Wall Street Journal*, November 9, 2005, p. A4.

41. See "States Take Lead on Policies for Immigrants," *Los Angeles Times*, June 9, 2003, pp. A1, A13.

42. "Driver's Licenses for Illegal Immigrants Divide Congress," *Wall Street Journal*, December 6, 2004, pp. B1, B4.

43. Quoted in "Should Illegal Immigrants Get Tuition Help?" *Wall Street Journal*, February 22, 2006, p. A4.

44. "Putting a Roof over Illegal Immigration," *Los Angeles Times*, May 11, 2006, p. A21.

45. "Arizona Stirs Up Immigration Stew," *Los Angeles Times*, November 6, 2004, p. A11.

46. "'Close the Borders,' Schwarzenegger Says," *San Francisco Chronicle*, April 20, 2005, pp. B1, B3.

47. "Slim Pickings in Farm Labor Pool," *Los Angeles Times*, August 14, 2005, pp. A1, A27.

48. "Uncommon Weapon in Immigration Fight," *Los Angeles Times*, March 7, 2006, pp. A1, A14.

49. "Local Authorities Take Border Patrol Control into Own Hands," *USA Today*, May 19, 2006, p. 8A.

50. "Mr. Fox, Cough Up $300,000," *Los Angeles Times*, May 12, 2006, pp. A1, A17.

51. "Border Watchers Capture Their Prey—the Media," *Los Angeles Times*, April 5, 2005, pp. A1, A23.

52. "Embracing Illegals," *BusinessWeek*, July 18, 2005, pp. 56–64.

53. Talcott Parsons, *The Social System* (New York: Free Press, 1951), pp. 218–19.

54. Walter Laqueur, *The Age of Terrorism* (Boston: Little, Brown, 1987), p. 72.

55. Brian M. Jenkins, "International Terrorism: The Other World War," in Charles W. Kegley, Jr., ed., *International Terrorism* (New York: St. Martin's, 1990), p. 30.

56. Jonathan R. White, *Terrorism*, 4th ed. (Belmont, CA: Thomson Wadsworth, 2003), p. 284.

57. For a review of terrorist activities against the United States prior to 9/11, see Paul R. Pillar, *Terrorism and U.S. Foreign Policy* (Washington, D.C.: Brookings Institution, 2001).

58. For a complete list of the consolidated agencies, see "Establishing New Agency Is Expected to Take Years and Could Divert It from Mission," *New York Times*, November 20, 2002, p. A12.

59. "Gaps in Security Stretch All along the Way from Model Port in Dubai to U.S.," *New York Times*, February 26, 2006, section 1, p. 26.

60. "9/11 Report Calls for a Sweeping Overhaul of Intelligence," *New York Times*, July 23, 2004, pp. A1, A10.

61. "Poll: Terror Threat Is Permanent," CBS News, September 10, 2005.

62. "How We Got Homeland Security Wrong," *Time*, February 2, 2004, pp. 33–38.

63. "U.S. Mayors Cite Lack of Money for Security," *Los Angeles Times*, January 23, 2004, p. A34.

64. See "New Terror Alert Brings No Change in States' Security," *New York Times*, May 25, 2002, pp. A1, A11.

65. See "Cities Confront High Cost of Security," *Wall Street Journal*, March 25, 2003, p. A2.

66. For a discussion of terrorist activities from cult-like groups, see Bruce Hoffman, *Inside Terrorism* (New York: Columbia University Press, 1998).

67. Frances L. Edwards, "Homeland Security from the Local Perspective," in William C. Nicholson, ed., *Homeland Security Law and Policy* (Springfield, IL: Charles C. Thomas, 2005), p. 133.

68. Stella Z. Theodoulou, "AIDS Equals Politics," in Stella Z. Theodoulou, ed., *AIDS: The Politics and Policy of Disease* (Upper Saddle River, NJ: Prentice-Hall, 1996), p. 3.

69. "States and Cities Lag in Readiness to Fight Bird Flu," *New York Times*, February 6, 2006, pp. A1, A16.

70. "Many States Are Not Confident in Disaster Plans, Survey Finds," *New York Times*, February 13, 2006, p. A16.

Notes to Chapter 9

1. Stanley Elkins and Eric McKitrick, *The Age of Federalism* (New York: Oxford University Press, 1993), p. 59.

2. Quoted in Walter Isaacson, *Benjamin Franklin: An American Life* (New York: Simon and Schuster, 2003), pp. 457–58.

3. Ibid.

4. In his book on Alexander Hamilton, Ron Chernow argues to do otherwise would have sent the Convention into a complete breakdown. See his *Alexander Hamilton* (New York: Penguin, 2004), pp. 229–39.

5. Daniel Boorstin makes this point in his *The Lost World of Thomas Jefferson* (New York: Henry Holt, 1948), pp. 194–95.

6. Theodore J. Lowi, Benjamin Ginsberg, and Kenneth A. Shepsle, *American Government: Power and Purpose*, 8th ed. (New York: W.W. Norton, 2004), p. 5.

7. See G. Ross Stephens and Nelson Wikstrom, *American Intergovernmental Relations* (New York: Oxford University Press, 2007), pp. 257–70.

8. James E. Anderson, *Public Policymaking*, 3rd ed. (New York: Houghton Mifflin, 1997), p. 50.

9. William L. Morrow, *A Republic, If You Can Keep It* (Upper Saddle River, N.J.: Prentice Hall, 2000), p. 300.

10. Shirley Anne Warshaw, *The Keys to Power*, 2nd ed. (New York: Pearson Longman, 2005), p. 2.

11. G. Alan Tarr, *Judicial Process and Judicial Policymaking*, 4th ed. (Belmont, CA: Thomson Wadsworth, 2006), pp. 290–91.

12. "By Any Measure, Earth Is at the Tipping Point," *Time*, April 3, 2006, pp. 34–61.

13. See Gary C. Bryner, *Blue Skies, Green Politics*, 2nd ed. (Washington, D.C.: CQ Press, 1995), pp. 155–57.

14. For example, see "In Alabama, a 'Hot Spot' in the Debate over Clean Air," *Washington Post*, June 2, 2002, pp. A3, A5.

15. "States Take the Lead," *U.S. News & World Report*, April 10, 2006, p. 36.

16. As examples, see "Bush Hits State's Emission Rules; He Backs Carmakers in Lawsuit," *San Francisco Chronicle*, October 10, 2002, pp. A1, A11; and "3 States Plan a Court Fight on Air-Conditioner Efficiency," *New York Times*, June 19, 2001, p. A19.

17. For a review of this case and the issues, see "Supreme Court Refuses to Hear the Schiavo Case," *New York Times*, March 25, 2005, pp. A1, A14.

18. "Health Leaders Seek Consensus over Uninsured," *New York Times*, May 29, 2005, pp. A1, A19.

19. "Health Costs Will Keep Rising, U.S. Says, Along with Government Share of Paying Them," *New York Times*, February 24, 2005, p. A21.

20. Clyde Prestowitz chronicles the transformation of American businesses to global enterprises in his *Three Billion New Capitalists: The Great Shift of Wealth and Power to the East* (New York: Basic Books, 2005).

21. David Osborne substantiates this thought through several case studies in his *Laboratories of Democracy* (Boston: Harvard Business School Press, 1988), pp. 8–9.

22. David C. Nice, *Policy Innovation in State Government* (Ames: Iowa State University Press, 1994), p. 145.

Index

Dahl, R., 30, 51
Davidson, R., 66
Death with dignity concept, 61, 130, 169
Declaration of Independence, 20–21, 23–24, 47
Democratic institutions, 51
Department of Homeland Security, 152, 168
Deutsch, K., 35
Devolution, 94
Dillon, J. F., 106
Distribution of power, 29–30
Doctrine of implied powers, 54
Domestic terrorism, 153–154
Downs, A., 84
Dred Scott v. Sandford, 55–56

Economic development agencies, 131
Economic impacts/outcomes, 15, 132
Eight Amendment, 45, 59
Eisenhower, D. D., 96
Elastic clause, 41
Elazar, D., 47, 120, 140
Electoral College, 28, 39, 75
Eleventh Amendment, 60
Elkins, S., 159
Emancipation Proclamation, 62
Employee incentives, 131–132
Environmental issues, 101, 134–135
  auto emissions, 134–135
  controlling natural resources, 165–166
  international policy, 146–147
  water pollution, 135
Environmental Protection Agency (EPA), 60, 63, 85, 96–97, 134–135, 146
Equal protection, 56, 58, 61
Equality, 31, 46, 48, 119, 163
  in defense of, 48–50
  of opportunity/outcome, 48
Ethridge, M., 143
Ex post facto laws, 41
Executive authority, 65–66. *See also* President
Executive Order, 62–64, 72
Executive Order 8802 (Fair Employment Practice Commission), 63
Executive Order 9981 (desegregation of military), 63
Executive Order 11246 (affirmative action), 63
Executive Order 12612 (national standards), 63

Fair Employment Practice Commission (Executive Order 8802), 63

Federal Bureau of Investigation, 87
Federal Emergency Management Agency (FEMA), 105, 152
Federal grants-in-aid, 68–70
  block grant-in-aid programs, 108–109
  as catalyst for control, 107–112
  categorical grant-in-aid programs, 107–108
  growth of, 109
  local power and, 112
  problem of formulas, 109–111
Federal Maritime Commission v. South Carolina Ports Authority, 60
Federal Register, 62
Federalism. *See also* Horizontal federalism; Vertical federalism
  bureaucracy and, 87
  conflict and, 94
  defined, 93
  international dimension of, 141–142
  leading theorists on, 21–23
    Baron de Montesquieu, 22–34
    Jefferson, 23
    Locke's "natural rights," 22
  national dominance style of, 36
  in other nations, 6
  Supreme Court rulings and, 52–54
Federalism grid, 7
Federalist Papers, 31
Federalist #10, 37
Federalist #23, 49
Federalists, 29–31, 36, 43–45
Feinstein, D., 83
Fifth Amendment, 45
First Amendment, 45
First Continental Congress (1774), 21
Fiscal federalism, 68–71
Fourteenth Amendment, 56, 58, 61, 130
Fourth Amendment, 45, 61
Fox, Vicente, 150
Franklin, Benjamin, 20, 160
Fredericksen, P., 137
Free to Choose (Friedman and Friedman), 114
Freedom, 23
Friedman, M., 114
Friedman, R., 114
Friedman, T., 144

Garcia v. San Antonio Metropolitan Transit Authority, 59
Gay rights, 16–17, 48, 97
Gerry, E., 47
Gingrich, N., 95

Larry N. Gerston is professor of political science at San José State University. For more than thirty years, his books on public policymaking, California government and politics, and other topics have carefully balanced the academic and nonacademic worlds. With one eye on esoteric political concepts and the other eye on the students attempting to grasp those concepts, Gerston has developed a knack for translation. His books have been praised as user-friendly without minimizing complex themes. In addition to his work at San José State University, Gerston is the political analyst at KNTV, the NBC television station in the San Francisco Bay area, where he appears on a regular basis.